imirce

migration and Ireland through time

Proceedings of the 6th National Monuments Service annual archaeology conference

Edited by Peigín Doyle

Word*well*

***IMIRCE*: Migration and Ireland through Time**

First published 2025
by Wordwell Ltd,
in association with National Monuments Service

Wordwell Ltd.,
Unit 9, 78 Furze Road,
Sandyford Industrial Estate,
Dublin 18, Eircode D18 C6V6
T: +353-1-2933568
www.wordwellbooks.com
ISBN 978-1-916742-12-3

Acknowledgements:
The publisher would like to acknowledge the collaboration offered by the authors of the separate papers to Peigín Doyle in producing this work, which reflects their individual contributions to the *Imirce: Migration and Ireland through Time* conference held at Dublin Castle on 07 October 2023 and the financial contribution of the Department of Housing, Local Government and Heritage toward the book's production costs.

Contributors:
Susan Arthure, Paul Duffy, Giselle González García, Edmund Gilbert, Kieran O'Conor, Geraldine Stout, Graeme Warren and Jacqueline Cahill
Consulting editor:
Sharon Greene
Commissioning editor:
Una MacConville
Editor:
Peigín Doyle
Production editor:
Nick Maxwell
Design:
Ger Garland
Layout:
© Wordwell Ltd.
Printer:
Sprint Books, Dublin

Note: Every effort has been made to identify the source or owners of images used in this book but in some cases this was not possible. Where images are subsequently identified corrections will be made in a later edition.

CONTENTS

FOREWORD

The annual archaeology conference of the National Monuments Service has become a key calendar event since it was first initiated six years ago. It is a stimulating occasion that attracts the interest of the archaeology sector and the wider public alike, having garnered a reputation for themes and presentations that are accessible, thought provoking and of high quality.

Since its inception, our National Monuments Service conference has explored a wide variety of connections between communities and archaeology on this island and beyond. Our 2023 conference – *Imirce*, meaning 'migration' or 'change of abode' – explored the very meaning of community and identity through the past. Where we have come from and where we settle shape us both individually and collectively and help to define our identity. Genetic data can help map movement of peoples, those migrations bringing with them various cultural identities, which have left enduring legacies.

People move, whether individually or collectively, for many and varied reasons, be it failure of crops or lack of food, natural disasters, trade, the search for better economic opportunities or to escape conflict or persecution. Reasons are not always obvious when viewed through the tunnel of time.

Archaeology can help us understand the how, why and when of these events, and show us how what has happened in the past shapes our future.

We thank Wordwell | *Archaeology Ireland* for their expertise and ability in bringing this conference together and for the enduring partnership with our National Monuments Service. We are extremely grateful to all the expert speakers for sharing their research with us and for making this conference such a success. We are delighted to bring to print their conference presentations, the results of excavation and research, in the field, the library or the laboratory, and share them with a wider audience.

We are committed through the national heritage plan – Heritage Ireland 2030 – to making our heritage accessible to everyone. Through such events as our annual conference – including making all talks accessible online and publishing the proceedings in richly illustrated books such as this – we share and celebrate knowledge of the past that enriches our present so much.

Michael MacDonagh
Chief Archaeologist
National Monuments Service

BROLLACH

Tá comhdháil seandálaíochta bhliantúil Seirbhíse na Séadchomharthaí Náisiúnta anois ina príomhimeacht bhliantúil ó cuireadh tús léi den chéad uair sé bliana ó shin. Is ócáid spreagúil í a mheallann spéis na hearnála seandálaíochta agus an phobail i gcoitinne araon, a bhfuil cáil bainte amach aici as téamaí agus cuir i láthair ar ardchaighdeán a bhfuil fáil orthu agus a bhfuil ábhar machnaimh iontu.

Ó cuireadh tús léi, pléadh réimse leathan nasc idir phobail agus an seandálaíocht ar an oileán seo agus thar lear ag comhdháil Seirbhíse na Séadchomharthaí Náisiúnta. Pléadh – Imirce – an bhrí dhíreach atá leis na focail ‘pobal’ agus ‘féiniúlacht’, mar a thuig ár sinsir iad, ag ár gcomhdháil 2023. Fágann an áit as a dtagaimid agus an áit ar chuireamar fúinn lorg orainn, mar dhaoine aonair agus mar bhaill ghrúpaí, rud a chabhraíonn linn ár bhféiniúlacht féin a shainmhíniú. Is féidir le sonraí géiniteacha a bheith ina gcabhair dúinn agus gluaiseachtaí muintireacha á rianú, agus na féiniúlachtaí éagsúla a rug siad leo agus na hoidhreachtaí marthanacha a d’fhág siad ina ndiaidh á n-imscrúdú.

Is iomaí cúis éagsúil atá le himirce dhaoine aonair nó mhuintireacha. D’fhéadfadh teip na mbarr nó easpa bia, tubaistí nádúrtha, trádáil, an tóir ar dheiseanna eacnamaíocha níos fearr nó chun coimhlint nó géarleanúint a fhágáil ina ndiaidh a bheith ina gcúiseanna imirce. Ní bhíonn cúiseanna soiléir i gcónaí nuair a dhéantar imscrúdú orthu trí lionsa an ama. Is féidir leis an seandálaíocht a bheith ina cabhair dúinn agus sinn ag iarraidh a thuiscint conas, cén fáth agus cathain a tharla na himeachtaí sin, agus is féidir léi a léiriú dúinn na slite a mbeidh tionchar ag imeachtaí a tharla fadó ar an todhchaí.

Gabhaimid ár mbuíochas le Wordwell | Seandálaíocht Éireann as a saineolas agus a gcumas an chomhdháil seo a thabhairt le chéile agus as ár gcomhpháirtíocht mharthanach le Seirbhís na Séadchomharthaí Náisiúnta. Táimid thar a bheith buíoch do gach cainteoir saineolaíoch as a gcuid taighde a roinnt linn agus as rath a chur ar an gcomhdháil seo. Tá lúcháir orainn a thabhairt chun cló a gcuir i láthair chomhdhála, na torthaí tochailtí agus taighde, ar an láthair, sa leabharlann nó sa saotharlann, agus iad a chomhroinnt le lucht léitheoireachta níos leithne.

Táimid tiomanta tríd an bplean oidhreachta náisiúnta – Oidhreacht Éireann 2030 – dár n-oidhreacht a chur ar fáil do gach éinne. Trí ócáidí amhail ár gcomhdháil bhliantúil – lena n-áirítear gach caint a chur ar fáil ar líne agus na himeachtaí a fhoilsiú i leabhair a maisíodh go galánta amhail an ceann seo – roinnimid agus comóraimid eolas ar an gcianaimsir a chuireann an oiread sin saibhris lenár saol sá lá ata inniu ann.

Michael MacDonagh
Príomh-Sheandálaí
Seirbhís na Séadchomharthaí Náisiúnta

CHAPTER 1

The Irish DNA Atlas: Providing a map of Irish genetics in and out of Ireland

DR EDMUND GILBERT

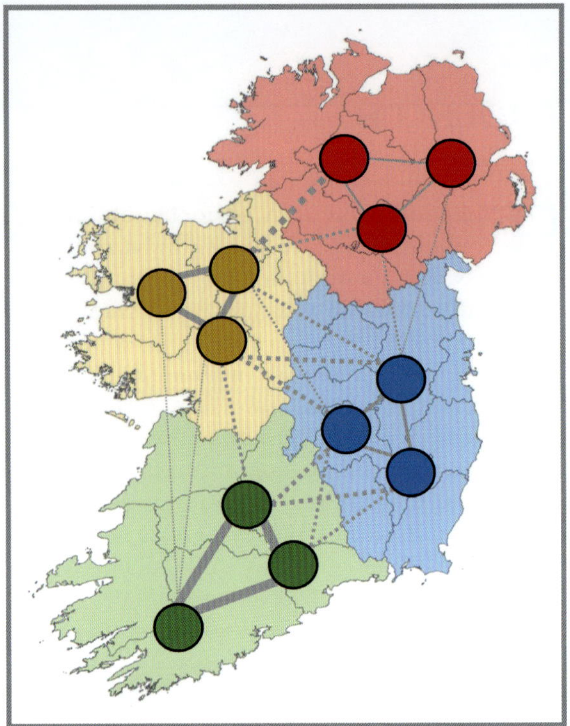

Dr Edmund Gilbert is a Lecturer in Human Population Genetics and Bioinformatics at the Royal College of Surgeons of Ireland. His current research focus is the impact that a population's history has on the current-day genetic variation, focusing especially on the Irish population. Here he discusses genetic evidence for historical migration into Ireland and for Irish migration out of Ireland to a number of north Atlantic locations.

We are very interested in the Royal College of Surgeons in Ireland (RCSI) in the genetics of communities, using that interest to study Irish history, and part of Irish history is, of course, the migration of people both into Ireland and outside of Ireland. Information on the DNA of a population is very useful in helping us to understand history. It provides some extra context, some additional evidence. However, although it helps us to contextualize, it is worth noting that it does not provide answers to how people think or how they act. We have been using predominantly modern DNA and the Irish DNA Atlas in our work, and there are a number of different tools available to us, which I will outline below.

I will begin with a brief discussion about the genetics of migration and the Irish DNA Atlas itself. I will move on then to looking at ancient migrations. Next, I will describe in more detail how we have used the Irish DNA Atlas in three specific instances, to help us to understand the links between Ireland and Scotland, then the links between Ireland and regions within the Viking world in the Viking migration period and, finally, some very recent work that was published in 2023 detailing Irish migration to Newfoundland, using evidence of DNA within the Newfoundland population.

Above: **Map of regional clusters of shared ancestry.**

Opposite page: **Scotland from Torr Head, County Antrim.**

The Irish DNA Atlas is quite a unique and interesting data-set. It is a DNA atlas of modern DNA, so a lot of the insights discussed here are based on our modern DNA. But, of course, part of understanding ancient migrations or migrations in history is being able to look at the DNA of people that lived in past times as well.

The project started in 2011 and is a collaboration between RCSI and the Genealogical Society of Ireland (GSI) and it is primarily funded by Science Foundation Ireland.

For most of our work, what we are trying to do is to identify genetic communities from their sharing patterns. These are groups of individuals who share more of their genetic identity with people within that group than they do outside of that group. Then we try to understand how those groups are related to other, different groups. So, for example, we can take a group of participants from a DNA research study and we can start recording the genetic links between them. Some people more than others share a lot more genetic material with other individuals and that usually is a sign that they share common ancestors or more recent common ancestors than those with whom they share very little DNA (although they still share some DNA).

What we can do, then, is provide some clustering or grouping of those individuals by their genetic sharing patterns, so we can identify genetic communities. We could use the information on these communities or clusters in downstream uses in genetic analyses but what we can also do is map them to different geographic areas. We can understand how different areas within regions of the world are genetically related to each other at the moment, but we can also go back in time and see how they relate to other regions. This, as a general overview, is what we do in our analysis and the primary motivations for why we want to collect these DNA samples and then analyse them.

GENETICS OF MIGRATION

Within Ireland we have had plenty of migrations to look at from a DNA perspective. We can examine the links between Ireland and Scotland, links between Newfoundland and Ireland, and, of course, with Norway and Iceland because there is history of Viking migrations too.

In studying the genetics of migration, we are looking at the migration of peoples with a different genetic ancestry. When we detect the effects of migration on the collective genome of a population, what we are doing, essentially, is detecting the descendants of those migrants and the genetic material their descendants have inherited from them. Different degrees of ancestry leave different genetic footprints. If the migrants came in relatively small numbers and they did not have much chance to transmit their own genetic material to subsequent generations, they might not leave a large genetic footprint. But if we have lots of individuals migrating over a long time, a flow type we call 'constant flow', or if there was one big burst or 'pulse' of migration, that is going to leave a genetic signature that we could investigate nowadays using modern DNA.

In terms of a genetic footprint, there may be a mixing together of the genes of different genetic ancestors, a process we call 'admixture'. So, we can consider whether a migration was a case of constant flow, as we suspect the linking between the north of Ireland and Scotland was – you can see Scotland from Ireland on a clear day – and then we can have a look at the genetic legacy of those migrations, so understanding how a population has a mixed ancestry from possibly two source populations. We can also see whether there is no source or genetic evidence of the migration and that could be an elite dominance model where we have a case of an elite that come over but they tend not to mingle with the population so they do not leave their genes very much as a footprint.

We study the genetics of migration by analysing DNA taken from present-day samples taken from the populations involved in or descended from those migrations. With the Irish DNA Atlas we primarily study modern DNA, which is relatively easy to collect. You just ask people if they would like to participate in a study. We might have some criteria from the Irish DNA Atlas that we look for when seeking volunteers, which I will discuss below. We then collect a saliva sample from the inside of the cheek. Because a saliva sample will contain the person's buccal or cheek cells, we can extract DNA from that and get a good DNA sample with which to genotype their genome, where the genome holds all of a person's genetic information. It is also possible to collect the genetic information by taking blood. However, although it is possible to take extra information or biomarkers from the blood, taking blood is more intrusive and the person usually needs to be onsite whereas nowadays we can send out a saliva collection kit in the post. A person can spit in a tube, which holds some preservative liquid, and that can be sent back to us and then we can extract DNA.

The other case is the extraction of ancient DNA from individuals from the time of the migration or before. Within the past ten years, we have seen an explosion of data that it is now possible to generate from people that lived thousands and thousands of years ago. One of the best places from which to collect DNA is from a little bone called the petrous bone that is inside the skull near the ear. This is an extremely dense bone and, because it is dense, the DNA survives there in appreciable amounts.

There are increasingly large data-sets of individuals from different time periods and different areas around the world with which we can directly analyse the genetics of an individual at the time the migrations were happening and relate them to the genetic

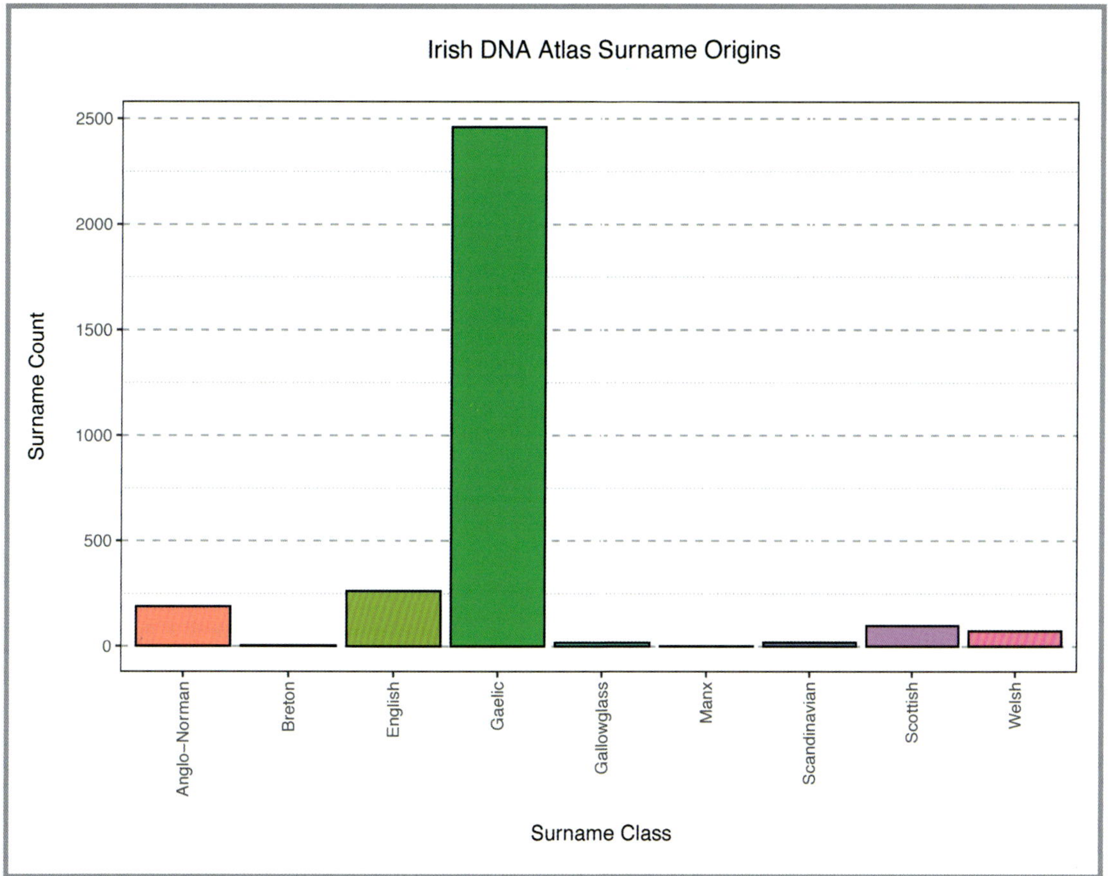

identity of people today. So, we can see whether people within Neolithic Ireland genetically speaking looked like the modern-day people of Ireland as well.

IRISH DNA ATLAS

Most of the results in the Irish DNA Atlas are based on modern DNA. Migrations that leave a genetic footprint can be detected through genetic sharing patterns. What we are doing when we are detecting genetic relationships between individuals or different populations is we are measuring sharing patterns or how much of the genome does an individual share in common with another individual. We can do this by a number of different ways. We can look at segments of the genome. A person's genome is inherited as blocks so when they generate gametes or reproductive cells, these have a mixture of their father's and their mother's genes but that is not random, that is inherited as different blocks across the

Above: **Irish DNA Atlas of Surname Origins.**

genome. We can identify those blocks and look at them being shared, the amount of genome shared in common, between individuals who are putatively unrelated.

We can also look at just the genetic variants in the cells that are shared in common, in other words, whether you share however many genetic variants out of a possible number that we are testing for. So, for each one of these different methods or the data that underlie them, we can use different methods from that data to estimate genetic sharing and admixture.

The Irish DNA Atlas is what we call a DNA cohort. So, it is a cohort, a group of individuals who share some specific defining feature, such as date of birth, but in our case, we are collecting DNA information on individuals. What we want is to collect individuals that have regional Irish ancestry, that is, ancestry from a specific area around Ireland and we are using this to investigate Irish genetics both from a disease perspective, to map disease, but also, at the moment, primarily from a historical perspective. We are collecting individuals who have great-grandparental information. What we want to do is collect individuals that have all eight of their great-grandparents born within a single area in Ireland, typically within a radius of about 50 kilometres. To take one example, one participant and their forebears lived on the Iveragh peninsula in Kerry. The participant provided a saliva sample through the post and we have collected the genetic data from that.

Since we started compiling the Irish DNA Atlas a couple of years ago, new participants have joined the project and we now have good coverage right across the island of Ireland. A cohort of about 500 recruited samples has been created to date. We have about 300 whole-genome sequences, 196 SNP-array data and 192 new SNP-array data coming in at time of writing. SNP-array genetic data is a common variant data, which is the sort of data that would be generated as part of a commercial family or ancestry kit service. Each person has several million mutations called single-nucleotide-polymorphisms (SNPs), where there are small, single letter changes in the genome. SNP-array data is used in studying slight differences or changes in entire genomes. The information helps in identifying genetic vulnerability to a disease and mapping the incidence of a particular disease, as well as ancestry investigations.

We have also got a wealth of genealogical data due to our collaboration with the Genealogical Society of Ireland. In the case of three individuals who participated, for example, we have their previous three generations, we know their birth places and we have the area within which their great-grandparents lived, which is within a radius of 30–50 kilometres. We also know the birth year of each of these individuals, both their parents, grandparents and great-grandparents. The great-grandparents typically were born around 1840 to 1850. So, this information really is capturing the genetic landscape of Ireland in the mid-nineteenth century.

Because of the collaboration with the Genealogical Society of Ireland, we also have some really interesting information on the genealogical surnames and the characterization of those surnames. We are able to group those surnames by geographical origin. Most of the Irish surnames are Gaelic-Irish in origin, with a mixture of Anglo-Norman English as well as Scottish surnames as well. The full range of surname origins were Anglo-Norman, Breton, English, Gaelic, Gallowglass, Manx, Scandinavian and Scottish. We are able to map where the great-grandparents were born and group them by their origin as well.

Coming back to migration, that is what the Irish DNA Atlas is and that is where we are getting this genetic data from.

ANCIENT MIGRATIONS

At this point I will provide some pre-Atlas insights into migration history prior to the periods that we have been studying, which have arisen from ancient DNA results. The work that we have been doing has been focused on migrations in the past 2,000 years but there have been migrations before that, which it is useful to cover here in brief, although I am neither an archaeologist nor an expert in ancient DNA. We had Neolithic farmers arriving around 4000 BC and genetically what we know is that these were the

Below: **Migration route of Neolithic farmers from Near East.**

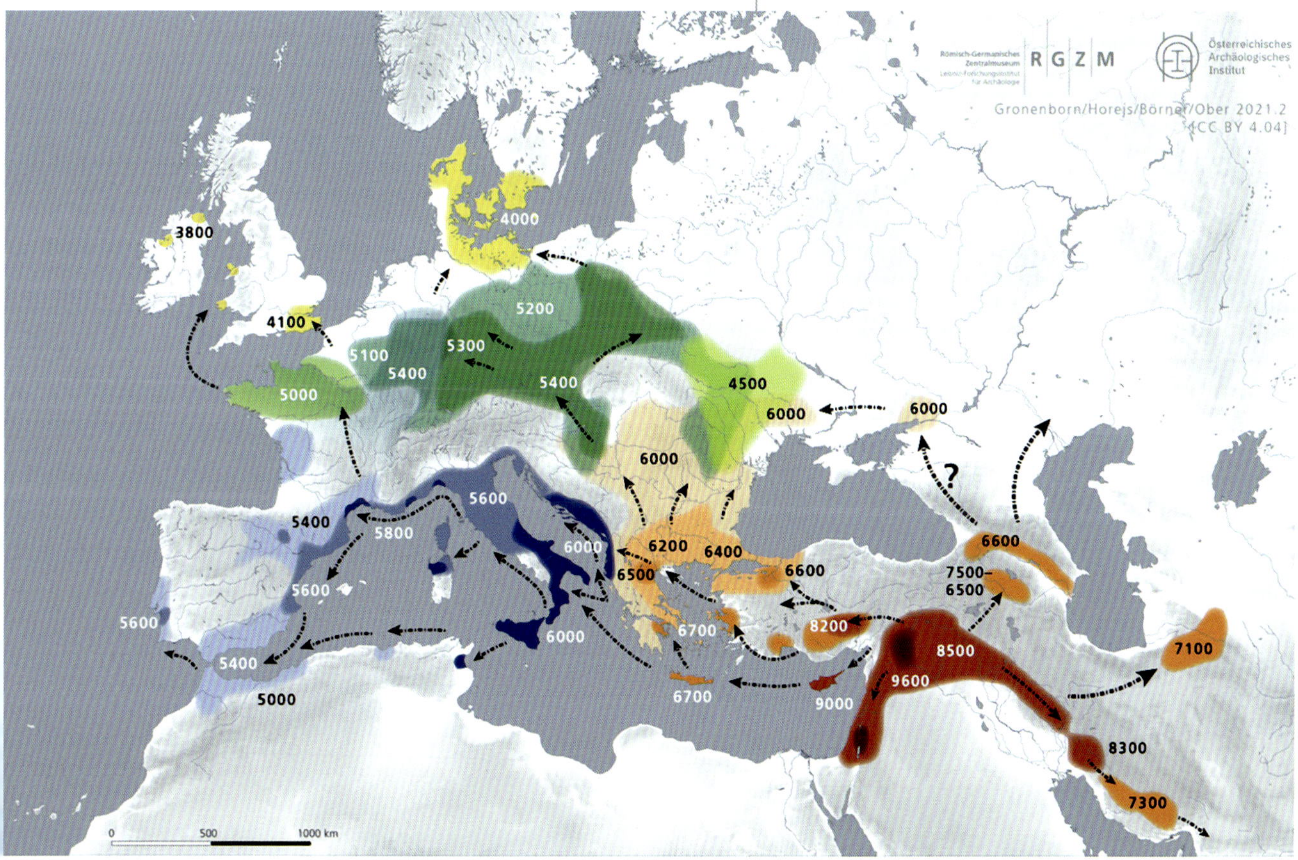

result of a wave of migrations coming from the Near East, probably from Anatolia in modern Türkiye (Turkey), via a number of different pathways through Europe, and they ended up in Ireland. At that point, these farmers were a genetic mixture between western hunter-gatherers as well as those original Near Eastern migrants.

When we look at the modern DNA landscape of Europe, we find that modern Sardinians share a very similar genetic profile to those first farmers within Europe. Sardinians have the Southern European or Near Eastern ancestry component and this continues to the present day, through geographic isolation it is thought. So, the first Irish farmers look very distinct genetically from the modern Irish.

Going forward into the Bronze Age, we have found evidence that there was a large migration around 2500–2200 BC of pastoralist people associated with the Yamnaya culture from the Eastern European steppe. They came in and brought a new ancestry component into Europe and that ancestry eventually ended up in Ireland as well, so in Ireland and Britain at that time the genetic profile shifted towards resembling what it looks like today.

European DNA can be thought of as a mixture between three original source populations: the hunter-gatherers that were there before the Neolithic revolution, the Neolithic farmers themselves, who were descended from the first farmers in the Near East, and then the Central / East European ancestry component that came in during the Bronze Age. When we see Irish samples from those different time periods, we find that the individuals with this new ancestry component

Below: **Flow of Yamnaya steppe pastoralists.**

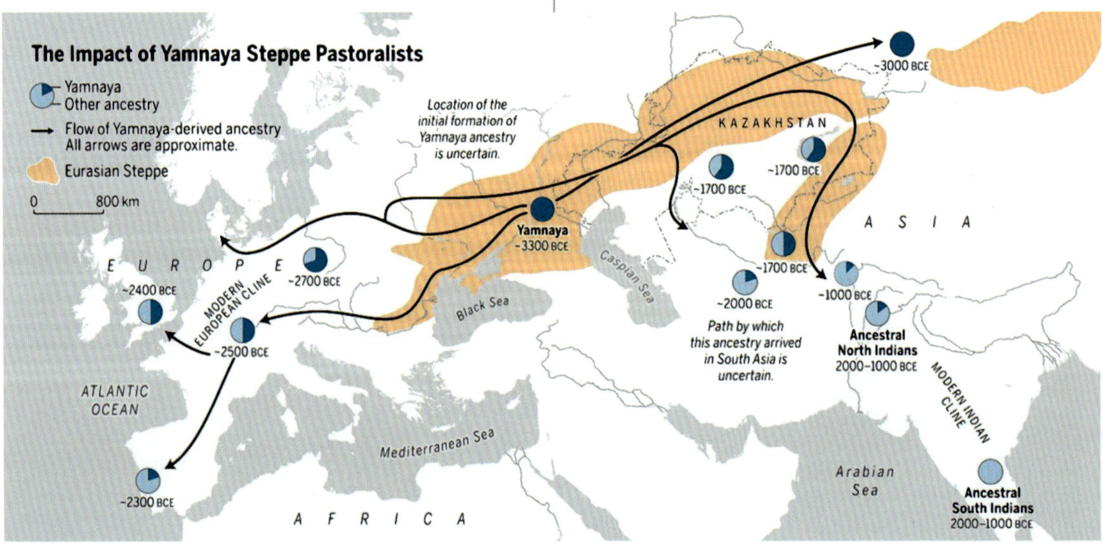

that have come from the East at the Bronze Age are the individuals that, genetically speaking, start to look like the modern Irish. Essentially, it looks like the modern Irish genetic landscape started to form from these Bronze Age migrants into Ireland and it looks like the individuals that we find are predominantly of this ancestry and not of the preceding Neolithic ancestry. So there seems to have been a population turnover of some degree in Ireland at this point.

This is where the Irish genetic landscape was formed to the point that we are studying now.

IRELAND AND SCOTLAND

The first specific case study I will look at is about Irish-British migration. I am going to focus on the northern Irish and I will deal specifically with the north of Ireland and Scotland, although we need to have a look at the links between Ireland and the area of south Wales as well. Previously, what we knew before we started on the Atlas project was that Ireland, obviously, was a little bit genetically distinct from neighbouring Britain, in the same way that England is genetically distinct from Scotland, just due to being different populations and being slightly geographically dissimilar from each other.

When we first started to analyse the data, we combined the Irish DNA Atlas with another data-set called the People of the British Isles Study, which is a similar study of individuals with regional British ancestry. Then we merged these data-sets and analysed all of these individuals together to understand the genetic landscape for Ireland in the context of neighbouring Britain. What we find is that there are a number of different communities around Ireland and they nicely map onto historical provincial boundaries.

We found there is an interesting selection of individuals in Ulster that we have grouped with other similar individuals in Scotland. In mapping these individuals, each one is represented by a coloured point on the map (See pp14/15) and each one of these points represents one individual based on their average grandparental or great-grandparental birthplace. The points are colour-coded according to the genetic community that our algorithm has placed them in. We can see even from the colour-coded clustering alone that there is a genetic link between the north of Ireland and Scotland. When we delve into this a little bit deeper, it looks like this is a recent migration. We dated it and, although the tools are not fully exact, it coincides with the period of the plantation in Ulster. It looks like this cluster, these individuals, when you look at their genetic profile, they are a mixture between Irish and British ancestries, although they are predominantly British ancestries.

Given that context, in order to investigate links with Scotland more fully, we contacted some collaborators in the University of Edinburgh, which had a much larger sample of Scottish genetics that we could include in our sample. In doing this, we massively increased our sample size in this study from about 100 individuals up to about 800 individuals. This allowed us to better refine where in Scotland these individuals of British ancestry in Ireland are linked to. What we found out was that it is, indeed, in the south-west of

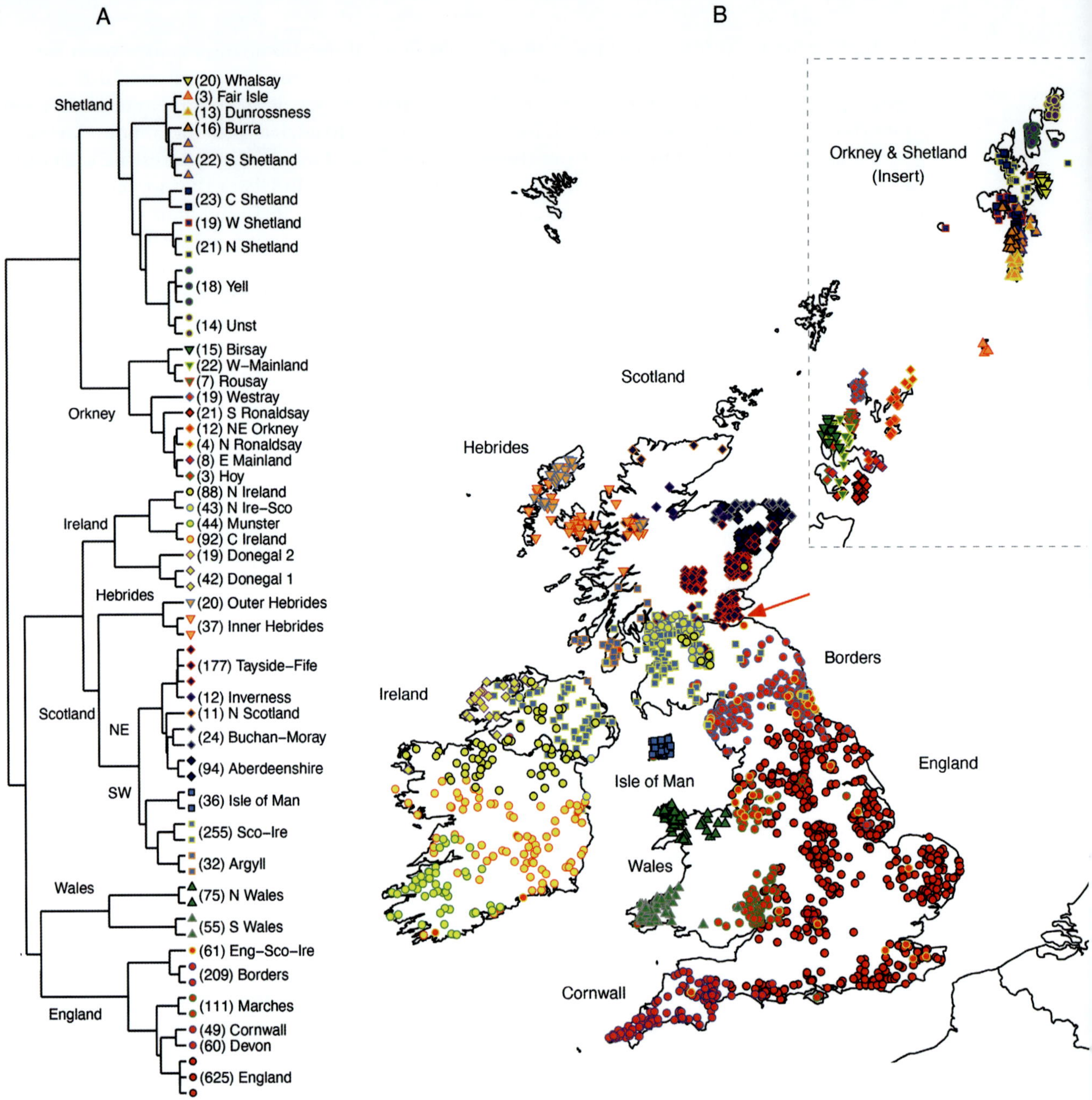

A
B
Shetland
(20) Whalsay
(3) Fair Isle
(13) Dunrossness
(16) Burra
(22) S Shetland
(23) C Shetland
(19) W Shetland
(21) N Shetland
(18) Yell
(14) Unst
Orkney
(15) Birsay
(22) W–Mainland
(7) Rousay
(19) Westray
(21) S Ronaldsay
(12) NE Orkney
(4) N Ronaldsay
(8) E Mainland
(3) Hoy
Ireland
(88) N Ireland
(43) N Ire–Sco
(44) Munster
(92) C Ireland
(19) Donegal 2
(42) Donegal 1
Hebrides
(20) Outer Hebrides
(37) Inner Hebrides
Scotland
NE
(177) Tayside–Fife
(12) Inverness
(11) N Scotland
(24) Buchan–Moray
(94) Aberdeenshire
SW
(36) Isle of Man
(255) Sco–Ire
(32) Argyll
Wales
(75) N Wales
(55) S Wales
England
(61) Eng–Sco–Ire
(209) Borders
(111) Marches
(49) Cornwall
(60) Devon
(625) England
Orkney & Shetland
(Insert)
Scotland
Hebrides
Borders
Ireland
Isle of Man
England
Wales
Cornwall

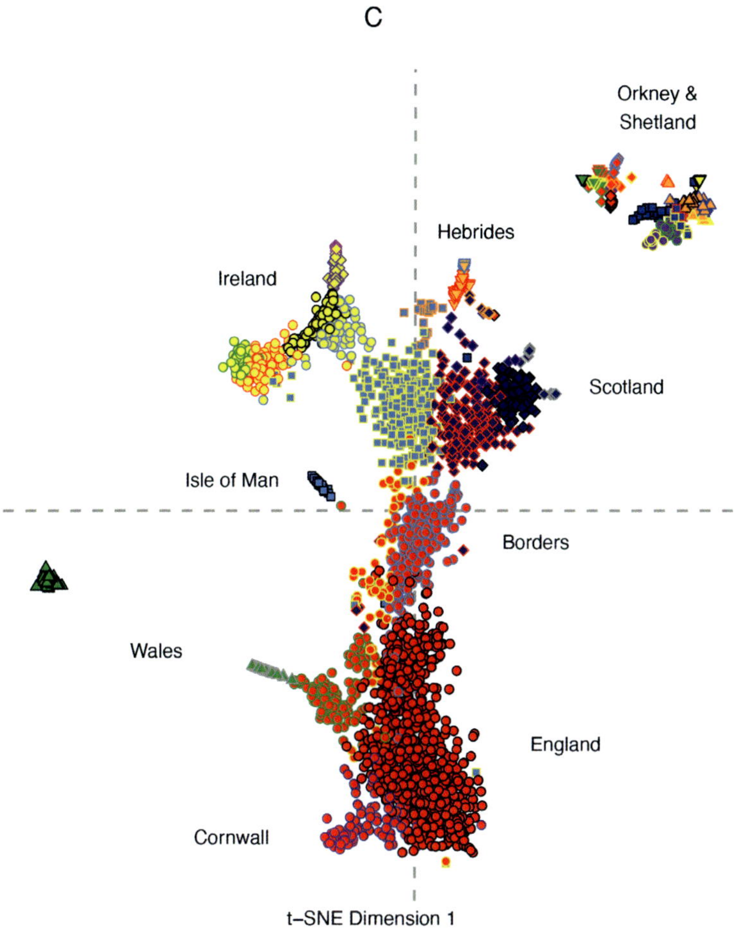

Scotland.

As part of a data-set from Scotland that we were analysing called Generation Scotland, which is a volunteer-based research study into individual and family health in Scotland, co-ordinated by the University of Edinburgh, we happened to sample genetic data of Irish migrants who had moved to Scotland but nevertheless were still predominantly of Irish ancestry. When we placed them in genetic clusters a lot of them were predominantly from Donegal. When we enquired with the Genealogical Society of Ireland, they pointed out that there was some historical precedent for that. So, while doing our own research we accidentally found this genetic signal that we had not been expecting but which is still recorded within the genetics of these participants.

When we had studied this much larger, more comprehensive, sample of individuals with ancestry from the north of England and from the south of Scotland, it looked like individuals who have British-looking ancestry in the north of Ireland are, indeed, largely from southern Scottish ancestry or they have links more like Scottish genetic samples. Interestingly, there is one individual in the Irish DNA Atlas from right at the top of Ulster near Rathlin Island who is actually clustered with individuals of Scottish ancestry from up in the Western Isles or Outer Hebrides of north-west Scotland.

We have some good evidence to suggest that we are also able to pick up genetic signs of Irish migration into Scotland that seems to be much older as well. Using these segments of shared genetic identity, what we are able to do is use them to look at different time periods or at comparative time periods and it seems that this link between the west of Scotland and Ireland is an older genetic signal than the movement of Scottish DNA into the north of Ireland and nicely

Opposite page and above: **Map of British Isles with genetic clusters.**

coincides with the migrations of Ireland into Scotland previously.

We want to expand this study and one of the ways that we are going to expand it is to combine the Irish DNA Atlas with larger data-sets like the UK Biobank, which is a massive health-related genetic data-set of about a half million individuals who are selected from Britain. Because the UK Biobank extends to half a million people, it has quite an interesting selection of individuals with ancestry from different parts of the UK. We are going to try to see whether access to this data bank can help us to look in more detail and answer the outstanding questions about the links between the Western Isles of Scotland and the north of Ireland.

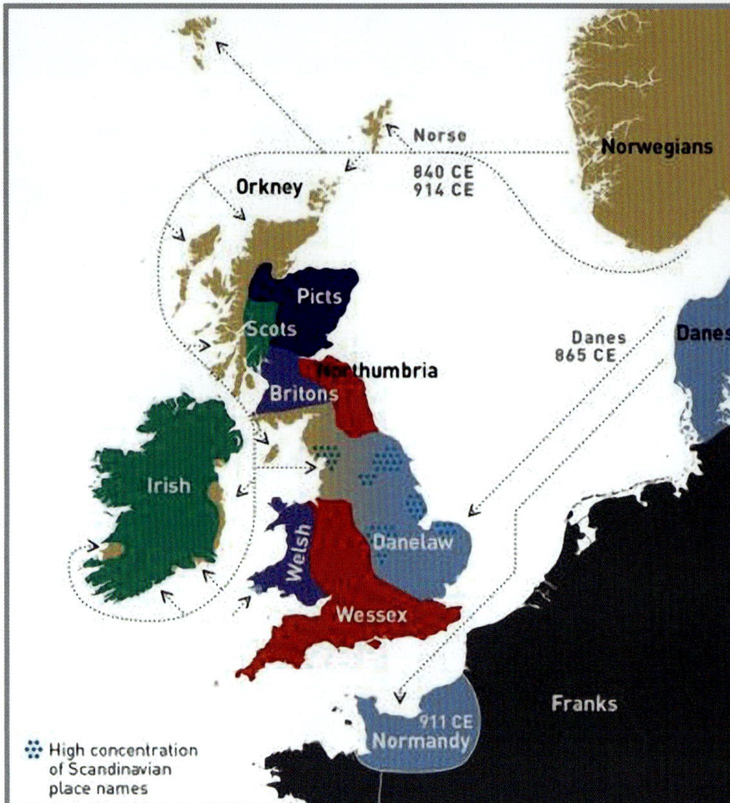

VIKING LEGACY

One aspect of genetics that we always get asked about is the genetic identity of Vikings in Ireland. In our Scottish study, we are also studying the genetic legacy of Vikings in Ireland because we would also be sampling the genetics of Orkney and Shetland as well, which are well-known places of Norse Viking settlement.

The Vikings that we are discussing here, who were interacting with the north of Britain and Ireland, were predominantly from Norway and, genetically speaking, the evidence is that this source is true and is mainly from the north and north-western shores of Norway.

In very early days of genetic analysis in Ireland, researchers in Trinity College Dublin (TCD) studied Y-chromosomes, the male sex chromosome that is passed only from father to son, and they looked at the Y-chromosomes of individuals with Norse-looking surnames. However, they did not find an enrichment of Norse-looking Y-chromosomes in males that carry Norse-looking surnames. So, that was some sort of evidence to suggest that maybe the genetic legacy or the genetic footprints of Norse settlement in Ireland are quite small.

Above: **Viking migration 800–950 CE.**

Opposite page: **Irish-British gene flow into Scandinavia.**

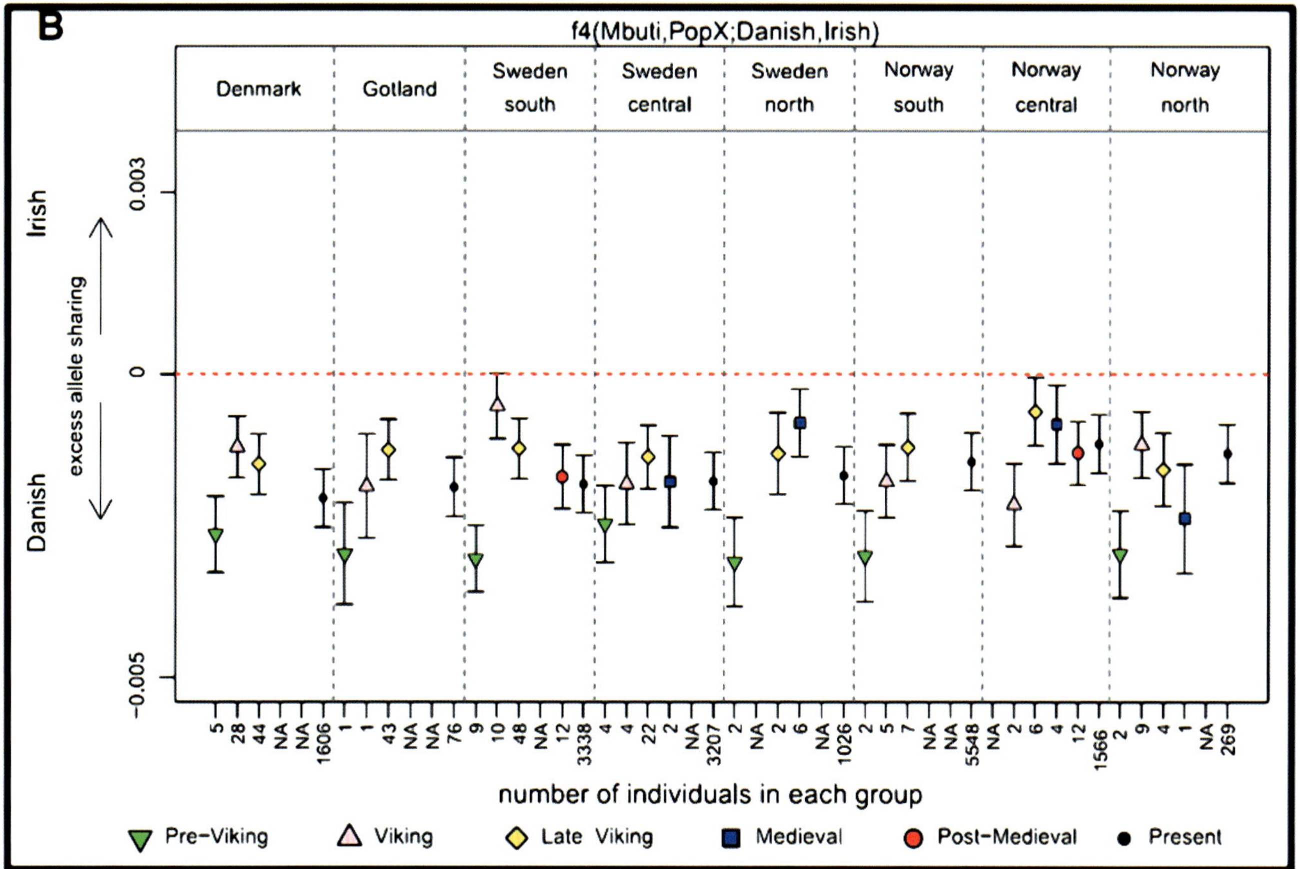

Moving on to 2017, however, our work suggested that there actually was some amount of Norse Viking ancestry in Ireland and that about 15–20 per cent of total ancestry most closely matched present day Norwegians. For reasons that I will explain below, that figure seems to be an overestimation. When we looked at this using a different methodology that is a little bit more nuanced and included British references this time, what we found was that the peak of Norwegian-looking ancestry within Britain and Ireland is found in Orkney and Shetland, which matches what we have also known in independent studies of Orkney specifically, although learning that Shetland was the peak maxima in Britain and Ireland was a new finding. In contrast, in Ireland the Norwegian-looking ancestry is minimal, so it looks like the genetic legacy of Norse settlement in Ireland has not followed through into the modern landscape of Irish genetics, which would be more in keeping with data from other genetic work.

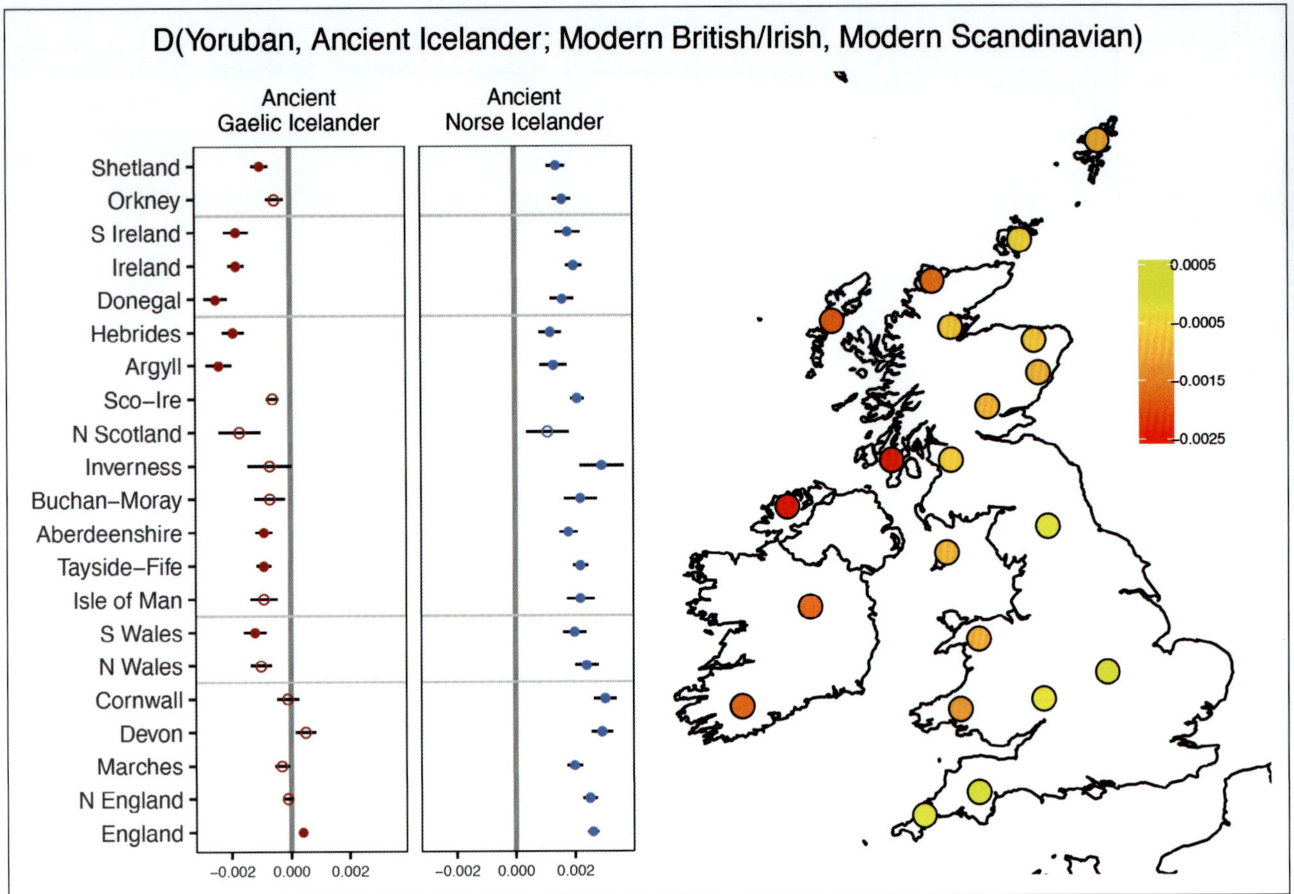

SCANDINAVIA

But there is a problem with estimating Scandinavian genes in Ireland and this is probably the source of our findings in 2017 that a fifth of ancestry in Ireland looked Norwegian. The normal theory is that we have Viking genes or Viking ancestry in Ireland and that, when we picked up Norwegian-looking ancestry in Ireland today, that was a legacy of some Norwegian Viking ancestry still existing in Ireland. But the problem is, we also know that Irish slaves were being brought over to Norway, and that Irish who had turned a'viking were going over to Norway and living their lives over there. So modern Norwegians

Above: **Source areas of Gaelic ancestry found in Iceland**

Opposite page: **Painting of Heliesun Harbour, southern Norway, 1800.**

may have Irish ancestry that has been passed on from these migrants. So, if we compare modern Norwegians to modern Ireland, what we will find if that Irish-migrant model is true is an enrichment of Norwegian-looking ancestry in Ireland but it is, in fact, Irish genes in Norway matching with Irish genes in Ireland.

Helping to answer this question, in collaboration with some researchers in Iceland and Norway we took ancient DNA of Scandinavians who had lived before and after the Viking period. We plotted the results across different time periods and different areas within Scandinavia, but here we focus on Norway. The results showed a flow of Irish genes into Norway in the Viking period. We could see that past the Viking period there was a pulse of Scottish or Irish-looking ancestry within areas of Norway and then it tapered off. Most importantly, present-day Norway still has a higher estimate of Irish or Scottish-looking ancestry than pre-Viking Norway did. So, it looks like there are Irish migrationary genes in Scandinavia today and it is likely that there is not much of a genetic legacy of those Norse Vikings in Ireland today.

IRELAND TO ICELAND

The last piece of this Viking puzzle is the question of Irish genes in Iceland. We know that Irish Vikings and slaves were brought to Iceland although Scandinavian ancestry predominates in present-day Iceland. Again, we entered into a collaboration, this time in

Iceland with deCODE Genetics. The Irish DNA Atlas was able to provide valuable modern Irish references to compare to the first migrants into Iceland. Researchers at deCODE put together a combined data-set of Irish, British and Scandinavian references and then placed ancient DNA taken from the first settlers of Iceland onto the modern variation. Through this we could see that there were first migrants in Iceland that looked Irish or looked British in ancestry, as well as a mixture of individuals that looked Scandinavian. This shows that some of the first settlers in Iceland indeed were Irish although it does not seem to be the case of 100 per cent male Norse and 100 per cent Gaelic, Irish or Scottish female.

Above: **Vestmannaeyjar Islands from Fljótshlið in Southern Region, Iceland.**

Opposite page: **In Newfoundland Irish ancestry comes from the south-east of Ireland and English ancestry from the south-west of Britain.**

We have learned something about the movement of Irish genes out of or movement of genes into Ireland around the Viking migratory period. We also wanted to look at where in Ireland were these people who had ended up in Iceland from. Where are the modern-day genetic regions in Scotland and Ireland that they were from? If we look around Ireland, are there areas of Ireland today where the DNA evidence looks like there are common descendants of those first Gaelic migrants to Iceland? It looks like for the individuals who were Irish or Scottish who ended up being the first migrants to or forming the first settlements in Iceland, their Irish or Scottish affinity seems to be predominantly from ancestry that is found today in the west of Scotland or the north of Ireland. That is not necessarily saying that they were from the north of Ireland or from the west of Scotland, it is just that the modern-day descendants of that historical community are found today in those regions.

A NEW FOUND LAND

Our most recent work involves looking at a diasporic Irish population in Newfoundland in Canada. In a collaboration with a genomics company called Sequence Bioinformatics based in Canada, we are investigating the European genetics in Newfoundland. We know that European settlement in Newfoundland was predominantly driven by English and Irish settlers in the late 1700s and early 1800s, mainly by fishermen who were going over there with their families.

We first looked at the genetics in

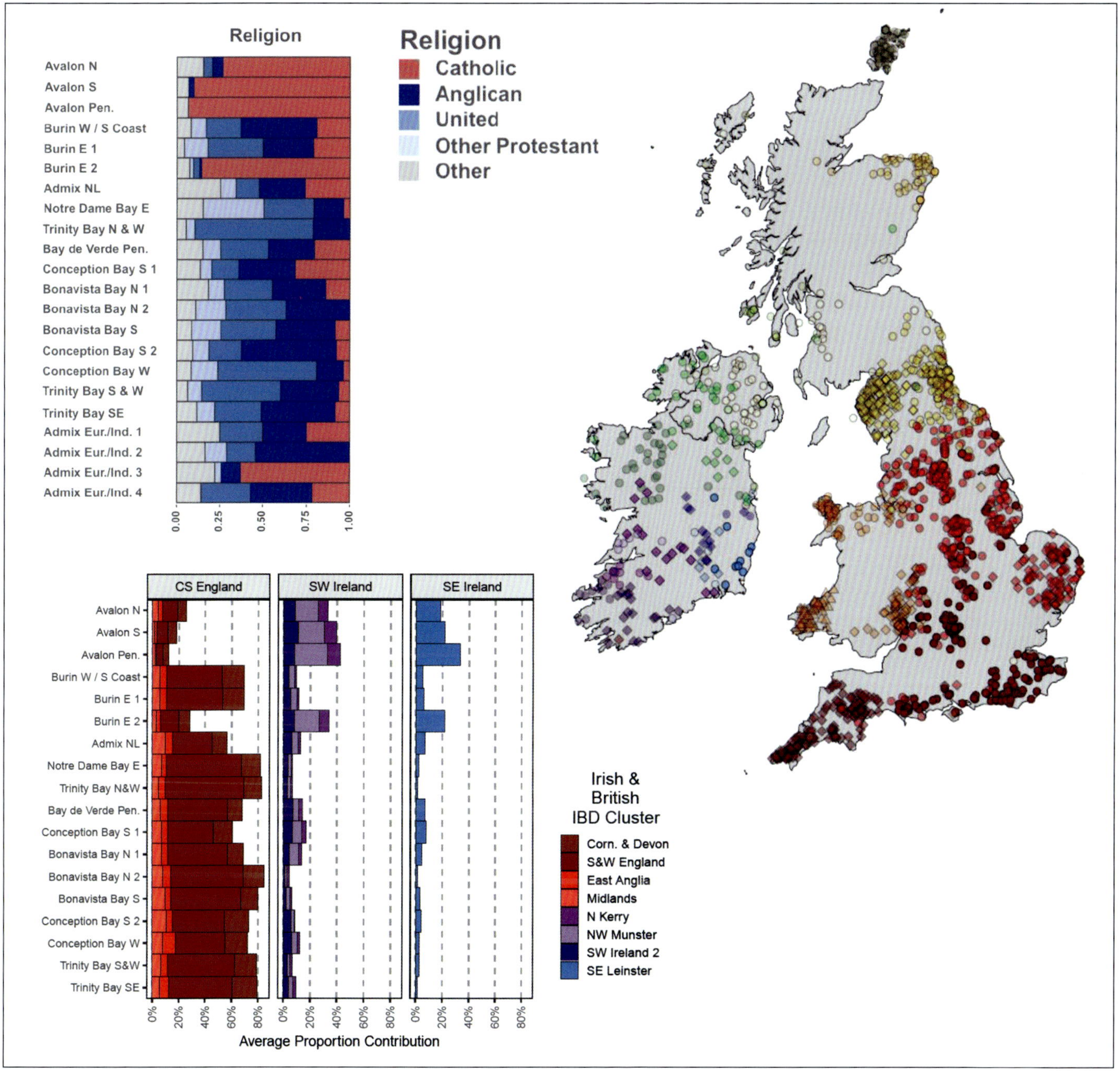
Religion
Avalon N
Avalon S
Avalon Pen.
Burin W / S Coast
Burin E 1
Burin E 2
Admix NL
Notre Dame Bay E
Trinity Bay N & W
Bay de Verde Pen.
Conception Bay S 1
Bonavista Bay N 1
Bonavista Bay N 2
Bonavista Bay S
Conception Bay S 2
Conception Bay W
Trinity Bay S & W
Trinity Bay SE
Admix Eur./Ind. 1
Admix Eur./Ind. 2
Admix Eur./Ind. 3
Admix Eur./Ind. 4
0.00
0.25
0.50
0.75
1.00
Religion
Catholic
Anglican
United
Other Protestant
Other
CS England
SW Ireland
SE Ireland
Avalon N
Avalon S
Avalon Pen.
Burin W / S Coast
Burin E 1
Burin E 2
Admix NL
Notre Dame Bay E
Trinity Bay N&W
Bay de Verde Pen.
Conception Bay S 1
Bonavista Bay N 1
Bonavista Bay N 2
Bonavista Bay S
Conception Bay S 2
Conception Bay W
Trinity Bay S&W
Trinity Bay SE
0%
20%
40%
60%
80%
Average Proportion Contribution
Irish & British IBD Cluster
Corn. & Devon
S&W England
East Anglia
Midlands
N Kerry
NW Munster
SW Ireland 2
SE Leinster

Newfoundland. We took individuals with ancestry from specific areas around the island of Newfoundland, as well as some individuals from the mainland in Labrador, but it was primarily from the island of Newfoundland. Then we clustered those individuals, as we always love to cluster our genetic data-sets, finding this tree or that dendrogram to organize those clusters by their groups. We grouped together three clusters, from the Avalon peninsula in south-east Newfoundland, clusters from the south coast and then a mixture of clusters from bays up in the north-east of the island.

In the case of the Avalon peninsula clusters, these were predominantly of individuals who self-identified as coming from a Catholic rather than a Protestant background: the idea is that the English migrants are probably of Protestant background and the descendants of Irish fishermen who came over are predominantly from a Catholic background. We can see that there is a hint of English versus Irish ancestry in these communities that we are detecting using modern-day DNA samples. Even though it has been five or ten generations since first arrival, it looks like these communities are still largely sticking to these historical groups.

The main question that we wanted to ask was where in Ireland did this Irish ancestry come from and where is it found within Newfoundland itself? We modelled the European descendants of the settlers within Newfoundland as a mixture of different Irish

Above: **A bay in Newfoundland.**

Opposite page: **Newfoundland genetic map. Mainly Irish ancestry on South Coast and Avalon Peninsula.**

and British regions using those clusters that we had previously identified. We found that the Newfoundland individuals from the south coast and the Avalon peninsula in general were a mixture of predominantly Irish ancestry, genetically speaking, which matches the self-reported Catholic background. The other clusters were a mixture predominantly of English ancestry. We found that the Irish ancestry in those individuals was predominantly from the south-east of Ireland, which nicely matches the historical records of migrants coming from ports like Wexford and Waterford. Further, it looks like people in Ireland generally were not funnelling through these ports, it was the people from areas *around* those ports that were moving. There is a similar story within England, where those migrants were coming from the south-west region.

CONCLUSIONS

Through these genetic studies we have been

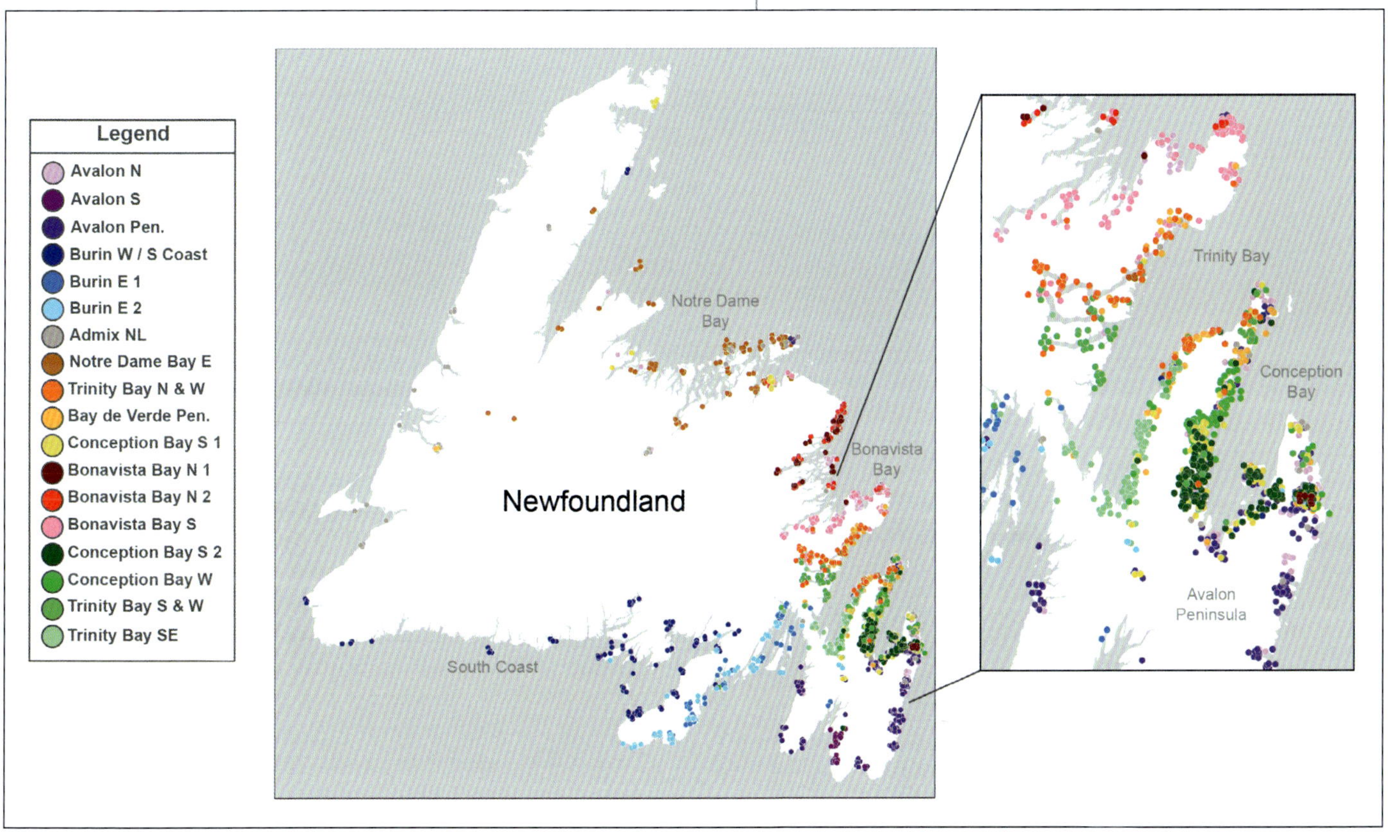

looking at diasporic populations essentially of Irish ancestry. There are a lot of people of Irish ancestry in North America, so that would be a potential area for future study, especially given that with the DNA Atlas it is possible to trace Irish ancestry back to different areas of Ireland. The links between Celtic populations, between Britain and Ireland and, for example, Brittany in north-west France also would be very interesting to look at. We want as well to look at how these genetic clusters and the impact of this genetic history affects human health today, for example, whether the disease genes in Newfoundland are Irish genetic disease genes. That might inform us about the genetics of disease within Ireland today. Lastly,

Above: **Luce Sands, near Stranraer, Scotland. Migration from Scotland into Ireland is believed to have been a 'constant flow' type.**

we are also working with other communities of Irish ancestry such as Irish Travellers, although that study is less a question of migration.

Acknowledgements

I would like to express my gratitude for the support I and my colleagues have received in our ongoing work from RCSI University of Medicine and Health Sciences, the National University of Ireland for its Fellowship Grant, Science Foundation Ireland (SFI) for their funding, Future Neuro – the SFI Centre for Chronic and Rare Neurological Diseases, SFI Centre for Research Training in Genomics Data Science, and our partners in the Genealogical Society of Ireland. We are indebted to the Irish DNA Atlas participants and participants in all other data-sets including the NL Genome Project in Newfoundland and Labrador; Generation Scotland; and ORCADES and VIKING Genes genetic epidemiology projects for Orkney. I want to thank deCODE in Iceland, SequenceBio in Newfoundland, the University of Edinburgh and our collaborators in Scandinavia.

BIBLIOGRAPHY

Benson, K. et al. 2021. The genetic landscape of polycystic kidney disease in Ireland. *European journal of human genetics* [Online]. 29 (5), pp827–838. Available from: https://doi.org/10.1038/s41431-020-00806-5. PubMed Identifier: 33454723 [accessed 11.1.24].

Ebenesersdóttir, S. et al. 2018. Ancient genomes from Iceland reveal the making of a human population. *Science* (New York, N.Y.) [Online]. 360 (6392), pp1028–1032. Available from: https://doi:10.1126/science.aar2625. PubMed Identifier: 29853688 [accessed 11.1.24].

Gilbert, E. et al. 2023. The Newfoundland and Labrador mosaic founder population descends from an Irish and British diaspora from 300 years ago. *Communications Biology* [Online]. 6. Available from: PubMed Identifier: 371176 [accessed 11.1.24].

Gilbert, E. et al. 2022. Revealing the recent demographic history of Europe via haplotype sharing in the UK Biobank. *Proceedings of the National Academy of Sciences of the United States of America (PNAS)* [Online]. 119 (25), e2119281119. Available from: https://doi.org/10.1073/pnas.2119281119. PubMed Identifier: 35696575 [accessed 11.1.24].

Gilbert, E. et al. 2019. The genetic landscape of Scotland and the Isles. *Proceedings of the National Academy of Sciences of the United States of America (PNAS)* [Online]. 116 (38), pp19064–19070. Available from: https://doi:10.1073/pnas.1904761116. PubMed Identifier: 31481615 [accessed 11.1.24].

Gilbert, E. et al. February 2017. Genomic insights into the population structure and history of the Irish Travellers. *Scientific Reports* [Online]. 7, p42187. Available from: https://doi.org/10.1038/srep42187. PubMed Identifier: 28181990 [accessed 11.1.24].

Gilbert, E. et al. December 2017. The Irish DNA Atlas: Revealing Fine-Scale Population Structure and History within Ireland. *Scientific Reports* [Online]. 7 (1), p17199. Available from: https://doi.org/10.1038/s41598-017-17124-4. PubMed Identifier: 29222464 [accessed 11.1.24].

Ó Dushlaine, C. et al. 2010. Population structure and genome-wide patterns of variation in Ireland and Britain. *European Journal of Human Genetics* [Online]. 18 (11), pp1248–1254. Available from: https://doi.org/10.1038/ejhg.2010.87. PubMed Identifier: 20571510 [accessed 11.1.24].

Rodríguez-Varela, R. et al. 2023. The genetic history of Scandinavia from the Roman Iron Age to the present. *Cell* [Online]. 186 (1), pp32–46. e19. Available from: https://doi:10.1016/j.cell.2022.11.024. PubMed Identifier: 36608656 [accessed 11.1.24].

CHAPTER 2

Raiders, Traders and Settlers in Late Iron Age and Early Medieval Ireland and Britain

DR JACQUELINE CAHILL

Dr Jacqueline Cahill is a Visiting Fellow at the Royal Agricultural University Cirencester, a Fellow of the Society of Antiquaries London, Vice-Chair of the Historical Studies Committee of the Royal Irish Academy and the former Project Director of the Discovery Programme's Late Iron Age and Roman Ireland project 2011–15. She founded the multidisciplinary Irish Isotope Research Group (IIRG) and has published widely on her research on the Iron Age and Roman period in Ireland and western Europe.

This paper discusses how archaeologists use scientific techniques to identify people who are believed to have migrated in the past and explores why this type of research is so important in contemporary investigations and how it is reshaping how we view the past. The concept of identity, how we see ourselves and how we represent ourselves through social signifiers and social mores, is key to our understanding of past peoples. Then, as now, these allow us to fit in or, indeed, stand out from others and are developed from our understanding of familial and societal expectations.

Exploring this remains central to my research because I am someone who has migrated twice in my lifetime and I am also the child of migrants. My father left Longford aged just 14. After travelling the world, he met and married my mother, who is from Mayo, and they settled in an Irish diaspora community in Manchester in the 1950s. In 1974 my father brought us back to live in Longford where we grew up. After I completed my Leaving Certificate examination in Ireland, like so many others of my generation I left Ireland to find work and join my siblings in England. So, I am both Irish and English, socially and culturally. For me the key question is what (if any) elements of my dual heritage would be left behind after my day and what would be recoverable archaeologically speaking. Exploring the nuanced and complex nature of dual heritage, which we can read retrospectively about migrants, is a core tenet in my archaeological research.

MOBILITY AND MIGRATION

The research that we do and some of the sciences that we use have only been included in archaeological research in the last 20-plus years. Much of the research and the sciences that I discuss in this paper could not have been achieved without the work of many scholars over many years and across different disciplines.

How do we use these scientific tools to look for individuals who we believe may have migrated? It is important to understand that, as far as archaeological research is concerned, origin and identity are two completely different things. Origin is fixed as chemical traces in our bodies but identities are fluid, they are malleable, and they can change many times

over our lifetimes. The social circumstances of our identities are very important in terms of archaeology although there are elements of the past that can never be recovered through archaeology alone, such as language, speech and accents. By applying these methods on the physical remains of people of the past and then combining our findings with what we understand from the archaeological context, we are trying to get closer to their lives. Our work is often driven by challenging previous interpretations or, perhaps, just digging a bit deeper.

Above: **Aerial view of Lambay Island.**

It is important to say from the very outset that the methods we use to analyse isotope ratios are very good at demonstrating where someone is *not* from. It is much more difficult to suggest where somebody *is* from. Something will have led us to a particular site or a specific burial, something about it that was different and unusual from what we might

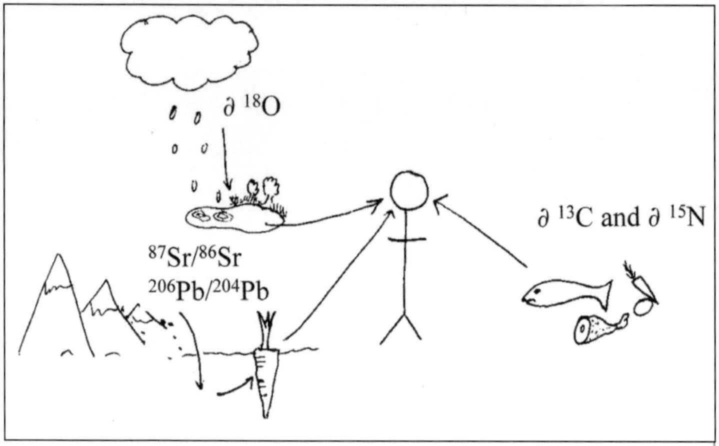

ANALYTICAL TECHNIQUES

Although the emphasis in this paper is on isotope ratio analysis, there is a whole host of different suites of scientific and environmental analysis that are now standard procedures and integral in terms of post-excavation research. DNA analysis, for example, is in many respects a sister method that can be used to refine results from isotope ratio analysis to understand if and how individuals are related and why they have come to be buried in the places where we have found them.

There are some common adages that we use in archaeology and one that is often used with isotope ratio analysis is: 'you are what you eat'. Everything that a person eats and drinks is absorbed in skeletal tissue even from before they were born, leaving a chemical signature in that person's body. We are looking to identify these traces through the measurement of the isotope ratios in a person's teeth and bones.

The principles of the scientific methods are very well published elsewhere and for a detailed methodology please see Cahill and Standish 2016. By way of a simplified overview here, suffice to say we sample from different parts of the skeleton. The enamel in our teeth is the hardest material in our bodies. It is made up of hydroxyapatite and it is used because the isotope ratios are fixed or locked in before the teeth mineralize around the age of 12. Everything that you have eaten and drunk up to that point creates a little chemical time capsule and it does not vary very much subsequently.

As with teeth, bone contains many chemical elements and as it remodels in our body

have expected, either from the location or the burial itself, and this will have sparked an interest in undertaking this type of analysis.

When we look at sites, we use exploratory frameworks to assess them. We ask ourselves a series of questions that will frame our investigations. What can we see at a local level and how does this fit into the broader archaeological, geographical or social context, especially when we are talking about things like migration and migrancy? Only when we are clear about the parameters of the research do we apply a whole suite of scientific analysis to the material itself. Then we bring everything together, including examining the evidence of the material culture, to offer a better understanding of who these people may have been and where they may have come from.

Above: **Useful isotopes.**

Opposite page: **Geological map of Ireland.**

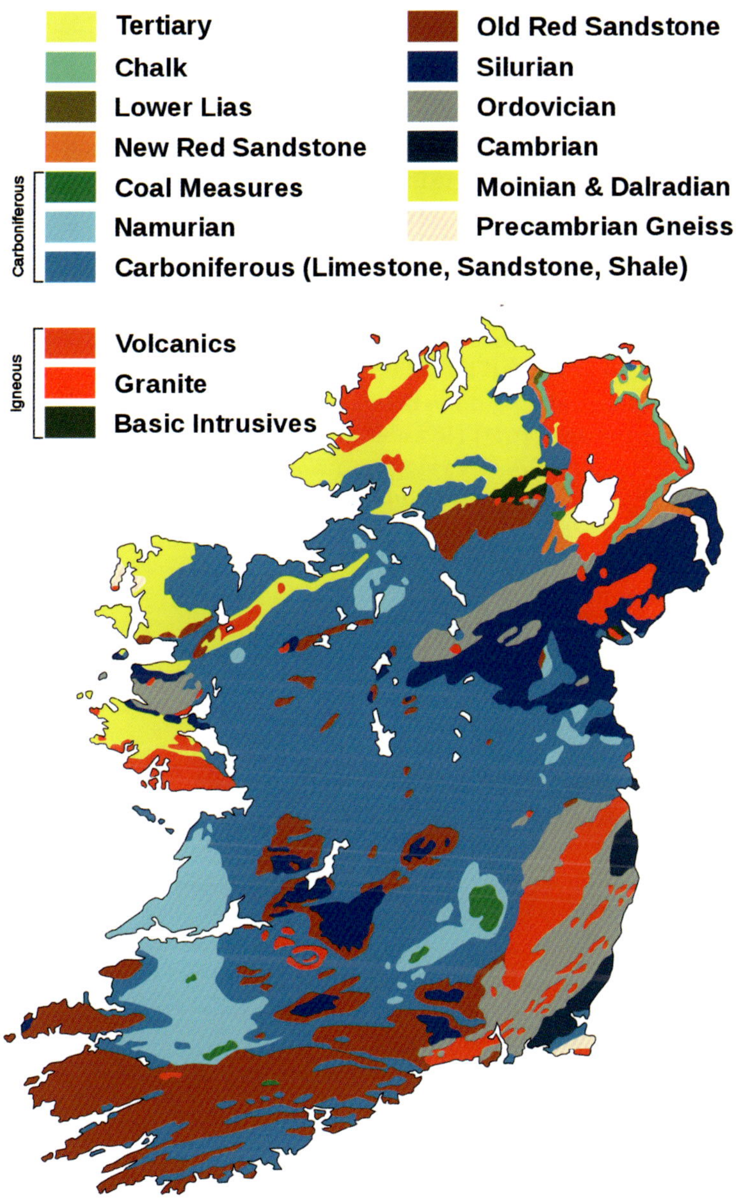

over our lifetime it can give us information on health and diet and, importantly for migration studies, any changes in likely geographical location. In particular, the smaller, thinner bones will remodel more quickly than the denser, bigger bones, on average over about 10 years, so they are indicative of location in later years. If we do a comparative analysis, we can see that, if the enamel and bone differ significantly, then perhaps the individual was not raised in the same area in which they were buried. This is how the analysis allows us to reconstruct movement and mobility (Lamb et al.)

We measure the ratio between specific strontium isotopes to determine a geographical location for an individual. Strontium is in everything from the rock underneath our feet to the food that animals graze on, everything that we grow and consume. The ratio varies geographically depending on the geological age of the rock. Where a person has lived will dictate the strontium ratios that are left in their skeleton and in their teeth and it is the relative weight of each, the ratio, that we can identify and map.

Carbon and nitrogen isotope analysis can tell us about food pathways and diet, the types of food people ate and the environmental conditions the food grew in. This can also tell us about individual or population mobility. Lead isotope analysis is frequently used not least because at certain times pre-industrialization there were periods when lead production left a much higher environmental record, for example, in the Roman period. We can also follow a lead isotope ratio from its source through objects made from this and map trade routes, such as the evidence for lead from the Mendips in the UK found in a cistern at Pompeii (Brill and Wampler 1967)

Oxygen isotope ratios are also used, in particular what we sometimes refer to as the 'heavy' oxygen isotope $d^{18}O$, the ratios of which are dictated by climatic evaporation and precipitation levels (rainfall) and ultimately drinking water sources. Analysis of sulphur isotope ratios has more recently been applied to help reconstruct past ecosystems and mobility. These are among the suite of isotopes that we can test and measure, and others are being added as the systems and the methods that we use are being refined.

In many respects, in the prehistoric and Early Medieval periods we have a series of burial types that we tend to regard as normative. In Ireland, there are certain types or forms of burial that we would expect to find when we are carrying out an archaeological excavation. If a burial varies from that form, it suggests that it may be an intrusive burial type for the timeframe that we are looking at. This is what may lead us to investigate it further, using scientific analyses to see if we can find out if an individual was local or possibly a migrant.

COMPARATIVE DATA-SETS

We have data-sets of geological, geographic and biosphere data that are extremely important in establishing baseline chemical signatures. We apply these data-sets in our analysis as the new sciences are developed. For us, for the work that we are doing, it is highly important that we all share data and then we can build out from that and refine the methods and refine the information that we have.

We use a geological data-set that has been produced for Ireland and this gives us the baseline signature of the rock type in the location that we are looking at. The reason for doing this is that even where there is, for example, a great swathe of carboniferous limestone there may be intrusions of markedly younger or markedly older rock that differs in its strontium ratios. The more data that we collect, the more we can refine our identification of a source area for strontium.

We also have a secondary set of data for Ireland, what we call biosphere data, thanks to work that is being done primarily at Trinity College Dublin (TCD) (Ryan et al. 2018). This is a collection of data based on samples of the vegetation that is growing in a region and helps us to refine the identification even further. So, when we compare the data derived from the individual we are studying with the biosphere data, it will give us an indication of where someone lived.

CASE STUDIES

NAVAN FORT

A recent paper published by Dr Richard Madgwick at Cardiff University and his colleagues (Madgwick et al. 2019) detailed the investigations they made into many animal remains from the 40-metre structure at Navan Fort in County Armagh, which we know is probably one of the most important ceremonial sites in Ireland. In conducting his analysis, Dr Madgwick used a lot of my own isotope results (Cahill Wilson 2010) plus the research that was published for the Discovery Programme (Cahill Wilson 2014, Cahill Wilson and Standish 2016). This highlights the value of collecting isotope data and the importance of sharing and publishing this data, so that we can build on the data that other people have already put together.

When carrying out this investigation, Dr Madgwick and his colleagues used the addition of sulphur isotope ratios. What they demonstrated by this wonderful piece of research was that the animals found around the 40-metre structure at Navan Fort were not just from Ulster, they came from all over Ireland, some of them over great distances. The animals did not take themselves to Navan and it is safe to say that through this analysis we have evidence of an influx of people from all over Ireland coming together at Navan Fort. We may not have the human skeletal remains

Below: **Navan Fort, County Armagh.**

that would match the sheer scale of the animal remains but certainly we can say that their results support the recorded historical significance of this site.

LAMBAY ISLAND

I want to briefly discuss the burials that were found at Lambay Island off the coast of north County Dublin, which bring us into the late Iron Age and the Early Medieval periods. The material from Lambay Island was found when a new harbour was built in the twentieth century. Some skeletons and some late pre-Roman Iron Age / Roman period material was found there. We did not have an opportunity to sample the skeletons from Lambay but I want to discuss this site in terms of why this science is offering us a different way to see the past.

Because of the nature of the material found, it has been suggested that these were the burials of refugees from Britain (Rynne 1976). Roman brooches can be closely dated by types in different periods and the Roman brooches that were found date to between AD 50–75. Because of this date, it has been suggested that perhaps these were people fleeing ahead of the Roman conquest in Roman Britain. In particular, the presence of a beaded iron torc of a type known from just before and after the Roman conquest, and found geographically in northern Britain, led to the suggestion that this linked the site to a people known as the Brigantes. The Brigantes did not give the Romans an easy job in terms of conquering the country, so it is entirely possible that some fled across the Irish Sea. However, we must be very careful about giving an origin and an identity to people based on one aspect of the

material culture alone. It is entirely likely that this was a settlement that began in the later Iron Age when we consider all of the material together and when we take into account what we now know about the very important site of Drumanagh promontory visible across the bay (Cahill Wilson et al. 2014).

DRUMANAGH PROMONTORY

As I mentioned above, we can also provenance metals through isotope analysis, in particular through lead, and I will come back to this point later in the discussion. The site of Drumanagh is a headland on which there are the remains of a large Iron Age promontory fort. Drumanagh has been steeped in politics and controversy because over a period of about 40 years it was systematically looted by metal detectorists, illegally moving material off the site. Given a great deal of the material was Roman in origin, it has been suggested that the fort might have been a Roman toehold

for an invasion of Ireland. We cannot know the extent of damage that has been done in terms of potential archaeology but thankfully, because of conversations that took place around the Discovery Programme's Late Iron Age and Roman Ireland (LIARI) Project, it is now in the care and conservation of Fingal County Council.

Drumanagh is much more likely to have been an emporium, a trading site, and there is currently not enough evidence to suggest it was the site of a Roman invasion. Given that much of the looted material appears to be linked to Roman (and Irish) horse paraphernalia, a small Roman cavalry unit may have been stationed there. The material from the site is not just Roman, however, a lot of the

Above: **Ornate terminal of the Attymon horse-bit; three-link Irish type in bronze, Raftery type E, found in County Galway.**

Left: **An orthoimage of the impressive promontory fort of Drumanagh at Loughshinny, County Dublin.**

Opposite page: **Lambay beaded torc.**

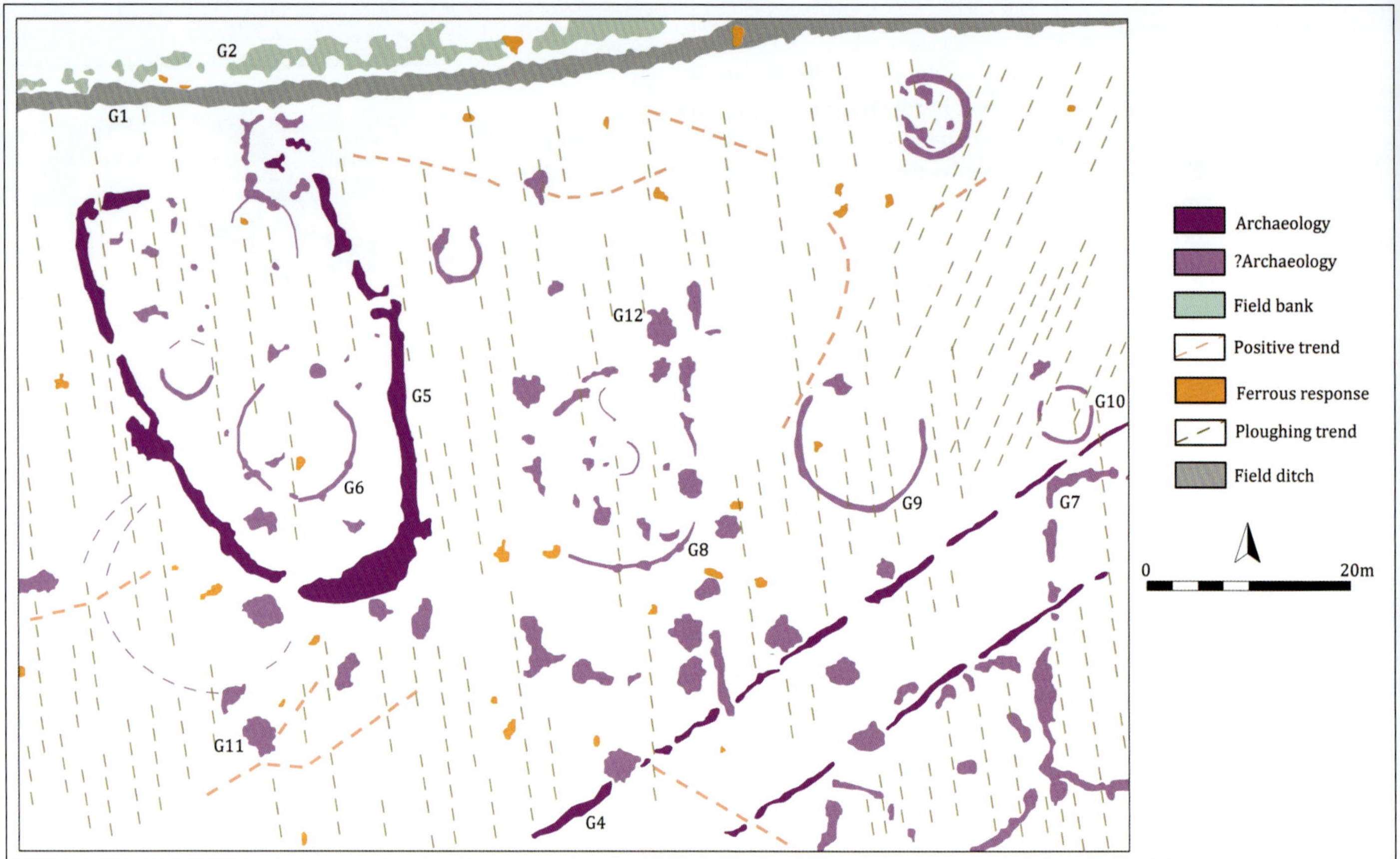

finds are regarded as quintessentially Irish, for example, the Irish-type horse bits being manufactured on the site. We also have Y-shaped pendants being manufactured and these have been reviewed quite recently by archaeologist Dr Rena Maguire, who is a specialist in ancient equitation, and she convincingly demonstrates that they are a type of horse bosal or noseband (Maguire 2021). We also have the moulds to make Romano-British bow-shaped trumpet brooches. As far as I am aware, there are no trumpet brooches in Ireland, so there remains the question of whether they were being made on the site and exported back to Roman Britain or Gaul.

Over 40 Romano British-type copper ingots were looted from the Drumanagh site, though

Above: **Area 1A (Drumanagh) interpretative plan showing principal geophysical anomalies.**

Opposite page: **The former copper mine known as 'Smuggler's Cave', Lane townland, Loughshinny, County Dublin.**

they are now in the care of the National Museum of Ireland. Some of them are stamped in a particular Romano-British style. Some of them were quartered, some of them were halved, and alongside the unfinished horsebits and Y-pendants and moulds for brooches it leads us to conclude that people at Drumanagh were manufacturing these items. The site is located beside an old copper mine at Loughshinny that we know was exploited in the seventeenth and eighteenth centuries and the copper exported to Britain.

Although we did not get a chance to sample the copper ingots themselves from

Drumanagh, we did sample the copper from the mine for analysis. We now have a discrete lead isotope ratio from Loughshinny and it is distinct from copper that was mined in Wales in the Roman period that is believed to have been the primary source of copper in Roman Britain. In future work we can trace this Irish copper from Drumanagh through the period and confirm if it was also being exported into the Roman world.

Above: **Small gold** *(left)* **torc end inscribed with punch dot or pontille SCBNS.MB and copper alloy leaf** *(right)* **lightly etched with ogham inscription, both from among second to fourth century AD Roman finds from Newgrange.**

Opposite page: **African Red Slipware.**

WIDER IRISH SEA CONTACTS

People often ask me what the Irish would have been trading with the Romans and why there is not more evidence for it. There are several reasons for this not least that, up until quite recently, Roman finds in Ireland were often treated as irrelevant or linked to the Grand Tour, when a wealthy person touring the Continent might have brought home a Roman-period souvenir of their travels. Ironically, it was the background research carried out in advance of the isotope analysis that highlighted for me a remarkable correlation between precious metals and minerals in Ireland and the clusters of Roman material that we find throughout Ireland. That and the distributional analysis that shows clear access points to such sites either in safe harbours or along navigable river routes well inland. We know that large hunting dogs were being traded as there is a classical reference to them being paraded through the streets of Rome in advance of games (Freeman 2001).

One of the key sites in this trading pattern was situated directly across the Irish Sea from the sites that I have just discussed. The site of Meols on the Wirral in Liverpool has suffered almost complete obliteration due to sea inundation and urban sprawl but many thousands of finds are in the Liverpool Museum. This port long predated the legionary fortress and naval base at Deva Victrix (Chester) and was the main trading base and likely stop off point for contact to and from Ireland in prehistory and the Iron Age.

We know that there is a relationship between Ireland and the Romano-British world in the later period because of the occurrence of a type of pottery called African

Red Slipware, which is late Roman pottery. This slipware is found dotted all around the south of Wales down into the Severn valley region and all along the eastern seaboard of Ireland. In fact, there is a lot of it at a site in Garranes, County Cork. Dr Katie Hemer of University College London studied a series of burial sites along the south coast of Wales (Murphy and Hemer 2022). Through her isotope analysis of these Welsh burials, Dr Hemer found not only people whom evidence suggests were from the Mediterranean world, she also found people whom she believes may have been from the west coast of Ireland.

Dr Hemer's work gives weight to the idea of this ebb and flow of migration to and fro across the Irish Sea. Another very important point Dr Hemer made is that we tend to think of traders, as opposed to raiders or settlers, as being very transient. People are imagined as coming, dropping off their wares, selling them and taking material back. Dr Hemer found in her analysis greater numbers of women, children and infants relative to the numbers of individuals at the sites she analysed, which suggests that some people were not necessarily returning to where they had originated.

During my doctoral research, I carried out an analysis of burials from a site at Bettystown, on the coast of County Meath, which I will call Bettystown 1, because there is another Bettystown site nearby. This analysis was done with permission of the former Keeper of Irish Antiquities at the National Museum of Ireland, Eamonn P. Kelly, who had excavated the site in the early 1970s and uncovered an Early Bronze Age cist and a sixth-century AD cemetery (Cahill Wilson 2010). He very kindly let me study his notes of the excavation and then date and sample some of the burials. When we sampled them, what was interesting was that some of the people who were in the local-type burials were not local themselves. They were migrants but they were buried in what we would expect to be an Irish-type funerary form. The flip side was true as well. Some of the burials we thought might be foreigners because of the non-local burial types turned out to have isotope ratios that were local.

So, the concept of identity in terms of how we represent ourselves or people represent us in death is much more complex. This site at Bettystown is particularly important because one of the burials that I sampled, because I thought he was a local individual buried in a typical type of burial of the period, turned out to have an oxygen isotope signature that would suggest he had come straight from the north African coast. African Red Slipware, which I mentioned above, comes from Tunisia, which would have been in the Roman provinces in northern Africa. An even more exotic type of Roman fine pottery tableware has been found in Ireland, called Phocaean Red Slip, which comes all the way from Türkiye (Turkey). We also have amphora types LL1 or B2, all clustered along these sites along the eastern and south-eastern seaboard of Ireland and western coast of Britain around the Irish Sea.

TRADING TO RAIDING

Something occurred around AD 367, which is known from the classical histories as the '*barbarica conspiratio*', the point at which, we are told, some sort of pact broke down between the Romans who were in Roman Britain and the people in Ireland, Scotland and Wales (Rance 2015). Across Europe we know that people were on the move, the Goths and Huns were pushing into Roman territory and challenging the military. The reason for this is quite simple. The control, the hold that Roman power had at its height on keeping people out and keeping people in their designated territory was waning. This was especially true in Roman Britain. The military garrisons stationed in Roman Britain were needed elsewhere and were significantly depleted by the mid-fourth century. Although there were moves to redeploy and rebuild with the forts known as the Saxon Shore Forts, the vast

Below: **_Barbarica conspiratio_ AD 367.**

Opposite page: **St Patrick depicted in _Legenda aurea_ manuscript (Jacobus de Voragine).**

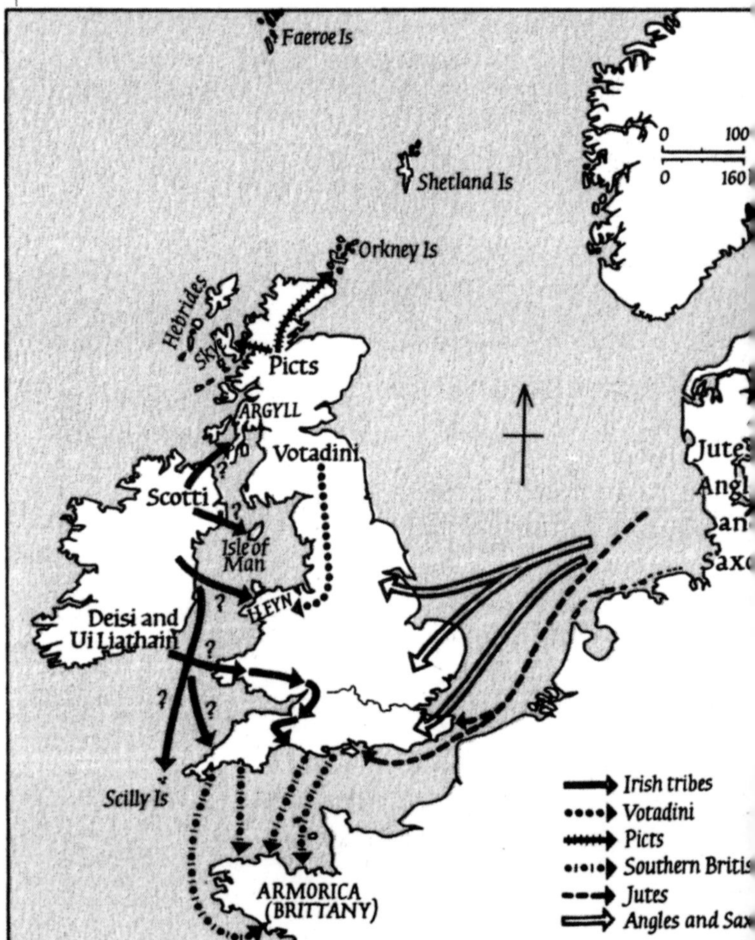

majority of the troops had probably already been moved to Europe. Hence the need for building additional military infrastructure that allowed for a minimal garrison on a lot of the strategic sites, and the local neighbouring peoples would have known this. The area of the Severn valley where many large, rich Roman villas were located would have become a target and this is where we think the raiding between Ireland and Britain occurred. Raiding essentially took over from the more benign trading that had existed between Ireland and Roman Britain. People as well as goods became commodified and the most famous Irish captive of all from Roman Britain was Patricius, latterly St Patrick. I think it is important to add that, whether you agree with the latest analysis, based on more recent scholarship, on whether Patrick was a slave or took himself off to Ireland, he regarded himself as an alien amongst Irish people (Flechner 2019).

'I live as an alien among non-Roman peoples, an exile on account of the love of God – he is my witness that this is so,' he wrote in his *Letter to the Soldiers of Coroticus*, a Brittonic warrior chieftain (Royal Irish Academy 2011).

Raiding became endemic as far as the known history of this period is concerned; it became part of the cultures between these neighbouring islands and, as Patrick wrote in his *Letter to the Soldiers of Coroticus*:

> On the day after that, I sent a letter by a holy priest (whom I had taught from infancy), with clerics, to ask that they return to us some of the booty or of the baptized prisoners they had captured. They scoffed at them.

SETTLEMENT EVIDENCE

Following on from the Discovery Programme Project, archaeologist Cóilín Ó Drisceoil (Ó Drisceoil 2016) and I returned to the prehistoric burial cairn and Iron Age hillfort site at Freestone Hill in County Kilkenny, a site that had been excavated in 1948–9 by archaeologist Gerhard Bersu (1889–1964), who had been himself a migrant or a refugee from Nazi Germany. His excavation uncovered three inhumation burials and 13 cremations (Raftery 1969). We decided to look again at some of the material and we did swathes of geophysics with colleagues at the RGK (German Archaeological Commission). Along with Freestone Hill, we undertook a programme of geophysics at another site, that of a destroyed barrow at Stoneyford, where a Roman burial was discovered in the mid-

nineteenth century (Bourke 1989). We believe we have located the burial site of the Roman cremation and we have discovered another potential barrow burial site there, which appears to be undisturbed. Notably, one of the enclosures highlighted on the geophysics is a very unusual banjo-type enclosure, which is regarded as Earlier Iron Age and quintessentially an English-type monument, so there is much more work to be done still on these sites (Rassman et al. 2022).

FURTHERING RESEARCH

The two-way trade evidenced in Ireland means that future research in this area needs to focus on the other side of the Irish Sea and on potentially Irish migrants settled in Roman Britain. With the help of the sciences, we can now look at this and reassess skeletal evidence from Roman and Late Roman Britain.

One site of particular importance will be the Roman temple complex at Nettleton Scrub in Wiltshire. Here, in the fourth century AD, something catastrophic happened. The archaeologists found skeletons literally buried where they fell. These were not formally buried, and some were lying face down. On analysis, they found that there were cut marks and sword marks on the bones. The archaeologists thought that this might have been a site of Roman or Irish settlers, or it might have been that the site was raided by Irish people. The material is housed in Bristol Museum and some dating and isotope analysis could offer answers to the question of who these people were and what happened there.

Moving on to the very big question that remains over the dating of literacy in Ireland, there is a good deal more work to be done in terms of looking at the origins of Irish writing, because the Roman material gives us a much earlier date than previously thought. We know that at least some people were literate as early as the first century AD, because a little seal box was found on Drumanagh that would have sealed correspondence like the wooden tablets that are found at the Roman Vindolanda fort on Hadrian's Wall, which was occupied by Romans between approximately AD 85 and AD 370.

We also seem to be able to push back earlier and earlier the origin of Ogham script. Ogham writing is mostly in the form of inscriptions on stone and is believed to date from the third or fourth century AD. An example of this is a little copper-alloy plate from Newgrange that was found in association with single deposits of Roman jewellery from the second to fourth century AD (Carson and O'Kelly 1977), which has an Ogham inscription scratched onto it. I am told that its translation and interpretation will form part of a new volume aiming to catalogue all Ogham in the National Museum of Ireland and I look forward to this (Ó Floinn pers. comm. 2023). This is one of the few non-monumental Ogham inscriptions that we have, and in type and form it is reminiscent of little leaf-shaped votive plaques that are common at sites such as Nettleton Scrub temple, mentioned above. Interestingly, the later Roman plate brooches found at Newgrange also have a direct parallel with similar finds from Nettleton.

Opposite page: **The Stoneyford Roman glass burial urn.**

I started at the outset by explaining why this type of research is so important to me, so let us return for a moment to ponder some of the evidence we have from Ogham inscriptions that relate to possible migrants who have been recorded for posterity. There are six important Ogham inscriptions, three of which have Roman names on them – *Sagittari*, *Mariani* and *Amatus*. Some people have raised the point that they are also Gaulish names and, in fairness, they are. However, whether Gauls or Romano Britons, these individuals are identifying as Roman by using Roman names. We also have something that is even more curious, which is three more Ogham inscriptions of people that have Roman-named fathers with Irish-named sons: Donaidonus, son of Marianus; Coimagnas, son of Vitali(us); and Maqiddeccedus, son of Marin(us). Here we have that question of identity literally written in stone for us (Thomas 1998).

To conclude, the sciences are challenging a lot of what we thought we knew. They are really pushing us to look again at the narratives of the past and see how we view mobility, how we view identity, and who we think of as migrants. As Katie Hemer has shown in her work, those transient traders often settled down and, it can be argued, so did raiders, all of whom, like me, were once migrants.

Acknowledgements

I want to acknowledge the scholars that have come before me and the work that they have done in collecting the information and the data that enable us to apply these data-sets in our analysis. Much of the research and the sciences that I describe in this paper could not have been achieved without the work of scholars over many years, not least Dr Elizabeth O'Brien, Professor Jane Evans, Professor Janet Montgomery, Professor Alistair Pike, Dr Chris Standish, Professor Gabriel Cooney, Professor Aidan O'Sullivan, Raghnall Ó Floinn, Conor Newman, Dr Ger Dowling, Coilín Ó Drisceoil, James Eogan and Ronan Swan at TII and Dr Katherina Becker. I am immensely grateful to have had the privilege of knowing and working with the late Professor George Eogan and Professor Barry Raftery. I am grateful to Dr Siân Thomas for reviewing a copy of this paper and I remain indebted to my fantastic former colleagues at the Discovery Programme.

BIBLIOGRAPHY

Becker, K. 2009. Iron Age Ireland – Finding an invisible people *IN*: Cooney, G., Becker, K., Coles, J., Ryan, M. and Sievers, S. (eds.) *Relics of Old Decency: Archaeological Studies in Later Prehistory, Festschrift for Barry Raftery*. Dublin: Wordwell. p353.

Bourke, E. 1989. Stoneyford: A First-Century Roman Burial from Ireland. *Archaeology Ireland*. 3 (3), pp56–57.

Brill, R.H. and Wampler, J.M. 1967. Isotope Studies of Ancient Lead. *American Journal of Archaeology*. 71, pp63–77.

Cahill Wilson, J. 2010. Becoming 'Irish': The materiality of transcultural identities in the Later Irish Iron Age: Unpublished PhD thesis. https://research-information.bris.ac.uk/ws/portalfiles/portal/34505553/525449.pdf.

Cahill Wilson, J. 2014. *Late Iron Age and 'Roman' Ireland: Discovery Programme Reports* 8. Dublin: Wordwell.

Cahill Wilson, J., Cooney, G., Dowling, G. and Elliott, I. 2014. Investigations on Lambay, Co Dublin *IN*: *Late Iron Age and 'Roman' Ireland: Discovery Programme Reports* 8. Dublin: Wordwell.

Cahill Wilson, J., Standish, C.C. 2016. Mobility and migration in Late Iron Age and early Medieval Ireland. *Journal Archaeological Science* 6. pp230–241.

Carson, R.A.G. and O'Kelly, C. 1977. A Catalogue of the Roman Coins from Newgrange, County Meath and Notes on the Coins and Related Finds. *Proceedings of the Royal Irish Academy*. 77, pp35–55.

Doyle, I.W. 2009. Mediterranean and Frankish pottery imports in early medieval Ireland. *The Journal of Irish Archaeology*. 18, pp17–62.

Flechner, R. 2019. *Saint Patrick Retold: The legend and History of Ireland's Patron Saint*. New Jersey: Princeton University Press.

Freeman, P.M. 2001. *Ireland and the Classical World*. Austin: University of Texas Press.

Hemer, K., Evans, J., Chenery, C. and Lamb, A. 2013. Evidence of early medieval trade and migration between Wales and the Mediterranean Sea region. *Journal of Archaeological Science*. 40, pp2352–2359.

Kelly, A. 2007. A Turkish import in County Meath. *Seanda, NRA Archaeology Magazine*. pp16–18.

Kelly, A. 2010. The discovery of Phocaean Red Slip Ware (PRSW) form 3 and Bii ware (LR1 amphorae) on sites in Ireland – an analysis within a broader framework. *Proceedings of the Royal Irish Academy*: Section C: Archaeology, Celtic Studies, History, Linguistics and Literature. 110 (1), pp35–88.

Lamb, A.L., Evans J.E., Buckley, R. and Appleby, J. 2014. Multi-isotope analysis demonstrates significant lifestyle changes in King Richard III. *Journal of Archaeological Science*. 50, pp559–565.

Madgwick, R. et al. 2019. Feasting and Mobility in Iron Age Ireland: Multi-isotope analysis reveals the vast catchment of Navan Fort, Ulster. *Scientific Reports*. 9 (1) 19792.

Maguire, R. 2021. *Irish Late Iron Age Equestrian Equipment in its Insular and Continental Context:* Queen's University Belfast Irish Archaeological Monograph 2. Oxford: Archaeopress.

Murphy, K. and Hemer, K. 2022. *Excavation of an early medieval cemetery at St Patrick's Chapel, St Davids, Pembrokeshire, Final Report*. Wales: Dyfed Archaeological Trust.

Ó Drisceoil, C. 2016. Roman Kilkenny *IN*: Stanley, M. (ed.) *Above and Below, the archaeology of roads and light rail*. Dublin: Wordwell, pp31–46.

O'Kelly, E. 1981–8. Excavations Bulletin 1977–1979: Summary Account of Archaeological Excavations in Ireland No. 57. Betaghstown. Iron Age cemetery. *The Journal of Irish Archaeology*. 4 (7).

Patrick. 2011. *Letter to the Soldiers of Coroticus* and *Confessio*. Dublin: Royal Irish Academy [Online]. Available from: https://www.confessio.ie/#. [Accessed 4 January 2024].

Raftery, B. 1969. Freestone Hill, Co. Kilkenny: An Iron Age Hillfort and Bronze Age Cairn: Excavation: Gerhard Bersu, 1948–1949. *Proceedings of the Royal Irish Academy: Archaeology, Culture, History, Literature*. 68, pp1–108.

Rance, P. 2015. The 'barbarica conspiratio' of 367–9: Barbarian Threats to Britannia in the Reign of Valentinian I at the conference: 'Oppidorum et limitum conditor: Valentinian I, War and Policy Making in the Fourth Century Roman West', Central University, Budapest, 21 November 2015.

Rassmann, K., Scholz, R., Voß, H-A, Ó Drisceoil, C. and Cahill Wilson, J. 2022. https://www.academia.edu/113230714/Following_in_the_footsteps_of_Gerhard_Bersu_at_Freestone_Hill_and_Stonyford_Co_Kilkenny_New_contributions_from_magnetic_surveys.

Ryan, S.E., Snoek, C., Crowley, Q.G. and Babachuk, M.G. 2018. 87 Sr/ 86 Sr and trace element mapping of geosphere-hydrosphere-biosphere interactions: A case study in Ireland. *Journal of Applied Geochemistry*. 92, pp209–224.

Rynne. E. 1976. The La Tène and Roman Finds from Lambay, County Dublin: A Re-assessment. *Proceedings of the Royal Irish Academy*: Archaeology, Culture, History, Literature. 76, pp231–244.

Thomas, C. 1998. Early Medieval Munster: some thoughts upon its primary Christian phase *IN*: Monk, M. and Sheehan, J. (eds.) *Early Medieval Munster Archaeology History and Society*. pp9–17.

Wedlake, W. J. 1982. *The excavation of the shrine of Apollo at Nettleton, Wiltshire, 1956–1971*. London: Society of Antiquaries of London.

CHAPTER 3

Encounters, Stories and Connections: Hunter-Gatherer Ireland

PROFESSOR GRAEME WARREN

Professor Graeme Warren of UCD School of Archaeology discusses how important it is to scrutinize the origins and possible biases contained within the frameworks that we use to understand the early populations of Ireland, and how these biases influence our perceptions of past people, their culture and ways of life.

The stories that we tell about where we come from shape who we think we are. This means that the ideas that we use to tell those stories shape our worlds today, sometimes in ways that we might not expect. In this paper, I want to think critically about the stories that we tell about the earliest inhabitants of this island, who lived here in the Mesolithic period – from roughly 10,000–6,000 years ago. I am not dealing with potential evidence for Later Palaeolithic activity (Dowd and Carden 2016) because it is only in the Mesolithic that we have enough evidence to be able to say something of substance about the character of people's lives.

In particular, many of the stories we have told about the nature and extent of contacts and connections in the Mesolithic of Ireland can be demonstrated to have developed from ideas that themselves developed during the period of European colonial expansion. Even more surprisingly, we will see that specific prejudices about Aboriginal Tasmanian populations have been extended as models for how Ireland's deep time hunter-gatherers are supposed to have lived. Reflecting on the ways in which we construct our stories of those lives,

Below: **Hunter-Gatherer Ireland.**

and considering the choices we make about the kinds of stories we tell, allows us to reconsider our approaches to encounters and connections. I demonstrate this through a consideration of Mesolithic architecture in terms of the choices made by hunter-gatherer populations.

BACKGROUND AND CONTEXT

Many aspects of the Mesolithic of Ireland have always been interpreted in the light of the island status of Ireland. Whilst there have been debates in the past about when a land bridge might have linked Ireland to Britain, the consensus now is that Ireland was an island from before the time that humans arrived here (Edwards and Craven 2017). The island status of Ireland in the Mesolithic has often been associated with some kind of isolation or difference and a lack of contact with other areas – often expressed as loss or impoverishment from an Irish perspective.

In Ireland, it is conventional to distinguish between an Earlier Mesolithic, from around 8000–6700 cal BC, and a Later Mesolithic, extending from 6700 to 4000 cal BC, although I suggest below that we may need to rethink this terminology. The settlement of Ireland occurred about 1,500 years later than in the neighbouring island of Britain. It is often assumed that this 'delay' was because Ireland was an island and especially because its terrestrial ecology was somewhat impoverished relative to its neighbours, especially in terms of large mammals. As such, key resources were believed to have been absent and new adaptations needed to be developed before people could settle here (Woodman 2015).

In the Earlier Mesolithic Ireland was part of a shared north-west European tradition of stone tool manufacture, with lithic technologies including the manufacture of microliths such as the examples from the Knowles collection, found at Glenone, County Derry/Londonderry (below).

In the Later Mesolithic, hunter-gatherers in Ireland shifted away from microlithic technologies to traditions of stone tool manufacture focusing on the production of large blades and flakes. People often talk about this in terms of 'Bann flakes' – named for finds from the river Bann in Northern Ireland. The term Bann Flakes was once used broadly to describe large flakes and blades in general but now has a more restricted, technical definition (Woodman et al. 2006). The Irish lithic industries of the Later Mesolithic are different than those of most neighbouring areas of Europe but are actually quite closely related to those of the Isle of Man (McCartan 2004). Ireland was not completely cut off from contact over the sea.

The transition from an Earlier Mesolithic that is like that of neighbouring areas to a Later Mesolithic that is more distinctive has long been a key feature of Irish Mesolithic studies, influencing, for example, early typological attempts to define the period (for review, see Moucheron and Warren 2022, Woodman 2015). It is also important to emphasize that explanations of this change often cast the Irish Later Mesolithic as something distinctive and Irish, a unique development which, in most accounts, is considered to be something that happened because of Ireland's island status, be that because of isolation or the limited diversity in the terrestrial eco-

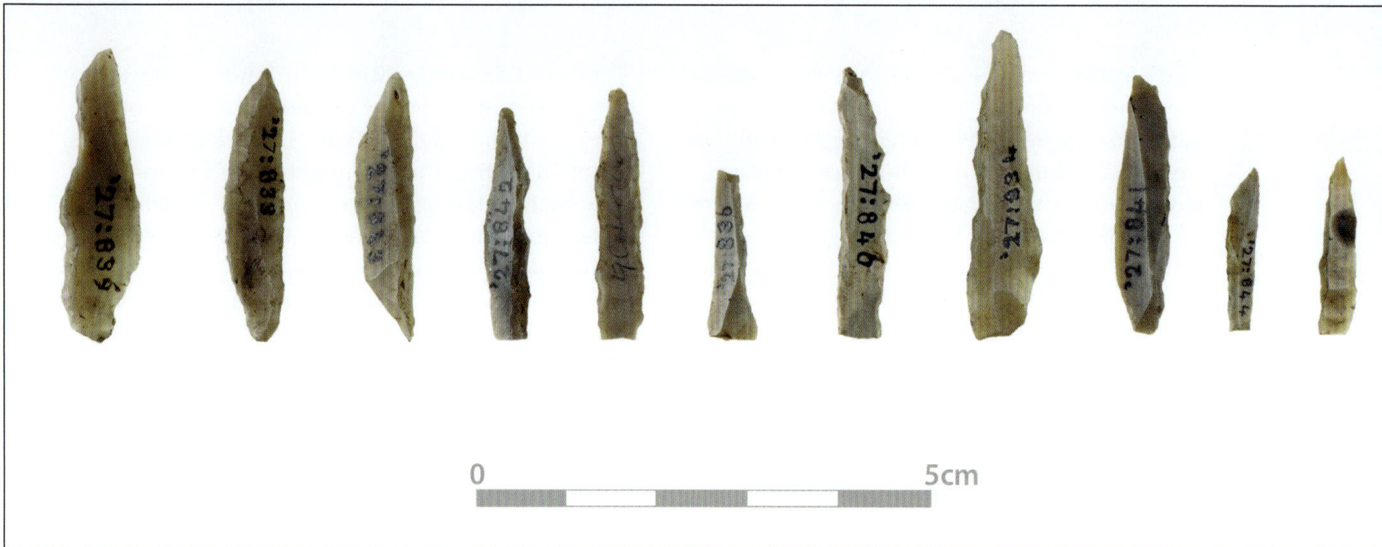

system in Ireland. But in all cases, the explanation for the change is sought on the island of Ireland and is considered to be an Irish problem (for a rare exception, see Costa and Marchand 2006).

TELLING STORIES

A key point to make about the stories we tell of the Mesolithic in Ireland is that for a long time there has been an absence of frameworks in which to place evidence that we find. In place of this, we often find generalized, stereotypical statements about hunter-gatherers.

In 1978, Peter Woodman published his PhD thesis as a British Archaeological Report called *The Mesolithic in Ireland* (Woodman 1978). (In the light of the themes of this paper, it is worth highlighting the book's subtitle: *Hunter-Gatherers in an Insular Environment.*) The next book-length overview of the Mesolithic in Ireland was published in 2015, Woodman's *Ireland's First Settlers: Time and the Mesolithic*. Thirty-seven years passed between those two publications. A lot of very good work was done in that intervening period and is published in excavation monographs, journal papers and conference proceedings but it is very scattered and, unless you are a specialist in the topic, it is hard to keep on top of such material. As a consequence, when archaeologists working in advance of road construction or other infrastructure development find and excavate Mesolithic sites, for many years they did not have an interpretative framework in which to place the evidence that they were finding. They do a fantastic job of digging Mesolithic sites but, ultimately, what they talk about in the publications are Mesolithic

Above: **Microliths of the Knowles collection, Glenone, County Derry/Londonderry.**

hunters and gatherers who live on campsites and who spend their time hunting and gathering. This is not their fault! It is because no alternative story is in place in which they can situate the material they have been excavating. In the absence of a framework, powerful stereotypes of hunter-gatherers persist.

One of my aims in publishing my 2022 book, *Hunter-Gatherer Ireland: making connections in an island world*, was to give researchers a way of placing the Irish Mesolithic material in context. I especially wanted to generate a context that placed emphasis on the connections between Ireland and other places and the choices that hunter-gatherers made in the past (Warren 2022a). The Heritage Council subsequently published a summary of some of the ideas of the book (Warren 2022b). The two substantial themes of this paper – firstly, the role of analogies with colonial-era Tasmania and, secondly, how important it is to ask different questions about Mesolithic architecture – both feature in *Hunter-Gatherer Ireland* and more detail and supporting references are provided there.

RETURN TO OLDER IDEAS

In the absence of overall stories about what was happening in the Irish Mesolithic, what we have seen in recent years has been a strange return to much older narratives that cast the period as isolated and impoverished and, in particular, ideas about the change from the Early to the Later Mesolithic that stressed regression or loss.

In the first half of the twentieth century, for example, Hallam Movius (1907–1987), talking about the Late Larnian culture of north-east Ireland (which would now be called Later Mesolithic), stated that:

> Late Larnian blades are coarse and clumsy, as if the industry, which originally was characterised by thin delicate blades, had lost its vitality to a certain degree (Movius 1942, 161).

He went on to say that:

> Just as a 'strand-looper' (sic) type of existence superseded a more vigorous hunting economy in the case of the Maglemose-Ertebølle transition in Northern Europe, a close study of the Larnian suggests that a similar transition took place in Ireland. But while the Baltic received exotic influences enriching the local cultures, the Irish development was more strictly indigenous (Movius 1942, 176).

I would dispute the claim that the stone tools characteristic of the Later Mesolithic are 'clumsy and crude'. But beyond this, there are a number of problems and fallacies embedded in these statements. Assuming that the complexity of an archaeological culture can be measured by the complexity of the stone tool assemblages it produces is a common mistake (Holdaway and Douglass 2012). A stone tool assemblage is as complicated as it needs to be for the task that people were choosing to undertake with those stone tools. It is not an abstract index of the complexity of a culture.

We can also note that the discussion of cultural 'vitality' and 'vigorous' economies in comparison to those of 'strand-loopers' contains very deep-set colonial concepts. Firstly, strandloper (not looper) was a Dutch term originally applied by Europeans to a diverse group of populations living on the coast of southern Africa from the fifteenth century onwards (Barnard 2007). It did not correspond to any single ethnicity or single economic practice but in European usage became both a racial and subsistence characterisation – often not recognizing that many 'strandlopers' had seen their traditional ways of life transformed by colonization. Secondly, Movius also clearly indicates that outside contact 'enriches' cultures, implying that 'more strictly indigenous' Irish hunter-gatherers could not benefit from this enrichment and, by contrast, must be considered impoverished. That outside influence was a benefit to other societies was a common justification for European colonial actions across the globe.

Whilst it might seem unsurprising that papers published in the 1940s contained prejudices about prehistoric populations and aligned isolation with loss, it is notable that many aspects of these ideas have come back into circulation, notably in two papers published by Felix Riede and colleagues in 2009 and frequently cited since (Riede 2009, Riede et al. 2009). In these, Riede was using Mesolithic Ireland as a case study in the relationship between a supposedly isolated island population and technological loss. Riede is explicit in stating that his work was 'prompted by' a 2004 population study by Joseph Henrich (2004) that itself focused on Tasmania. Henrich argued that Tasmania was isolated from Australia and was characterized by considerable technological loss including the loss of some fishing technologies, the ability to make cold weather clothing and possibly the ability to make fire (the latter an oft-repeated narrative about Tasmanian Aboriginal populations). Henrich argued that this was because of demographic collapse in an isolated community and that, as population levels declined in Tasmania, people lost the ability to maintain complicated technologies. We will come back again to the question of Tasmania below but it is important to note that narratives of cultural and demographic decline in Tasmania prior to European colonization are now recognized to be a 'myth of extinction' that enabled genocide and dispossession (Ryan 2012, Taylor 2017). They are also demonstrably factually false.

Riede extended Henrich's model into the Irish context, suggesting that because Ireland was isolated from Britain 'by a treacherous stretch of water' (2009, 318) the island was prone to demographic collapse, which would lead to the loss of complex technologies. (In terms of a comparison of Irish and Tasmanian 'isolation' it is worth noting that sea distance today from Tasmania to Australia is about 250 kilometres, that from Ireland to Britain currently 19 kilometres.)

Riede's language parallels that of Movius in claiming a 'targeted loss of more complex technologies (composite tools, organic technology, etc.) . . . maintenance of or even improvement in simple technologies' and describing a 'regionally restricted and much cruder macrolithic set with few formal tool types' (Riede et al. 2009, 318, 316). In order to demonstrate that the technological change coincided with a demographic one, Riede used a model of the available radiocarbon data as a proxy for population, suggesting that a decline in numbers of radiocarbon dates at about the time of the transition was evidence of demographic loss. The radiocarbon dataset available at the time was far too limited to be able to sustain those inferences (see Warren 2020). In work I carried out with Rowan McLaughlin and Robert Chapple (Chapple et al. 2022), we modelled a set of about 450 Mesolithic dates and showed an increase in radiocarbon dates during the period in which Riede's more limited data showed a decline. So, there are no empirical grounds now for the argument that Riede put forward.

Another part of the story of Ireland's supposed isolation has come from ancient DNA analyses carried out on two Mesolithic people. The genetic sequences of these individuals are distinct from their British or European neighbours, which is often interpreted as a sign of isolation. (I think it is important to be clear, the genetic data is not evidence of isolation. It is evidence for *no interbreeding* between those populations, and that is not necessarily the same thing.) Another feature of the Irish Mesolithic genetic data is that there is very little evidence for inbreeding within Irish populations. Cassidy argues that this is '. . . remarkable, given that the Mesolithic population of the island is typically estimated as no more than 3,000–10,000 people' (Cassidy 2020, 34). Here the population of Ireland in the Mesolithic is clearly being presented as being low.

It is worth exploring where this estimate comes from. Cassidy cites Woodman's 2015 book as the source for that population estimate. I cannot see that number in the book, though I might have missed it, but I can see that Woodman says 3,000 to 5,000 people. Woodman based his estimates of the Irish Mesolithic population on estimates made of the Aboriginal hunter-gatherer population of contact-era Tasmania. In particular, he is using estimates by archaeologist Rhys Jones (1941–2001). Rhys Jones' source for these estimates of population were the notes and journals of George Augustus Robinson (1791–1866), the so-called 'Chief Protector of the Aborigines'.

Below: **George Augustus Robinson.**

George Augustus Robinson's job was to remove Aboriginal communities from Tasmania and to relocate them on a small island off the coast of Tasmania itself (Ryan 2012). It is also worth pointing out that Rhys Jones had a problematic relationship with indigenous communities of Tasmania, especially because of his role in the production of a 1978 film *The Last Tasmanian*, which many people thought a damaging continuation of colonial-era narratives that Aboriginal Tasmanians were dying out (Ryan 2012, Taylor 2017).

So, in two recent cases, discussions of Mesolithic Ireland as isolated, technologically simple and with low population levels can be demonstrated to be based on comparisons with contact-era Tasmania, including data obtained during the process of colonization. This raises questions about the ethics of using these comparisons and about the validity of the data that was gathered.

POPULATION NARRATIVES

Firstly, embedding Tasmania in our narratives of Mesolithic Ireland and its contact and connection with other places is not, I think, ethically justifiable practice. Observations about Tasmanian communities were not neutral scientific observations, they were a form of scientific racism (Ryan 2012, Taylor 2017). During the nineteenth century, European descriptions of Tasmanians cast them as being one of the most primitive societies that could be imagined and they were mapped directly onto the prehistory of Europe as examples of how people here used to live (Taylor 2017). These ideas that Tasmanians were very primitive and very simple were used to justify the genocide and displacement of Tasmanian populations who, it was argued, were stuck in the past and were incapable of change. In this, they were presented as unlike their European colonizers, who had once lived like Tasmanians but had progressed to a more advanced form of social organization. The pervasive narratives of supposed cultural and demographic decline in Tasmania, or 'myths of extinction', provided justification for 'benevolent' European interventions in their lives. In short, in the nineteenth century, Europeans used indigenous Tasmanian communities as a model for what our past had been like, what we were supposed to have evolved and developed away from. This analogy caused those communities harm but academic researchers in the twenty-first century are now doing that again. It is hard to see how this might be ethically justified.

The other points of concern are that these comparisons may not even be good science or that the data may not be reliable. Many of the population estimates that were made by Augustus Robinson, for example, are what Mucher (2021) describes as a 'demographics of removal' – data obtained to enable a process of dispossession. Estimates made of population size, and assessments made of technological complexity at this time of colonial dispossession systemically underrepresented the scale of these communities and of their achievements overall (Milks 2020).

Let us look again at the population figures. Accepting the problems with the primary sources outlined above, most researchers working in Tasmania now estimate the population at time of contact with Europeans as having been about 6,000 to 10,000 (Ryan 2012).

Given that Tasmania is 81 per cent of the size of Ireland, we now have an estimated population of 7,500–12,500 in the Irish Mesolithic. Being source critical more than doubles Woodman's 3,000–5,000 figures. It is important to stress that I do not believe in these types of population estimates and, of course, Mesolithic populations varied over time. My argument here is simply that understanding the context from which our ideas come is critical. Removing a colonial-era estimate from our models of the Irish Mesolithic provides a very different vision.

The oft-claimed loss of complex technologies in Tasmania, including fire and fishing for example, we now recognize to be false. Aboriginal communities understood the creation of fire to be an act bound up in significant rituals (Taylor 2008). They did not show it to western observers. That is a very different thing to not having the capacity to undertake it. Recent archaeological work on Tasmania shows not a process of cultural decline over the pre-contact period but a time of transformation and change, a period of innovation and new practices (Griffiths 2018).

If you look at the Irish Mesolithic without a lens of loss and isolation, you can also see lots of very different things going on. Our 'indigenous developments', for example, include innovations like Moynagh Points, finely-manufactured ground stone points that are first produced in the very last stages of the Irish Mesolithic and are the focus of research being carried out at UCD by Deborah Buchanan (below). Our lithic technologies from the Later Mesolithic include so much more than just 'Bann Flakes', with a wide range of poorly understood core tools also present, such as the chert pick from Lough Kinale, County Longford (page 52). At Fanore

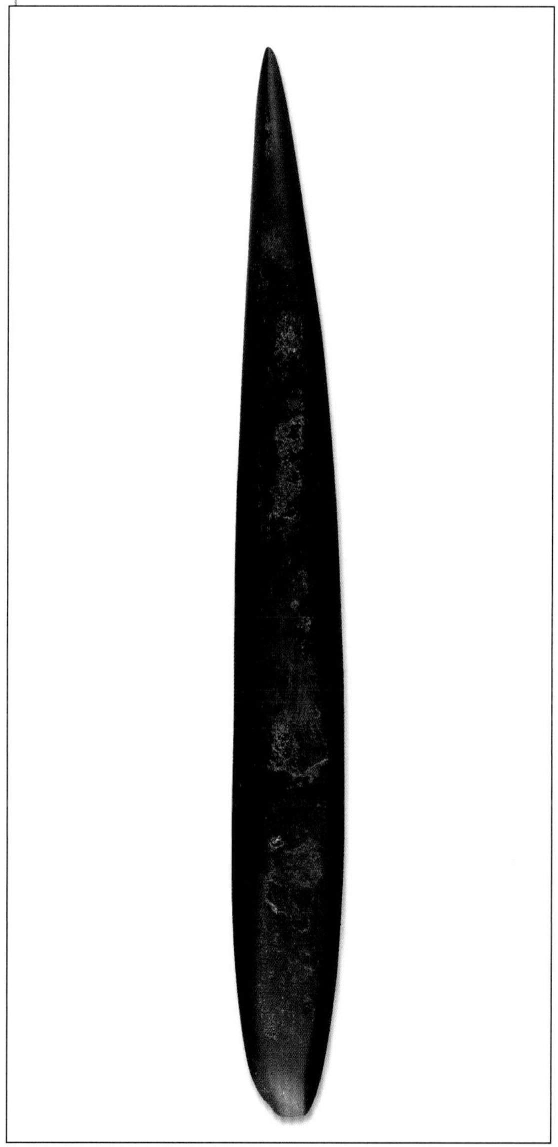

Right: **Moynagh Point from Cloonaragh, County Roscommon.**

in County Clare, Michael Lynch's excavations have identified Later Mesolithic cowrie shell beads (below right). These kind of perforated cowrie shells are well known in the Mesolithic of north-west Europe. The ones at Fanore, which are very late within the period, are contemporary with the use of perforated cowrie shells in shell midden contexts in Scotland as well. They are unequivocable evidence for contact, connection and shared practices between the Mesolithic people of Ireland and of Britain.

GEOGRAPHICAL SCALE

Finally, in addressing this idea of the Mesolithic of Ireland as being isolated and different, we also can make connections by changing our geographical scale. In *The Mesolithic in Britain* (Conneller 2021) Chantal Conneller redefines the chronology of the Mesolithic period in a new framework that covers Britain as a whole. What is really interesting and really important here is that this provides a context for the changes that are taking place in Ireland. In a forthcoming paper, Conneller and I (Conneller and Warren, forthcoming) suggest that we need to align the British and Irish terminologies. In brief, the Early Mesolithic in Britain, *c.*9400–8200/8000 BC, which is best-characterized by the site at Star Carr in North Yorkshire and its related bone, wood and antler technologies, is absent in Ireland. However, the Early/Earlier Mesolithic, *c.*8000–

Top: **Later Mesolithic chert pick from Lough Kinale, County Longford.**

Above: **Perforated Trivia arctica (cowrie shell) beads from Fanore More 2, County Clare.**

Opposite page: **(Top) Site map showing Later Mesolithic features at Newrath 34, County Waterford. (Bottom) Site drawing of Curraghprevin 3, County Cork, showing Later Mesolithic features.**

(Top) Eogan, J. and Shee Twohig, E. (eds.) 2011. Cois tSiúire: *Nine Thousand Years of Human Activity in the Lower Suir Valley: Archaeological excavations on the route of the N25 Waterford City Bypass*. Dublin: NRA Scheme Monographs 8. Image by Headland Archaeology Ltd. Courtesy Transport Infrastructure Ireland. (Bottom) Hanley, K. and Hurley, M.F. (eds.) 2013. *Generations: the archaeology of five national road schemes in Cork. Volume 1: prehistoric sites*. Dublin: NRA Scheme Monographs 13. Image by ACS Ltd. Courtesy Transport Infrastructure Ireland.

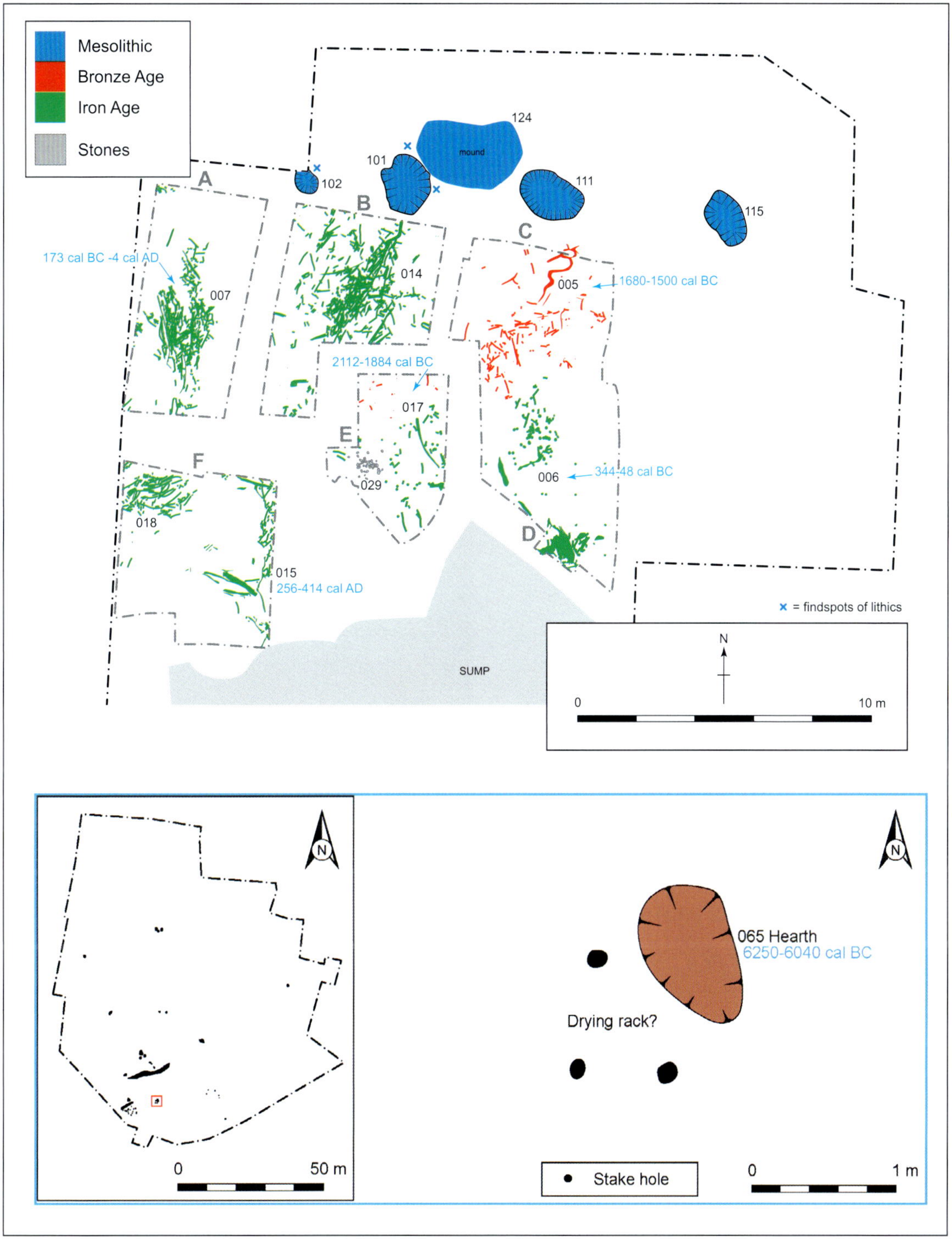
Mesolithic
Bronze Age
Iron Age
Stones
124
mound
101
102
111
115
A
B
C
D
E
F
173 cal BC -4 cal AD
007
014
005
1680-1500 cal BC
2112-1884 cal BC
017
029
006
344-48 cal BC
018
015
256-414 cal AD
SUMP
= findspots of lithics
N
0
10 m
0
50 m
065 Hearth
6250-6040 cal BC
Drying rack?
Stake hole
0
1 m

6700 BC in Ireland, which we do have, is exactly the same as the Middle Mesolithic in England, *c.*8200/8000–7000 BC. Both are characterized by large pit houses such as the kind at Mount Sandel in Derry/Londonderry (Woodman 1985) or East Barns, Scotland (Engl and Gooder 2021), pit alignments and very similar forms of technological practice.

The Late Mesolithic in Britain, *c.*7000–5200 BC, sees a significant increase in regional diversity within the Mesolithic in terms of stone tool technologies. In this sense, the transition to the Late/Later Mesolithic that takes place in Ireland *c.*6700 BC can actually be seen just as a more extreme manifestation of a trend to regional diversification that is happening throughout the Irish and British Isles. It is not a unique problem that we need to deal with as an Irish issue, it is part of a general historical trend taking place in the Mesolithic in this region.

The Final Mesolithic in Britain, *c.*5200–3900 BC, sees increased evidence of connections with the Continent and the arrival of some new, distinctive stone tool types along with it. At the moment, we do not have very strong evidence in Ireland of an equivalent. There is distinctive change in the very final part of the fifth millennium but nothing that will go back to about 5000 BC.

CHANGING STORIES: BUILDINGS AND TENTS

So far, I have shown that the origin of the concepts by which we make sense of the Mesolithic past requires careful consideration and that, if we are not careful, we run the risk of recreating colonialist stereotypes and misrepresentations of hunter-gatherers. I now want to look at how changing the types of questions that we ask can give rise to different stories about the Irish hunter-gatherer past, and that those stories can foreground the choices made by those communities.

In recent years, John Waddell (Waddell 2020) and Peter Woodman (Woodman 2015)

Above: **Reconstruction of Mount Sandel-type house at UCD Centre for Experimental Archaeology and Material Culture.**

have argued that the massive growth in the number of archaeological excavations that were carried out through the 2000s and generally since the 'Celtic Tiger boom' has not really helped our understanding of the Mesolithic past. This might seem surprising, because to take only one decade, that of 2000 to 2009, 71 sites excavated in that period have been radiocarbon-dated to the Mesolithic, most of them in advance of development (Chapple et al. 2022). That is nearly 60 per cent of all the sites *ever* radiocarbon-dated to the Mesolithic. Surely so many sites must have some significance to our understanding of the past?

Woodman argues that often this significance is limited, stating that:

> Though some of the sites are extremely important, the contribution from excavations associated with infra-structural (sic) developments . . . is not as great as might have been expected. Their contribution seems to have been more in documenting a presence across the landscape (Woodman 2015, 79).

And Waddell follows suit:

> Extraordinary expansion of archaeological work in the commercial sector over a decade ago (*c.*1997–2007) has confirmed the island-wide presence of hunter-foragers but has not appreciably advanced our knowledge of the period (Waddell 2020).

It is worth examining the logic behind these statements in detail. Woodman acknowledges that some important sites have been excavated in advance of development. Of the 25 key sites that he suggests create the 'framework' for the Irish Mesolithic (Woodman 2015) five (20 per cent) are associated with infrastructure: the fish-traps and platform at Clowanstown, County Meath; the Mesolithic hut site at Drumakeely, County Antrim; the cremation burials at Hermitage, County Limerick; fish-traps at North Wall Quay Docks, Dublin; and the flint assemblage at Toomebridge, County Antrim.

But most of what we find on road scheme excavations and infrastructural excavations is not outstanding. Most Mesolithic sites in Ireland are characterized by a spread of stone tools and occupation soil, maybe a hearth, a few pits, maybe some stake-holes – it is subtle and not the type of archaeology that grabs the attention. Yet that is repeatedly the type of archaeology of this period that we keep finding – and it is the type of material that Waddell and Woodman seem to suggest only adds dots to our distribution maps but has little other value.

Rather than bemoaning Irish archaeology for not having found enough of the spectacular and for being dominated by the mundane, surely we should try and develop questions that allow us to better understand the mundane, which is, after all, most of our data? Indeed, it is only once we find ways of making sense of this quiet, ephemeral archaeology, these scatters of pits, of stone tools, these stake-holes, that we can contextualize the more spectacular and unusual.

One way we can do this is by thinking about hunter-gatherer architecture or, if you like, mobile architecture. I have used a

Norwegian typology devised by Silje Freitheim for Mesolithic buildings, in which buildings are categorized as houses, composite buildings and tents (Fretheim 2017). Houses are defined as large, permanent or near-permanent dwellings that could have been re-occupied over a long period of time, such as a Mount Sandel-type pit house. Composite buildings are ones that have some kind of facility left on site but are not left completely constructed, for example, a location where someone has left the poles to construct a tepee-type structure. When you arrive on site, you have to cover those with skins or vegetation but you do not take the poles away with you. There are some examples of those buildings in Ireland as well (Warren 2022a).

But here I want to focus on tents. As Fretheim points out, tents are 'portable buildings, built to be easily assembled, disassembled, and transported'. Other than in exceptional circumstances, tents will leave little or no archaeological trace. Even when they are used extensively, it will be rare to find evidence for tents when they are used. This will especially be the case in sites that see repeated activity, where we are not seeing a straightforward footprint of any one phase but a mixture of all of multiple episodes of activity, making it even less likely that the footprint of a tent would be found. As stated above, the dominant evidence for the Mesolithic in Ireland, and especially the Later Mesolithic, is not of clear footprints of buildings but spreads of materials, a few stake-holes or accumulated occupation soil from multiple activities. Our evidence is wholly coherent with tents being the preferred architecture of Mesolithic hunter-gatherers in Later Mesolithic Ireland. This reliance on tents is also in keeping with a range of evidence that suggests that the Later Mesolithic was characterized by a high degree of routine mobility.

At this point, the reader may be thinking that I have gone a really long way around in order to just say that hunter-gatherers lived in tents. And of course, our powerful stereotypes of hunter-gatherers mean that we might simply have assumed this: as they are mobile people, we imagine that hunter-gatherers lived in tents. That is just what hunter-gatherers do. Perhaps but it is worth asking *why* hunter-gatherers in Ireland chose to live in tents or lightweight structures when we know that they could do other things. Buildings like Mount Sandel demonstrate that they had other architectural options available to them. Why tents?

SHARING AND TRUST

This is where turning to look at the comparative ethnography of highly mobile hunter-gatherers is interesting and useful. Many recent hunter-gatherer communities live in very small groups, the communities present in any one place at any one time might only be 20, 25 or 30 people. These are societies that are generally characterized by extensive sharing between community members and an emphasis on personal autonomy, leading many to be described as egalitarian. Although these communities are very small, they are characterized by a great intensity of interaction and sharing of space. This is what Nurit Bird-David (2017, 214) calls 'pluripresence', or the way in which:

> Throughout the day, every day, the fewness

of these people, all relatives, impresses itself on the observer – especially the depth of each person's presence to the others, the constant exposure of each not just to one or a few others but to almost all of the others, all of the time, throughout a lifetime.

When you are in these settlements, when you are in these communities, you are present to everyone else around you and they are present to you. You can sense your fellow residents – through all of the senses. This emphasis on shared presence is no accident. David Friesem and Noah Lavi (2019) suggest that:

> the rule of thumb among hunting and gathering societies is that houses are open or semi-open structures, built with very light and easily modified materials. Above all, the house design and site structure among foragers seems to manifest a social preference to ensure maximum sharing, co-presence and living-together.

Living in this way, where your presence to others is manifest all of the time, appears to be key to social relationships and fundamental practices such as sharing. Thomas Widlok (2016) puts it simply as 'sharing needs to be placed on the side that is opposite the house'; in other words, the absence of the house creates the social conditions under which sharing can take place. By sharing space and sharing presence you can build trust.

Barry Hewlett and colleagues (2019) show that living so closely in contact with others changes your body and your disposition. They demonstrate that when people are always aware of the presence of others, and when they physically share space so closely, often sharing physical contact, this proximity changes individuals hormonally: it *makes people feel better about themselves and others*. This then makes them more likely in turn to spend time with other people. The positive feedback loops created by this enable trust to be established. They also point out that if these are ways of living that generate trust, then in contrast, 'Modern living removes the conditions for intimacy and trust'. The choices we are making about how we live today remove those possibilities.

Therefore, I suggest that hunter-gatherers in the Mesolithic of Ireland *chose* to live in tents not just because this was what hunter-gatherers do but because living in tents, living in light, open structures where they shared space with their fellow residents, allowed them to create and maintain a particular form of social world. In particular, this was a choice that generated trust amongst those commu-

Below: **Porphyritic andesite found at Belderrig, County Mayo, but probably from Antrim.**

nities and that allowed them to maintain sharing and egalitarian practices. Living in tents allowed them to live well together.

Above: **Excavation of a Later Mesolithic and Neolithic site, Belderrig, County Mayo, carried out by UCD School of Archaeology.**

SOCIAL CONTACTS

Alongside the idea of people living in small communities bound by trust, it is important to correct common stereotypes that assume that those small communities of hunter-gatherers were defined by a biological extended family and that, beyond this group, foragers otherwise were quite isolated. That is incorrect. As Douglas Bird and colleagues show, '(f)oragers do not live in small-scale societies' (Bird et al. 2019). Ethnography demonstrates very clearly that, although those small units of 20 to 30 people exist, they are highly fluid in composition, they may include people from great distances away and they may even include people from different language groups. Over the course of people's lifetimes, the number of social contacts that foragers had could easily have been in the thousands. These contacts and connections, these links with different people in different places, are enabled through kinship, understood here not as the typical western emphasis on biological relatedness but the more expansive social kinship characteristic of hunter-gatherers, where most of the community is bound together through kinship relationships of some kind.

We have hints of this in the Irish data as well, with many Later Mesolithic sites showing very small amounts of lithic raw material that had come from over 100, and in some cases 200, kilometres away. For example, a piece of porphyritic andesite excavated at the Belderrig site in north County Mayo probably came in from Antrim. These are the sorts of journeys that people might make visiting, making contacts, making connections. Again, these visits and connections are enabled by mobility and movement and a fluid social world where people were bound to each other by recognizing their shared beings.

SUMMARY

At the start of this paper, I said that I wanted to think about how we tell stories about where we have come from and about how people have moved around Ireland and the contacts and connections that were there in the Mesolithic. I think we need to pay really careful attention to concepts that are hidden away in the ways we think about our evidence. I have shown that in two cases, the first being models of isolated populations characterized by technological loss and the second overall population estimates, interpretations of the Mesolithic period in Ireland have been reliant on outdated, incorrect and damaging analogies made to contact-era Tasmania. Some of the sources for these ideas can be described as scientific racism. It is unsurprising that these stories about the Mesolithic in Ireland have stressed that the hunter-gatherer settlement of this island was characterized by impoverishment and isolation. These were the stereotypical views of colonial powers in the nineteenth century – the sources for some of the ideas used to interpret the Mesolithic past. I have suggested that this is neither good scientific practice nor ethical.

In place of this, I have suggested that we can find other approaches to our material. These attempt to tell stories about the choices that people made in the past and how these generated material evidence. Rather than focusing on the rare and unusual, trying to understand the everyday allows us to think about the kinds of societies people lived in. I have suggested that in the Later Mesolithic these choices were about maintaining a physical space for interactions that emphasized co-presence and an awareness of mutuality. Out of this, practices such as sharing and a limit on the development of inequality arose.

I want to close with one other point. We have choices about the ways in which we narrate the lives of long dead hunter-gatherers. Our choice to write about these people – who did not ask us to imagine their lives – carries responsibility. I wonder why we would choose to tell stories that emphasize loss, and describe a fairly miserable, isolated existence. I have tried to recount a story about hunter-gatherers making choices in order to create a social world that emphasized trust and sharing and the relationships between different people in those communities. That, I think, is probably a better story to be telling of our encounters and connections in the past.

Acknowledgements

I am grateful to *Archaeology Ireland* and the National Monuments Service and all of the organisers of 'Imirce: Migration and Ireland through Time' for the invitation to speak and to Wordwell for their work on transforming a spoken word paper into text. To a large extent, this paper draws on research carried out for my book *Hunter-Gatherer Ireland*. I want to acknowledge and thank all of those who made that research possible, too many to name here. Please refer to the Acknowledgements in that book for details. I am grateful to Sadhbh Warren, the National Museum of Ireland, Michael Lynch and Transport Infrastructure Ireland for permission to reproduce images.

BIBLIOGRAPHY

Barnard, A. 2007. *Anthropology and the Bushman*. Oxford: Berg.

Bird, D.W., Bliege Bird, R., Codding, B.F. and Zeanah, D.W. (2019). Variability in the organization and size of hunter-gatherer groups: Foragers do not live in small-scale societies. *Journal of Human Evolution*. 131, pp96–108.

Bird-David, N. 2017. Before Nation: Scale-Blind Anthropology and Foragers' Worlds of Relatives. *Current Anthropology*. 58 (2), pp209–226.

Chapple, R., McLaughlin, R. and Warren, G.M. 2022. '...where they pass their unenterprising existence...': change over time in the Mesolithic of Ireland as shown in radiocarbon-dated activity. *Proceedings of the Royal Irish Academy*. 122, pp1–38.

Conneller, C. 2021. *Mesolithic Britain*. London: Routledge.

Conneller, C. and Warren, G.M. (submitted). Insularisation and isolation? Aligning the Mesolithics of the British and Irish Isles. *Proceedings of the Royal Irish Academy*.

Costa, L.J. and Marchand, G. 2006. Transformations des productions lithiques du premier au second Mésolithique en Bretagne et en Irlande. *Bulletin de la Société préhistorique française*. 103 (2), pp275–290.

Dowd, M. and Carden, R.F. 2016. First evidence of a Late Upper Palaeolithic human presence in Ireland. *Quaternary Science Reviews*. 139, pp158–163.

Edwards, R. and Craven, K. (2017). Relative Sea-level Change Around the Irish Coast *IN*: Coxon, P., McCarron, S. and Mitchell, F. (eds.) *Advances in Irish Quaternary Studies*. Paris: Atlantis Press. pp181–216.

Engl, R. and Gooder, J. 2021. 'A home by the sea': the excavation of a robust Mesolithic house of the late 9th millennium BC at East Barns, East Lothian. *Scottish Archaeological Internet Reports* 96 [Online]. Available from: doi:https://doi.org/10.9750/issn.2056-7421.2021.96. [Accessed 5 April 2024].

Fretheim, S.E. 2017. *Mesolithic dwellings: An empirical approach to past trends and present interpretations in Norway*. Thesis for the Degree of Philosophiae Doctor: Norwegian University of Science and Technology, Trondheim.

Friesem, D.E. and Lavi, N. 2019. An ethnoarchaeological view on hunter-gatherer sharing and its archaeological implications for the use of social space *IN*: Lavi, N. and Friesem, D.E. (eds.)

Towards a Broader View of Hunter-Gatherer Sharing. Cambridge: MacDonald Institute for Archaeological Research. pp85–96.

Griffiths, B. 2018. *Deep Time Dreaming: Uncovering Ancient Australia.* Carlton: Black Inc.

Henrich, J. 2004. Demography and Cultural Evolution: How Adaptive Cultural Processes can Produce Maladaptive Losses: The Tasmanian Case. *American Antiquity.* 69 (2), pp197–214.

Hewlett, B.S., Hudson, J., Boyette, A.H. and Fouts, H.N. 2019. Intimate living: sharing space among Aka and other hunter-gatherers *IN*: Lavi, N. and Friesem, D.E. (eds.) *Towards a Broader View of Hunter-Gatherer Sharing.* Cambridge: MacDonald Institute for Archaeological Research. pp39–56.

Holdaway, S. and Douglass, M. 2012. A Twenty-First Century Archaeology of Stone Artifacts. *Journal of Archaeological Method and Theory.* 19 (1), pp101–131.

McCartan, S. 2004. The Mesolithic in the Isle of Man: an Island Perspective *IN*: Saville, A. (ed.) *Mesolithic Scotland and its Neighbours: The Early Holocene Prehistory of Scotland, its British and Irish Context and some Northern European Perspectives.* Edinburgh: Society of Antiquaries of Scotland. pp271–284.

Milks, A. 2020. A Review of Ethnographic Use of Wooden Spears and Implications for Pleistocene Hominin Hunting. *Open Quaternary.* 6 (1), p12.

Moucheron, M. and Warren, G.M. 2022. The Mesolithic in the Proceedings of the Royal Irish Academy: An overview. *Proceedings of the Royal Irish Academy: Archaeology, Culture, History, Literature.* 122, pp1–18.

Movius, H. (1942) *The Irish Stone Age: Its Chronology, Development and Relationships.* Cambridge: Cambridge University Press.

Mucher, C. 2021. 'Born of the Soil': Demography, Demographic Narratives and American Origins *IN*: Mackenthun, G. and Mucher, C. (eds.) *Decolonizing "Prehistory": Deep Time and Indigenous Knowledges in North America.* Tucson: University of Arizona Press. pp. 51–70.

Riede, F. 2009. Climate and Demography in Early Prehistory: Using Calibrated 14C Dates as Population Proxies. *Human Biology.* 81 (2/3), pp309–337.

Riede, F., Edinborough, K. and Thomas, M.G. 2009. Tracking Mesolithic Demography in Time and Space and its Implications for Explanations of Culture Change *IN*: Crombé, P., Van Strydonck, M., Sergant, J., Boudin, M. and Bats, M. (eds.) *Chronology and Evolution within the Mesolithic of North-West Europe: Proceedings of an International Meeting, Brussels,* 30 May–1 June 2007. Newcastle: Cambridge Scholars Publishing. pp177–194.

Ryan, L. 2012. *Tasmanian Aborigines: a history since 1803.* London: Allen & Unwin.

Taylor, R. 2008. The polemics of making fire in Tasmania: the historical evidence revisited. *Aboriginal History*, 32, 1-26. Melbourne: Melbourne University Press.

Taylor, R. 2017. Into the Heart of Tasmania: a search for human antiquity. Melbourne: Melbourne University Press.

Waddell, J. 2020. Early Demographic Ebb and Flow in Pre-census Ireland. *Emania.* 25, pp53–59.

Warren, G.M. 2020. Climate change and hunter gatherers in Ireland: problems, potentials and pressing research questions. *Proceedings of the Royal Irish Academy: Archaeology, Culture, History, Literature.* 120C, pp1–22.

Warren, G.M. 2022a. *Hunter-Gatherer Ireland: making connections in an island world.* Oxford: Oxbow.

Warren, G.M. 2022b. *Our Ancient Landscapes: Hunter-Gatherers in Ireland.* Dublin: An Chomhairle Oidhreachta / The Heritage Council.

Widlok, T. 2016. *Anthropology and the Economy of Sharing.* London: Routledge.

Woodman, P.C. 1978. *The Mesolithic in Ireland: Hunter-Gatherers in an Insular Environment.* British Archaeological Reports, British Series 58.

Woodman, P.C. 1985. *Excavations at Mount Sandel 1973–77, County Londonderry.* Belfast: HMSO.

Woodman, P.C. 2015. *Ireland's First Settlers: Time and the Mesolithic.* Oxford: Oxbow.

Woodman, P.C., Finlay, N. and Anderson, E. 2006. *The Archaeology of a Collection: the Keiller-Knowles collection of the National Museum of Ireland.* Dublin: Wordwell.

CHAPTER 4

Archaeological Remains of Coffee Plantations: A history of pre-Famine Irish migration to Cuba

GISELLE GONZÁLEZ GARCÍA

Giselle González García is a PhD candidate in History at Montreal's Concordia University and School of Irish Studies. Her primary areas of interest are Irish migration to colonial Cuba, Irish coffee plantations in Cuba, material culture, memory studies, and global Irish diaspora studies. Here, she brings the reader to Cuba's eastern region and examines the Irish presence on the island and, in particular, in its coffee industry.

In February 2020, I visited Santiago de Cuba, the country's second main city, to research archival sources and material remains of an Irish historical presence in that region. Once there, I noticed a coffee shop that was located in a very central position at Plaza de Martes, one of the city's main squares, which had the name of a coffee plantation that I was researching. This was La Gran Sofía café and it was named after La Gran Sofía plantation, which I knew had once been owned by a native of Dublin, James Jenkinson Wright (1788–1845). From this estate, I found out later, he had often written letters to his aunts and cousins who lived in Dublin in which he discussed his conversion to Catholicism – he was from a Quaker family – and his experiences as a coffee planter and slave-owner in Santiago (González García 2020).

What was most striking to me at the time of my 2020 visit to this café was that it was decorated with images of the archaeological remains of its namesake. What they were trying to do, through pictures on the walls and decoration, was to identify this café as part of the French cultural legacy of the city. It turned out, this was one of many new establishments in Santiago that had been opened in 2015 to mark the five-hundredth anniversary of the foundation of the city. Arguably, this café commemorates La Gran Sofía as an important part of the coffee legacy of the region but not James Wright, its Irish owner.

La Gran Sofía is only one of 171 archaeological remains of coffee plantations identified in the mountains of La Sierra Maestra in a relatively small part of Cuba's eastern region (López Segrera 2010). Thus far, I have found that at least 28 of those were actually linked to Irish immigrants who arrived in Cuba in two different waves. For the purpose of this paper, I have separated these migrations into two groups to be able to describe specific characteristics of each. I will try to provide some answers to the following questions: how did Irish immigrants arrive and settle in early nineteenth-century Santiago de Cuba, in the south-eastern part of the

Opposite page, above: **Map of Irish properties in Cuba, including the estimated area where the coffee plantations were located.**

Opposite page, right: **Map of Irish coffee plantations in La Sierra Maestra.**

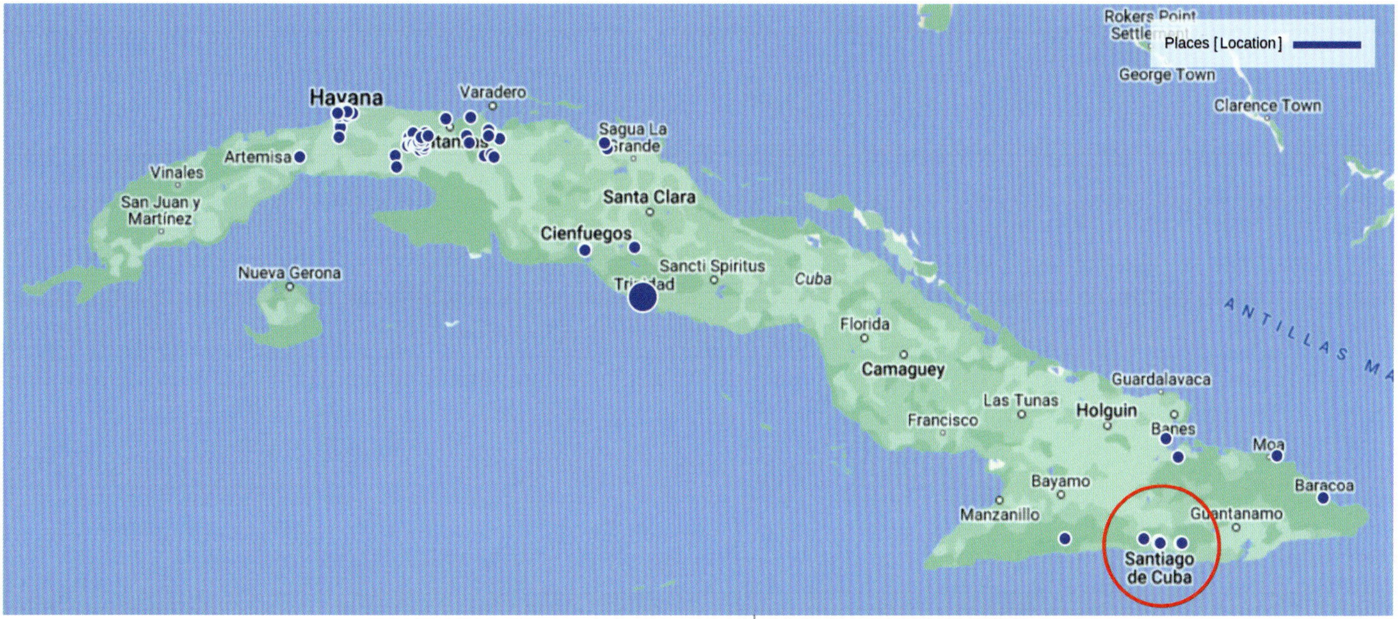
Places [Location]
Rokers Point
George Town
Clarence Town
Havana
Varadero
Artemisa
Vinales
San Juan y Martinez
Sagua La Grande
Santa Clara
Cienfuegos
Nueva Gerona
Sancti Spiritus
Cuba
Florida
Camaguey
Guardalavaca
Las Tunas
Holguin
Francisco
Banes
Moa
Baracoa
Bayamo
Manzanillo
Guantanamo
Santiago de Cuba

Places [Location]
La Maya
Boniatico
Platanillo
Santa Cruz
Estrella Roja
Sabanilla
Loma del gato
Arroyito
El Cristo
El Cujabo
Corea
Bell
El Recuerdo
Bell
La Candelaria
Cabañas
Yerba de Guinea
Arroyo Negro
Las Yaguas
La Juba
Kindelan
Santa Ana
San Juan
Micro 8
Reparto Sagarra
Reparto Vista Alegre
Santiago de Cuba
Reparto Vista Hermosa
Abel Santamaría
El Ramón
Kindelan
Santa Bárbara
Bell
Soledad
Kindelan
Humanidad
Creagh
Rincón
O'Callaghan & Wanton
Santa Rosa
Kindelan
El Olimpo
Kindelan
La Idalia
Wright
Kentucky
Wright
Santa Rita
Casimba
Wright - El Santiago
Wright - La Carolina
Poblado de Sevilla
Bell
Perseverancia
Africa
Wright
La Gran Sofía
Los Coquitos
Las Guásimas
Poblado de El Brujo
Firmeza
La Caridad
Siboney
Map data ©2024 Google - nodegoat

island? Why did they take an interest in coffee planting specifically? Why are these archaeological remains relevant today and why should they be studied at all? What do they tell us about Irish migration?

As my area of study is History rather than Archaeology, I focus here on the historic aspects of this subject and present the information about these plantations that I have gathered to date.

HISTORICAL CONTEXT

For hundreds of pre-Famine Irish immigrants,

Above: **Morro Castle and entry to the Port-City of Santiago de Cuba (1855).**

Opposite page: **A view of nineteenth-century Santiago de Cuba by artist Winslow Homer.**

Cuba was an island of opportunities. These often lay in the burgeoning sugar and coffee industries that dominated the island's economy during the first half of the nineteenth century. In 1807, Santiago de Cuba was a small – but rapidly growing – city that had a local elite, which hoped to compete with Havana in the west of the island. In 1791, due to its geographical proximity to the neighbouring French colony of Haiti/Saint-Domingue, Santiago de Cuba became the recipient of multiple waves of thousands of refugees who fled from turmoil caused by the revolution there. It was this largely 'French' influx that local historians have credited with

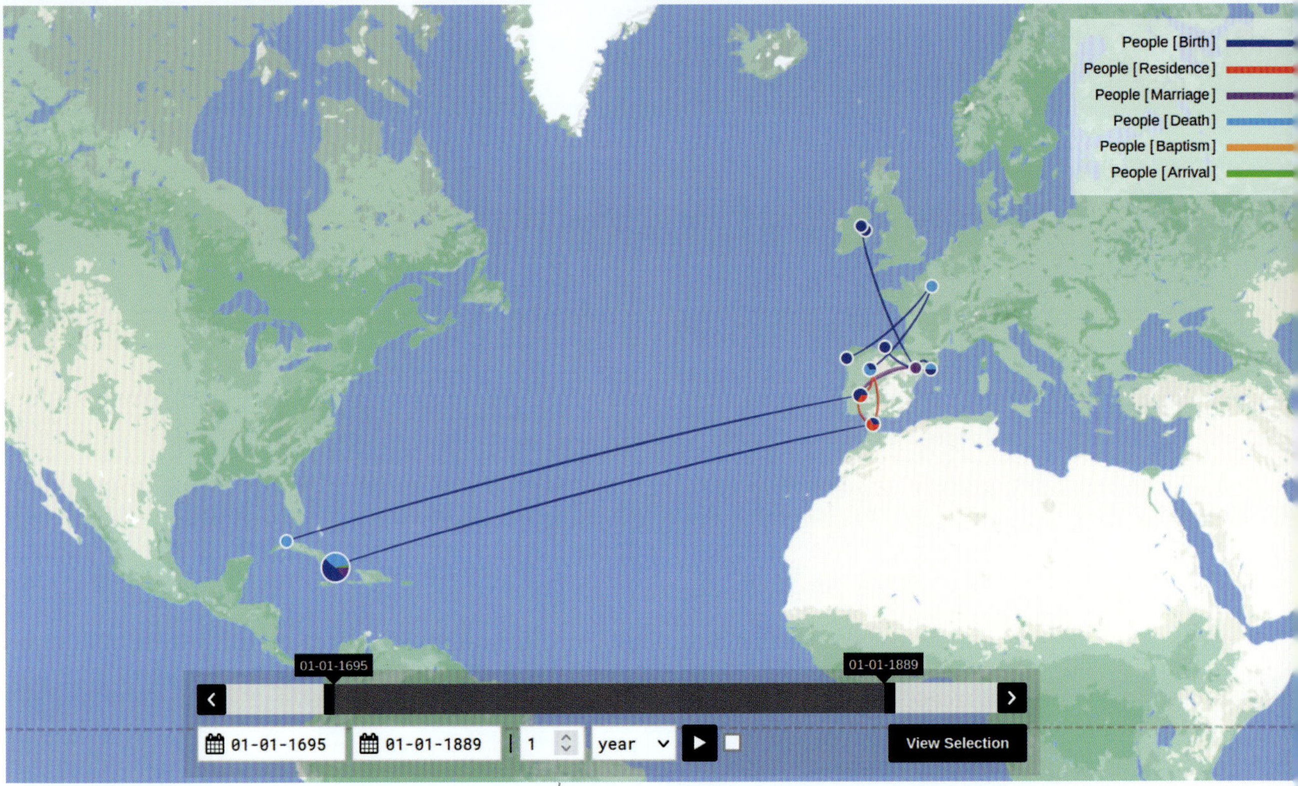
People [Birth]
People [Residence]
People [Marriage]
People [Death]
People [Baptism]
People [Arrival]
01-01-1695
01-01-1889
01-01-1695
01-01-1889
1
year
View Selection

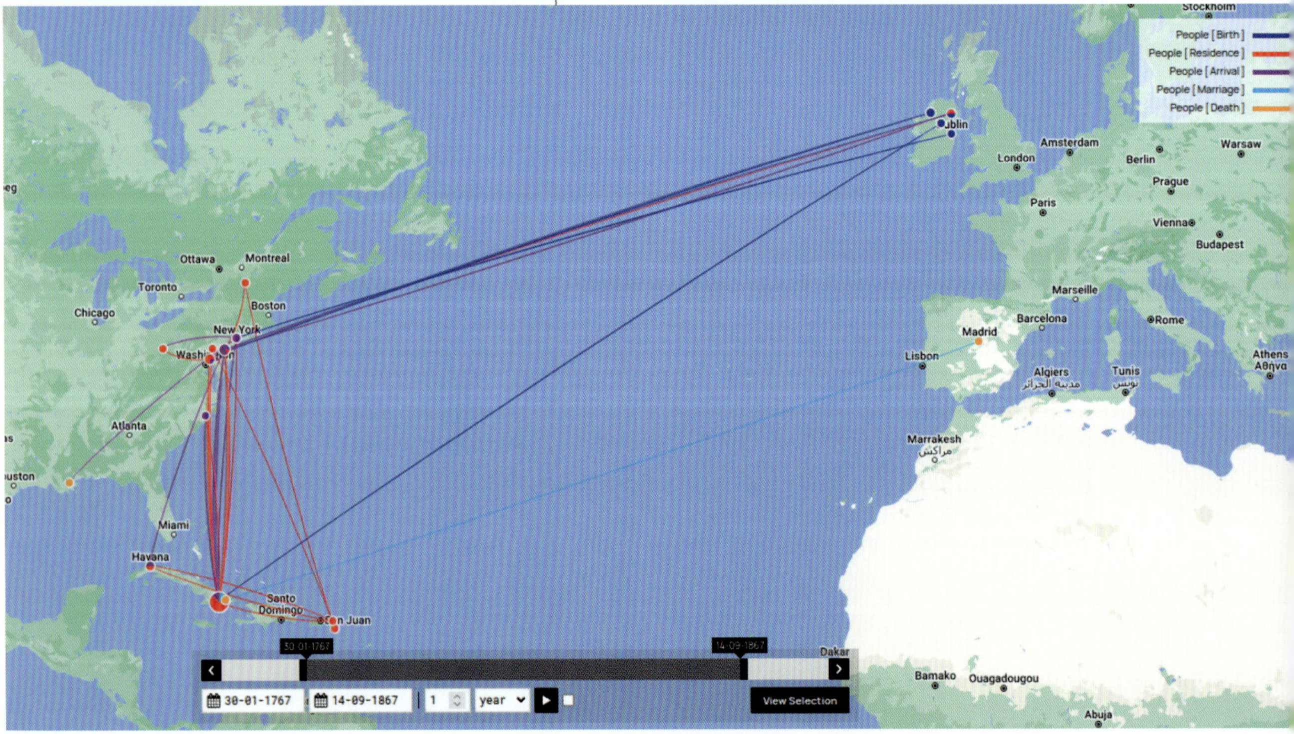
People [Birth]
People [Residence]
People [Arrival]
People [Marriage]
People [Death]
Stockholm
Dublin
London
Amsterdam
Berlin
Warsaw
Prague
Paris
Vienna
Budapest
Marseille
Barcelona
Rome
Madrid
Lisbon
Athens
Αθήνα
Algiers
الجزائر
Tunis
تونس
Marrakesh
مراكش
Ottawa
Montreal
Toronto
Boston
Chicago
New York
Washington
Atlanta
Miami
Havana
Santo Domingo
San Juan
Dakar
Bamako
Ouagadougou
Abuja
30-01-1767
14-09-1867
1
year
View Selection

the inception of a coffee industry that dominated world markets in subsequent decades (López Segrera 2010).

The participation of Irish immigrants in these processes has been overshadowed by the much higher numbers of French ones. However, although the number of Irish immigrants was small – I estimate that they were less than one per cent of the population – they still made a significant impact in the area by becoming part of the city's planter and merchant elite, and by expanding the international reach of the local economy through the export of staple goods. They also exerted a considerable influence in local institutions and local politics (González García 2020). For example, by the 1830s, two of the biggest coffee plantations – La Gran Sofía and Kentucky – were owned by the Irish immigrant James J. Wright (Archivo Histórico Provincial de Santiago de Cuba, Protocolos Notariales). He was a Quaker turned Catholic who was, at times, British consul, coffee planter, slave owner, merchant, and commercial agent for different enterprises based in Cuba, the United States and Britain. He was not the only one.

'WILD GEESE' IRISH

An Irish presence in Santiago de Cuba dates back to 1665 (Fernández Moya 2007). The first group that settled in the area developed a sense of symbolic Irish identity expressed through their naming practices (González García 2020). They had a hand in creating a local elite into which immigrants from the second group inserted themselves in the early decades of the nineteenth century. Members of the first group started to arrive in the late seventeenth century and continued to do so until the late eighteenth century. They had ties to the Irish 'Wild Geese' families that had fled to continental Europe after the 1607 Flight of the Earls and Plantation of Ulster, after the Cromwellian conquest of Ireland in 1649 and the Treaty of Limerick in 1691. Throughout the eighteenth century, the Irish 'Wild Geese' numbers were replenished following a very intricate policy of recruitment (Recio Morales 2010). In Spain and in Spanish America, many of these families became staunch supporters of colonial domination and the maintenance of a slavery regime (Fanning 2016). Members of this group constructed an Irish identity that was intrinsically linked to Roman Catholicism and was based on a 'special relationship' with the Spanish monarchy. They constructed a 'special status' that allowed members of this group to insert themselves into the local elite cohorts and to effect social climbing strategies (Provencio Garrigós 1994, Recio Morales 2012).

Cuban records show that they were mostly military men who used marriage effectively to access wealth and land ownership. They also claimed nobility, which was a coveted status sought by a Cuban-Creole planter class that was consolidating its sphere of influence on the island and was expanding its economic power.

As examples of families in this group, there

Opposite page, above: **Irish 'Wild Geese' migratory routes to Cuba.**

Opposite page, below: **Migratory routes of second group of Irish immigrants to Cuba.**

were the Duany family, originally from County Sligo; the Kindelán family, who were from County Meath and had left Ireland after the Cromwellian invasion; the O'Naghten family, who came from Athlone and the border areas between counties Roscommon and Westmeath; and the MacCrohons, who were from Galway. Other examples include the Garvey and Creagh families, whose specific regional origins in Ireland have not been determined yet.

PRE-FAMINE MIGRANTS

By contrast, the second group of Irish immigrants to Santiago was composed of a wider cohort of transnational and trans-imperial adventurers. Their arrival in Cuba coincided with the consolidation of the social climbing strategies of the Santiago-based 'Wild Geese' during the administration of first-generation Irishman Sebastián Kindelán O'Regan (1757–1826), who was Political and Military Governor of the Santiago province during the key years for the development of the coffee industry, from 1799 until 1810. Kindelán not only enabled the development of coffee plantations through a tax exemption policy but he became a planter and slave owner himself, alongside his wife, third-generation Irish Ana Manuela Mozo de la Torre Garvey (1780–1840) (Orozco Melgar 2007).

Below: **Signature in 1818 of Sebastián Kindelán O'Regan (1757–1826).**

Opposite page: **Letter written by James J. Wright, Santiago de Cuba, to Martha Wright, Dublin (February 28, 1834).**

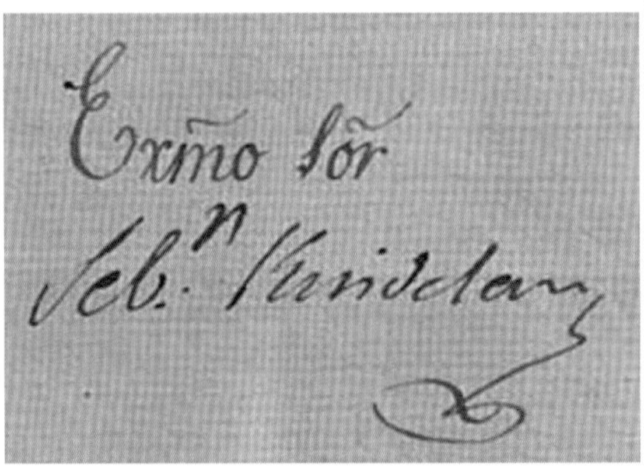

The members of the second migration group began to arrive in the first years of the 1800s and they had no links to Spain, no special relationship with the Spanish Crown and initially no stake in Roman Catholicism. This marked a shift in the route that was bringing Irish immigrants into Cuba, from Spain and continental Europe to North America and, particularly, to the Atlantic coastal cities of the United States. This group's members experienced an important transformation in their identities. They reinvented themselves ideologically and politically by drifting further away from republicanism and becoming conservative endorsers of slavery and Spanish colonial domination. In terms of religion, they adopted Spanish Catholicism by effecting strategic conversions but they were not fully embraced as such and were often the subject of suspicion by Spanish colonial authorities and the local population (González García 2020).

Moreover, although their political loyalties lay with Spain and the Spanish-American empire in theory, in practice the economic interests of many of these Irish immigrants

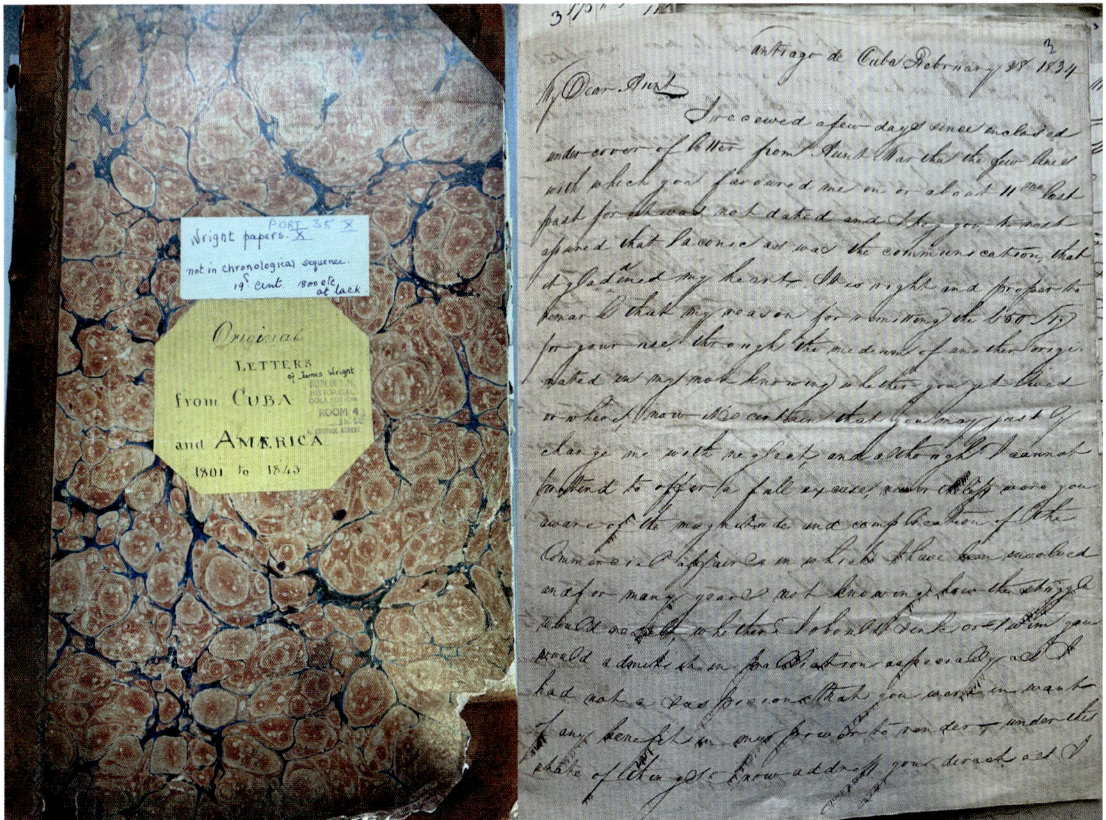

were actually best served in the establishment of an informal commercial relationship that prioritized the interests of the more attractive, and geographically closer, United States. Their focus in North America differentiates them from the 'Wild Geese' Irish. The migratory origins of this group can be traced to Baltimore and Philadelphia specifically. Several of their members were actually Irish Quakers who became Catholics and then subscribed to a pro-slavery ideology and articulated a paternalistic discourse that was similar to the one often found in the old south of the United States to justify slavery.

In Santiago de Cuba, these Irish Quakers followed specific strategies for integration. These were: religious conversion, naturalization (i.e. they became Spanish subjects), creation of an intricate business network, engagement in the African slave trade and in the purchase of rural and urban properties in and around Santiago. Some case studies of Irish men that fit this characterization were Dubliner James Jenkinson (*Santiago*) Wright (1788–1845), to whom I referred earlier and whose family originally had settled in Ballinclay, near Gorey in County Wexford; Armagh native Richard Maxwell (*Ricardo*

María) Bell (1777–1847); brothers William (*Guillermo*) B. and Samuel Wanton (?-1842), originally from Ballintra, in County Donegal; Simon and Cornelius (*Cornelio*) O'Callaghan; and Philip (*Felipe*) Boylan, who was from County Cavan. Of this group, only Bell and O'Callaghan established family units in Santiago; the others acted more as individuals and kept close kinship ties with the United States and Ireland (Archivo Histórico Provincial de Santiago de Cuba, Protocolos Notariales).

By 1827, these two groups, the Irish Wild Geese and the later, predominantly Quaker, migrants, had merged into an elite cohort. They interconnected and created a web of close alliances and fierce competition. Moreover, these Irish immigrants in Santiago de Cuba interacted closely with French, English and Scottish immigrants. Often, the coffee plantations that they purchased were developed alongside French settlers or in partnership with them. Many of these plantations retained their original French names, for example, La Gran Sofía had originally been named Sophie. This gives us a hint as to why they are recorded as part of a French cultural legacy, thereby obscuring Irish migratory experiences.

COFFEE PLANTING

Historians generally agree that coffee was introduced to Cuba around the year 1748 (García Álvarez 2008). However, it did not emerge as a significant plantation crop until the early decades of the nineteenth century. Two main geographical areas became coffee hubs, one in the west of Cuba and one in the east. This had to do with local climate conditions in those areas and with the natural elevation of the terrain, which is required for growing coffee. In western Cuba, the area south-west of Havana was particularly settled for this purpose, creating a coffee belt around the towns of El Wajay (today, Guajay), the Vuelta Abajo region in La Sierra del Rosario, and in Matanzas (Van Norman 2013). In the west, the land was significantly more expensive.

In contrast, in 1790, just a year before the Haitian revolution, only five or six estates existed in eastern Cuba (López Segrera 2010). There was plenty of land available to be developed into coffee plantations there. A decade later, the price of land in the east was still significantly cheaper than in the west but planters in eastern Cuba were deficient in knowledge, lacked the workforce or had limited access to the experience required for extensive investment in coffee. This allowed refugees from Saint-Domingue (p65) to leverage their capital and know-how to ensure their permanence in Cuba as refugees. In a short span of time, from 1800 until 1807, they acquired vast expanses of land, trafficked thousands of enslaved Africans and laid down the first coffee plantations in La Sierra Maestra (Bandera Merlet 1982).

However, in 1810, in the context of the invasion of Spain by Napoleon Bonaparte's forces, as part of the Peninsular War (1808–1814) and wider European campaigns, French people were asked to leave Spanish domains. The vacuum left by their departure created an opportunity for the local Cuban-Creole elite and for Irish and other migrants to invest in coffee planting.

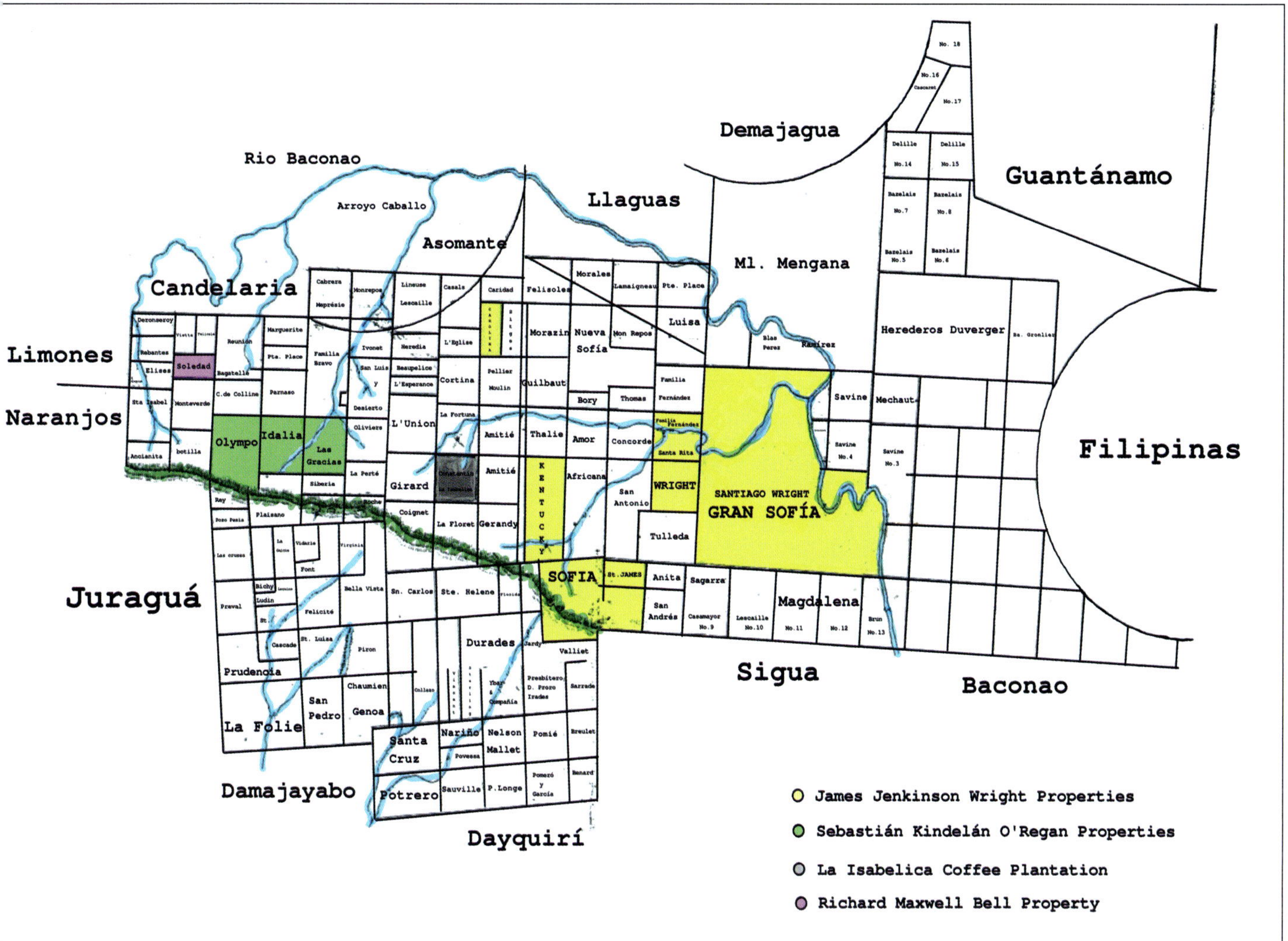

Above: **Land plots and jurisdictional divisions in La Sierra Maestra. Based on the 1832 map of the terrains bought by Prudencio Casamayor in the zone between Guantánamo and Juraguá.**

UNESCO HERITAGE

Although an Irish presence was widespread all over the island of Cuba and they were involved in coffee planting in both of the regions I have mentioned, in this paper I will refer only to the plantations located in eastern Cuba because today these plantations are recognized as a UNESCO World Heritage site (González García 2023). In total, I have

identified 40 Irish coffee plantations linked to Irish immigrants and their descendants island-wide, 12 located in the west and 28 in the east. From the 28 that I have found in the east, I was able to retrieve the precise geographic co-ordinates of only 17. Locating the majority of these estates was a very difficult process because it involved cross-referencing archival manuscripts that are not in good condition with historical maps and also with the documentation submitted by Cuban authorities to UNESCO in the 1990s (UNESCO).

Above: ***Cafetal La Ermita en las lomas del Cusco*** **[La Ermita coffee plantation in the hills of Cusco].**

Furthermore, few of these estates have been studied in detail and their study is significantly hindered by several factors. Firstly, after Hurricane Sandy in 2012, the access roads to where they are located in the mountains were significantly damaged.

Secondly, historical manuscript sources are inaccessible due to structural damage suffered by the building that houses the Provincial Archives in Santiago. Lastly, the few manuscript records that have been digitized by local researchers show the extent of the deterioration of these valuable sources. Some of them have become completely unreadable. Yet, from these scarce sources that I was able to access, courtesy of Santiago's Centre for Interpretation of the Coffee Cultural Heritage, I could discern a certain modus operandi for Irish planters in the city.

SLAVERY AND TRADE

Many of the Irish-born immigrants that established themselves in Santiago de Cuba from 1810 to 1814 became involved in the slave trade, an enterprise that was legal until 1820 (González García 2020). However, there is evidence that, even after it became illegal, several Irishmen, like James Wright and the Wanton brothers, continued to be involved in the trade in order to counter the significant losses that they had suffered due to crop failures in 1824 and 1825. Even when crops did not fail, other planters, such as Richard Maxwell Bell, would not only sell the products of their own plantation but they would also buy the products of other local planters and try to become their commercial agents (i.e. some sort of middle men). Many of these immigrants preferred to reside in their haciendas on their coffee plantations in the mountains but others still purchased homes adjacent to the docks in Santiago, which was a convenient location. This indicated a change in mentality in which business took precedence over comfort. Residing near the docks broke also the custom followed by the established local elite who preferred to live near the more fashionable plazas or squares. For example, the 'Wild Geese' families like the Kindeláns and Duanys had their urban residences at the Plaza de Dolores, one of the principal squares (Orozco Melgar 2007).

Although immigrants like Wright and Bell were exporting coffee produced on their own plantations, they also became middlemen to other planters and in the international market. They not only purchased coffee, they also bought muscovado sugar, molasses, tobacco, rum and other tropical products. Occasionally, Wright and his partners made purchases from planters not based in the east but based in the middle of the island in areas like Trinidad and Cienfuegos. They also had a network of people in what was called at the time Cumberland Harbour, which today we refer to as Guantanamo Bay (Archivo Histórico de la Ciudad de la Habana, Moses Taylor Collection).

A valuable source that gives us details of the day-to-day operations of Irish coffee plantations is the Moses Taylor Collection held at the New York Public Library, with copies at the Historical Archives of the City of Havana. These records show that planters like Wright, for example, could participate in the commission trade and enlist their own ships, if they had contacts abroad that they could rely on. Once shipped, the products were received, redistributed and sold by a network of agents and representatives. These agents' role was to procure insurance for the cargo, to enlist reliable captains to command the vessels, and to provide information on the demand for a specific product and the movements in its price. They were also responsible for sending gold and silver to facilitate payments because there were no financial institutions established in Cuba at the time. Therefore, people like James J. Wright, who had their own merchant houses, had to act as their own banks (Archivo Histórico de la Ciudad de la Habana, Moses Taylor Collection).

Below: **Santiago de Cuba street scene. Watercolour by American artist Winslow Homer.**

Opposite page: **La Isabelica coffee plantation museum today.**

The network of agents that Wright, for example, put together extended back to New York, Philadelphia, Baltimore, Boston and the United Kingdom. Wright had a very close association with the famous Baring Brothers' bank in London that had managed the Louisiana Purchase of French territory by the United States in 1803 (Barings Archives, Series House Correspondence 4/4.6.6, 1842). Even in the middle of the island, they had their own agents in the shape of Wittram & Co. In this way, they were able to create a transnational business model that was outwards oriented but much of their success relied on personal relationships and on kinship and social networks.

ARCHAEOLOGY OF PLANTATIONS

Turning now to discuss the archaeological remains of Irish plantations, the Office of the City's Conservators (CCO) of Santiago de Cuba has had a particular interest in studying the legacy of what they call 'French' immigration to Santiago and the shift to a coffee culture that radically transformed the whole province, socially and environmentally. As an institution, the CCO is invested in preserving, restoring and rescuing sites like La Gran Sofía because they are symbolic spaces associated with the fusion of cultural elements that led to the construction of a Cuban nation and a Cuban identity. This is how they present their projects. However, like other areas of the country, in reality the academic research that they undertake goes hand-in-hand with the promotion of tourism, an industry on which the current Cuban economy is highly dependent (López Segrera 2010). As such, coffee plantations that have been linked to Irish immigrants have been included in tourist routes like the Ruta del Café (Coffee Routes) and they plan to make them accessible to visiting tourists. To make the sites attractive, the CCO has planned the restoration of the best-preserved plantations and they have subdivided the area into two visitor circuits, North and South. Interestingly, three out of the five 'French' coffee plantations that they included in the South Circuit, which are La Idalia, Siberia, La Isabelica, Las Mercedes and La Gran Sofía, have a direct Irish connection in their histories. Several others in this area actually belonged also to Irish immigrants and their descendants and are located close to the pre-designed tourist route.

Why are these archaeological remains of coffee plantations attractive and useful in promoting tourism? What can we learn from visiting the sites? How easy is it to actually

ESTATES OWNED BY THE KINDELÁN-MOZO DE LA TORRE-GARVEY FAMILY				
Family Group	**Owner**	**Plantation Name**	**Product**	**Value** (in pesos)
Kindelán	Sebastian Kindelán O'Regan	Santa Ana	Coffee	128,691.00
Kindelán	Sebastian Kindelán O'Regan	Trinidad del Olimpo	Coffee	62,676.50
Kindelán	Sebastian Kindelán O'Regan	Santa Bárbara del Guayabal	Coffee	1,058.00
Kindelán	Sebastian Kindelán O'Regan	La Caridad de las Gracias	Coffee	86,313.00
Kindelán	Sebastian Kindelán O'Regan	San Cayetano de Aguadores	Sugar	2,792.00
Kindelán	Sebastian Kindelán O'Regan	Humanidad		
Kindelán	Sebastian Kindelán O'Regan	Concepción de la Idalia	Coffee	22,535.00
Garvey	Ana Manuela Mozo de la Torre Garvey	La Lima	Sugar	
Garvey	Ana Manuela Mozo de la Torre Garvey	Marcos Sánchez	Sugar	
Garvey	Ana Manuela Mozo de la Torre Garvey	Trinidad del Olimpo	Coffee	

Compiled from Archivo Provincial de Santiago de Cuba (Protocolos Notariales, 1814, 1819, 1845).

access them and are there no concerns with the impact of mass tourism on the sites themselves? Taking Circuito Sur (South Route) as an example, I visited La Isabelica coffee plantation in 2020. La Isabelica is considered a model plantation in that it has been preserved as a museum since the 1960s.

Even this popular site was challenging to get to in 2020. The visitor has to travel on the mountain road that leads to La Gran Piedra, a huge volcanic rock that is a landmark tourist attraction in the area. This road then ends abruptly and from there to La Isabelica Coffee Plantation Museum there are approximately two kilometres of rough terrain. Back in 2020, I wanted to go all the way to La Gran Sofía coffee plantation, which is located eight kilometres east of La Gran Piedra, near Pico Mogote, six kilometres approximately from La Isabelica. However, when I reached the area, the locals advised me against the hike, which shows how difficult it is to access and visit plantations like La Gran Sofía.

During this same research trip, I interviewed Dr Yaumara López Segrera, who was then the director of the Centre for Interpretation of the Coffee Cultural Heritage. Dr López Segrera reported that La Gran Sofía was by far one of the most formidable plantations in the area but that, even with their resources and logistics, they had trouble getting to the site. When I asked her why this particular plantation was so fascinating to her, she stated: 'we were in awe of how big its slave barracks were', because, unlike sugar, coffee did not necessitate a numerous labour force. Dr López Segrera estimated that around 100 enslaved people were held at La Gran Sofía. However, in one of his letters to Dublin, James Wright reported as much as 300, a number that is comparable to the wealthier sugar plantations in the west.

Certainly, James Wright became one of the biggest landowners in the area. I am convinced that it was land ownership more than anything else that cemented his status and that of his cohort of Irish immigrants.

From 1812 to 1827, alongside his partners Antonio Vinent Ferrer and Henry Shelton, Wright managed to own eight different coffee plantations in close proximity to La Gran Sofía. These were named La Gran Sofía, Santiago, which also appears with the names of St James or St Jaime, Kentucky or El Kentuckito (Little Kentucky), La Carolina, Andalucía, El Potrero, and Santa Rita (Archivo Histórico Provincial de Santiago de Cuba, Protocolos Notariales). Of the eight, I have only managed to find the geographical co-ordinates of five.

After Wright, the Kindelán-Garvey family, which had a 'Wild Geese' origin, owned a total of seven different estates, six dedicated to coffee and one to sugar, of which I have only been able to locate five on the maps. These are, Trinidad del Olimpo, Santa Ana, Santa Bárbara del Guayabal, Humanidad and Concepción de la Idalia. These had a combined value of 300,000 pesos, which was a considerable fortune at the time (Archivo Histórico Provincial de Santiago de Cuba, Protocolos Notariales).

Another Irish immigrant from Lurgan in County Armagh, Richard Maxwell Bell, was listed as the owner of six plantations, two of which specialized in coffee. These are El Recuerdo, Soledad, Santa Elena de la Demajagua, La Perseverancia, Santa Ana and La Candelaria de Guayama (Archivo Histórico Provincial de Santiago de Cuba, Protocolos Notariales). Of these six plantations, I have only found the locations of four. Under the tenure of Bell's son, La Perseverancia, a sugar plantation located in

Below: **Remains of slave barracks at the archaeological site of coffee plantation La Gran Sofía, identified by Dr Yaumara López Segrera and her team *c.*2010.**

Bottom: **The main house at the archaeological site of coffee plantation La Gran Sofía, identified by Dr Yaumara López Segrera and her team *c.*2010.**

Opposite page: **Estates owned by the Kindelán-Mozo de la Torre-Garvey family.**

Tí Arriba, was reportedly valued at 294,954 pesos. Although it was destroyed during the War of 1868, the land where La Perseverancia was located is owned today by the Cuban state and it is in very bad condition, according to their own reports to UNESCO. However, this land is prized because of its 'potential archaeological value'. Bell's Santa Elena coffee plantation also had a significant enslaved population, amounting to 250 people.

As part of my research, I found a very interesting letter sent on 31 October 1842. It was from Charles Clarke, who was at the time British Consul in Santiago, writing to the mayor of Lifford in County Donegal. He wrote the following:

> Sir, A Mr. Samuel Wanton, some years back formed a partnership with a Don Juan Morales in the purchase of a Coffee Estate called Santa Rosa situated in the district of Santiago de Cuba. Wanton has died as has also Morales, and I am informed that the Heir to the former is Mrs Margaret Wanton who resides in the Town of Balintra [sic], County of Donegal, Ireland. (National Archives at Kew Gardens, Foreign Office, 453, p300).

I have thus far not retrieved any information about this Wanton family from County Donegal. However, Cuban sources indicate that they retained the property of the Santa Rosa estate until at least the beginning of the twentieth century.

OBSCURED IDENTITY

A considerable proportion of the material heritage of the coffee plantations is today in an archaeological state with structures partially or completely buried. To local historians, these sites of memory evoke a fascinating history of migration but not necessarily an Irish one. Their curation of this heritage for the general public as 'French' has obscured the participation of Irish migrants in a historical process of expansion of a plantation economy that was sustained by the enslavement of thousands of Africans and gave rise to the cultural and economic renaissance of an entire region from the late 1790s until the early 1840s. The 28 Irish coffee plantations I have identified in the east, 17 of which I have actually been able to locate, stand as material evidence of the interconnected history of our two island nations – Ireland and Cuba – extending on opposite sides of the Atlantic world and the Atlantic economy.

The success of Cuban exports at the time was credited to a generically 'homogenous' North American group of merchants and this umbrella term is frequently found in Cuban historiography but it does not differentiate Irish people from Scottish, from Irish-Americans, from Anglo-Americans and others. Thus, the experiences of the Irish in Cuba have been at best a curious footnote in the work of very prominent historians. My work, and that of other scholars (Brehony and Finnegan 2019, Burton 2019, Chinea 2007, Rodgers 2009), addresses this historiographical gap and contextualizes the nuanced history that situates a pre-famine Irish diaspora on both sides of processes of colonialism and empire building.

The Cuban coffee industry started to

decline in the late 1840s due to the rise of Brazilian and Javan coffees, which were cheaper to produce than Cuba's. As for the Irish coffee estates, many suffered significantly during the earthquake of 1852 and were further damaged during the anti-colonial wars for Cuban independence from 1868 to 1878 and from 1895 to 1898. The industry never recovered to its pre-war levels. But the remains of these coffee plantations are still there in the mountains waiting to be studied.

Acknowledgements

I want to thank Dr Yaumara López Segrera and the *Centro de Interpretación de la Cultura del Café* (Centre for the Interpretation of Coffee Culture Heritage) in Santiago de Cuba, for their kind help in my research and in preparing this paper. I am also grateful to Professor Emeritus Kerby A. Miller, the Historical Library of the Society of Friends (Dublin Meeting), the staff at the Barings Archives and the National Archives in London, Dr Jane Ohlmeyer at Trinity College Dublin, the School of Irish Studies at Concordia University in Montréal, and MITACS Globalink.

BIBLIOGRAPHY

Bandera Merlet, I. 1982. *El Gobierno de Sebastián Kindelán en el Departamento Oriental, 1799–1810*. Bachelor Thesis, Universidad de Oriente, Santiago de Cuba.

Brehony, M. and Finnegan, N. (eds.) 2019. *Cuba y Irlanda: Historias Entretejidas / Cuba and Ireland: Entangled Histories*. Havana: Ediciones Boloña.

Burton, G. 2019. Richard Robert Madden, A Twelvemonth's residence in the West Indies *IN*: Brehony, M. and Finnegan, N. (eds.) *Cuba y Irlanda: Historias Entretejidas / Cuba & Ireland: Entangled Histories*. Havana: Ediciones Boloña.

Chinea, J. 2007. Irish Indentured Servants, Papists and Colonists in Spanish Colonial Puerto Rico, ca. 1650-1800. *Irish Migration Studies in Latin America*. 5 (3).

Fanning, T. 2016. *Paisanos: the forgotten Irish who changed the face of Latin America*. Dublin: Gill Books.

Fernández Moya, R. 2007. The Irish Presence in the History and Placenames of Cuba. *Irish Migration Studies in Latin America*. 5 (3).

García Álvarez, A. 2008. Auge y decadencia del café en Cuba colonial. *Stvdia Zamorensia*. 8.

Gonzaléz García, G. 2020. *Caught between Empires: Pre-Famine Irish Immigrants in Santiago de Cuba, 1807–1847*. MA Thesis. Concordia University Montréal.

Gonzaléz García, G. 2023. Coffee Plantations and Irish Migration to Santiago de Cuba: A Historical Case Study of Radical Environmental Transformation *IN*: McGaughey, J. and Walker, T. (eds.). *Environmental Migration in the Face of Emerging Risks: Historical Case Studies, New Paradigms and Future Directions*. Cham: Springer International Publishing.

López Segrera, Y. 2010. *Del Paradigma Tecnológico al Paisaje Arqueológico: presencia francesa y cultura del café en el sudeste cubano en la primera mitad del siglo XIX*. PhD Thesis. Universidad de Oriente, Santiago de Cuba.

Orozco Melgar, M.E. 2007. *Los acentos de una mujer*. Santiago de Cuba: Editorial Oriente.

Provencio Garrigós, L. 1994. 'Clase', poder y matrimonio: Configuración de un élite dirigente: La Sociedad Económica de Cuba de Amigos del País. *Contrastes: Revista de historia moderna*. 9.

Recio Morales, Ó. 2010. *Ireland and the Spanish empire, 1600–1825*. Dublin: Four Courts Press.

Recio Morales, Ó. (ed.) 2012. *Redes de nación y espacios de poder: La Comunidad irlandesa en España y la América Española, 1600–1825 / Power Strategies: Spain and Ireland, 1600–1825*. Madrid: Albatros Ediciones.

Van Norman, W. C. 2013. *Shade-Grown Slavery: The Lives of Slaves on Coffee Plantations in Cuba*. Nashville: Vanderbilt University Press.

CHAPTER 5

Under a Southern Sky: The Irish settlement of Baker's Flat in colonial South Australia

DR SUSAN ARTHURE

Dr Susan Arthure teaches and researches in archaeology at Flinders University, South Australia. She recently completed her PhD on the archaeology of the Irish in colonial South Australia. Her research interests include the social identity of the Irish in Australia, folk traditions and folklore, and experimental archaeology. Here, she outlines the history and archaeology of a South Australian Irish settlement called Baker's Flat that was established in the mid-nineteenth century and retained its Irish identity for upwards of a century.

Baker's Flat is located near a small town called Kapunda, about 80 kilometres north of the state capital, Adelaide, in an area of South Australia known as the Mid North. Some years ago, when I first set foot on Baker's Flat, I walked across a paddock scattered with ceramic and glass fragments and the occasional pile of stone rubble. Next to many of the rubble piles were pepper trees (*Schinus molle*), large trees that in Australia are markers of nineteenth-century colonization. Next to them were small, thorny bushes that resembled Irish hawthorns. For the first time in my three decades living in Australia, I felt a sense of Irishness in my surroundings.

What did I feel that others did not, what did I see? I was certainly biased by the knowledge that had been shared with me that this had been the site of an Irish community in

Below: **Location of Baker's Flat in the south-east corner of the Mid North region, South Australia.**

Opposite page: **Baker's Flat landscape, the distant tree line defines the course of the river Light. (Right, above) Pepper tree with thorny bush at its right; (below) blue-and-green banded ceramic shard, found on surface.**

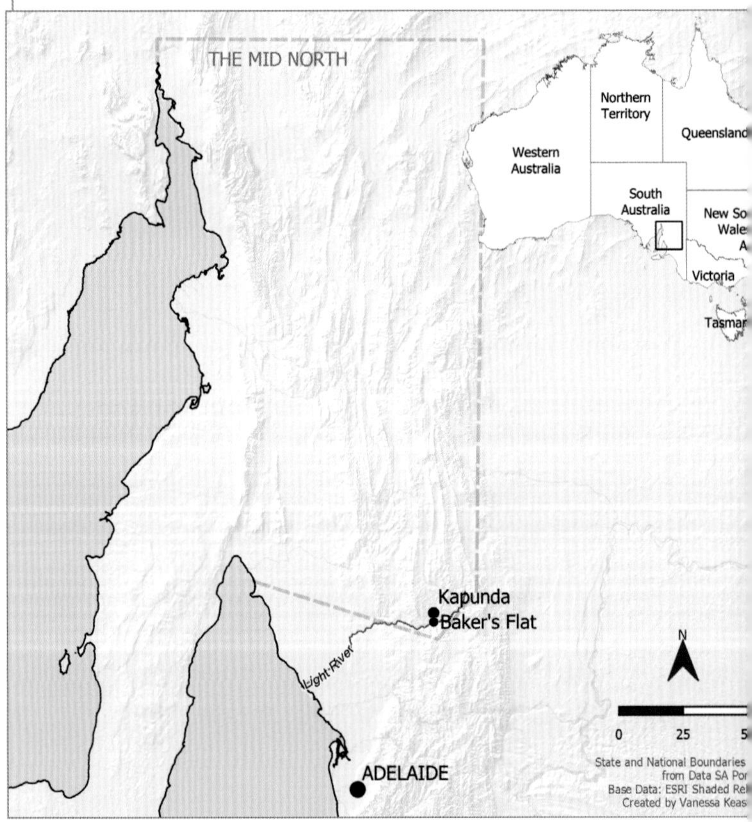

the nineteenth century (D. Lonergan, S. O'Reilly, P. Swann pers. comm. 2012). It was also the banded-design ceramics found on the surface that reminded me of Carrigaline pottery, and the thorny bushes that reminded me of the hawthorn. So, I set out to investigate the Baker's Flat site and the people who had lived there.

First, to offer some historical context, the colony of South Australia was established in 1836, essentially a Victorian-era colony. Deliberately designed to replicate a slice of England in the Antipodes, it was based on a scheme called the Wakefield Scheme, where men who were already wealthy could increase their wealth simply by buying land and waiting for it to increase in value (Pike 1967, Sendziuk and Foster 2018). It was a utopia for land speculators and capitalists. In fact, the Irish land reform campaigner Michael Davitt, who visited South Australia in 1895 as part of a fundraising tour, described it as 'a landlord's Utopia' (Davitt 1898).

Into this heady mix of largely English money and speculation came small numbers of poor Irish Catholics. The numbers were small because South Australia was well known for its antipathy towards Catholics, especially if they were poor and Irish (Nicol 1983, Pike 1967). In 1854, however, some of these Irish Catholics arrived at Kapunda, seeking work in a booming copper mine there. They settled down on a large parcel of land that was lying idle and unused by the legal owners. It was conveniently located close to the mine and was also available for free – no rent or other costs. This land parcel of *c.*490 acres (*c.*60 hectares) was known as Baker's Flat, and

although they were essentially illegal occupiers, the Irish took it under their full control.

Quickly they formed what was described as 'a close, fiercely Irish community' (Nicol 1983). There are estimates of about 500 people living on Baker's Flat when the copper mine was at its peak in the 1860s and 1870s (Charlton 1971) and they were seen as having a very strong Irish identity (Maloney 1936, Nicol 1983). Their Catholic faith was robust and enduring. They danced to Irish music by firelight on a common area in the Baker's Flat site known as the 'dance floor', and they played hurling on Sunday afternoons

(Maloney 1936). They also built houses that looked like Irish houses; a series of photographs from 1906 shows a cluster of houses built in the Irish vernacular style.

COURT CASE

Rectilinear in design, these houses were single storey and had steep thatched roofs. Visually, they would have appeared Irish and the records of a court case hint at more (*Forster et al. vs. Fisher* 1892). The *Forster et al. vs. Fisher* case began in 1892 and continued for a decade. It pitted the Irish illegal occupiers of the land against the lawful owners, who happened to be some of the most powerful men in the colony at that time. If you walk around Adelaide today, you can see the libraries, buildings and streets named after these men, a cohort that held control in South Australia and against whom the Irish were going up with everything they had.

In the court records, there are suggestions that the Baker's Flat Irish had adopted a traditional Irish way of managing land and community – the *clachan* and rundale system – where houses are clustered together and the land is managed co-operatively. This cluster of houses is obvious in an 1893 survey plan, which was prepared for the legal owners in the *Forster et al. vs. Fisher* case (1892) for an ultimately unsuccessful sale of land. The plan shows a large cluster of little black rectangles – houses and outbuildings – in the north-west corner of the site. It should be noted that it is not entirely accurate because the unfortunate surveyor, James Chapman Lovely, carried out

Right: **Records of the *Forster et al. vs. Fisher* court case.**

Opposite page: **Baker's Flat houses in 1906, depicted in a series of photographs taken by John Kauffmann, published in the *Christmas Observer*, 13 December 1906, Adelaide.**

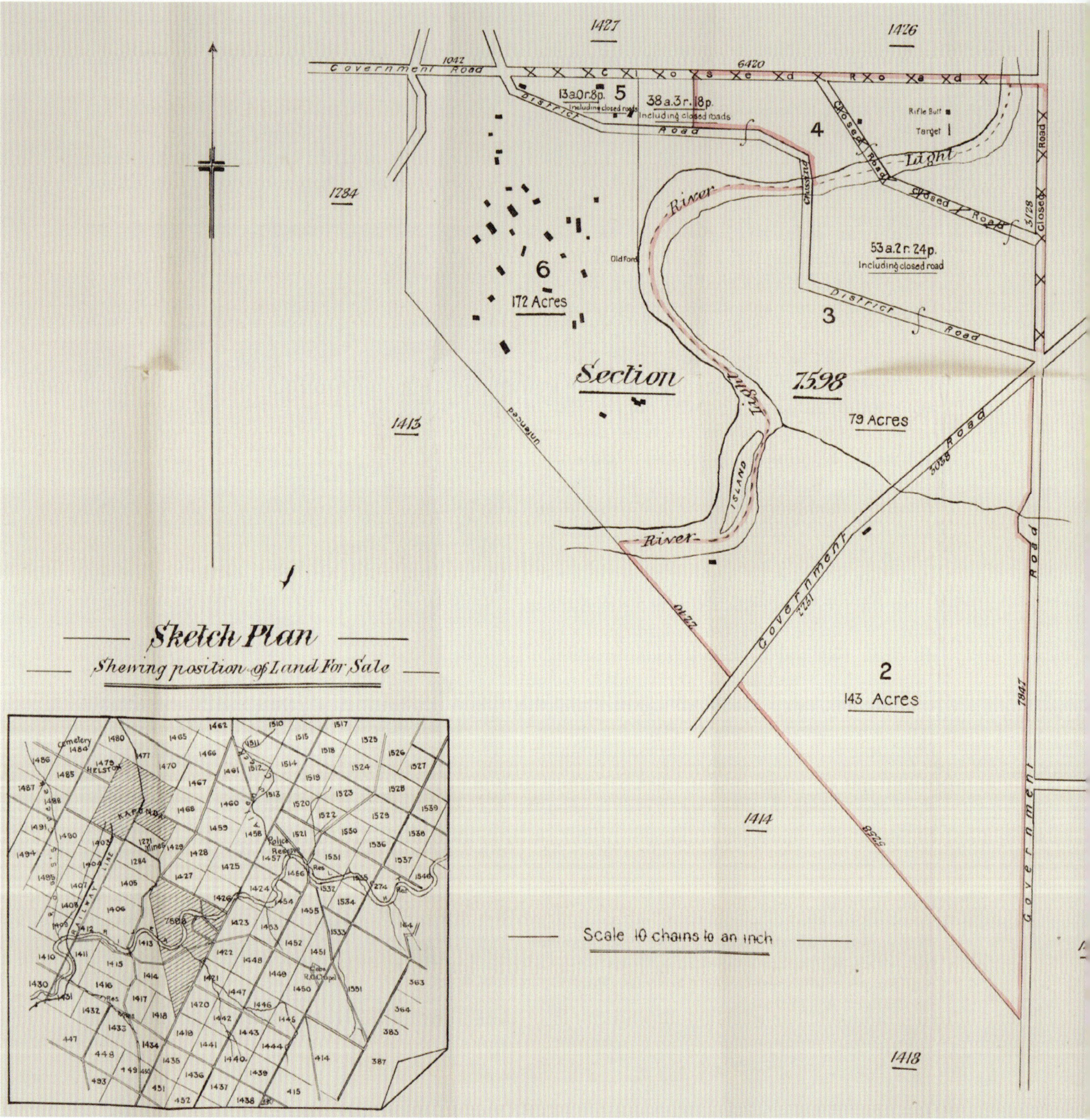

Sketch Plan
Shewing position of Land For Sale
Scale 10 chains to an inch
Government Road
District Road
Closed Road
River Light
Section 7598
6
172 Acres
5
13 a. 0 r. 8 p.
Including closed roads
38 a. 3 r. 18 p.
Including closed roads
4
Rifle Butt
Target
53 a. 2 r. 24 p.
Including closed road
3
79 Acres
2
143 Acres
Island
Old Ford
Crossing
Unfenced
1427
1426
1784
1413
1414
1418
Cemetery
Helston
Kaponga
Railway Line
Police Reserve
R.C. Chapel

the survey under duress. He was in danger of being thrown into the river Light, which flows through Baker's Flat, at any moment by the Irish (this had happened to a previous survey party). Although he tried to convince them that he was there to survey the land for a railway line, they were wise to that pretty quickly and he ended up leaving the settlement at speed and completing the survey from a nearby hilltop (*Forster et al. vs. Fisher* 1892).

These court records and the photos are important because clachans are difficult to recognize for outsiders. For somebody observing Baker's Flat from the outside, such as those wealthy landowners and English settlers in the neighbouring area, the settlement would have appeared disordered, chaotic, illegible. It is difficult to see order in what appears to be a haphazard cluster of dwellings and hard from the English landowners' perspective to see anything other than chaos in animals roaming freely without fences. Certainly, this is the story that was recorded in newspaper articles at that time – chaos, tumbledown huts, wretched hovels, cows, goats and geese all running wild in no apparent order (e.g. *Adelaide Observer* 1877, *Kapunda Herald* 1902, *Kapunda Herald and Northern Intelligencer* 1864, 1866, 1874, *South Australian Register* 1860).

RESEARCH METHODS

How does one begin to investigate an historic site where there is very little written down in the published histories? Until my archaeological research began, only about 500 words in total had been published about Baker's Flat, starting with a compilation of edited articles in 1929 (Tilbrook 1929). These were then recycled over and over again in anything that was published about Baker's Flat from that point on. As a result, there was little new material recorded and most of what was written bought into that stereotype of wretched hovels and lawlessness. Soon after the last people had left or died (in the early twentieth century), the entire community faded out of memory, recalled by only a couple of people in Kapunda.

And how to set about exploring what seems to be a strongly Irish settlement hidden in plain sight in a strongly English colony? Following some initial historical background research, I carried out a geophysical survey in 2016 with a small team of archaeologists. This was designed to collect subsurface data that might indicate the original footprints of dwellings or outbuildings, fences, enclosures, old paths or roadways, and the dance floor where people had played hurling and danced by firelight. Using a magnetic gradiometer and ground-penetrating radar, we surveyed a 2.4-hectare grid, with the location of the survey grid being based on historical data and local knowledge.

Based on the geophysical survey results, our Flinders University team of archaeology staff and students carried out excavations over two field seasons across eight broad areas of interest. Eight trenches were opened excavating more than 120 square metres. Then came the cataloguing and analysis of almost 20,000 artefacts in the laboratory, comprising 1,186 ceramics, 2,153 pieces of glass, 15,911 pieces

---

Opposite page: **Survey plan of Baker's Flat, Section 7598, drawn in 1893 in preparation for a sale.**

Summary of archaeological fieldwork and research methods used in the Baker's Flat project.	
METHODS	
Geophysical survey	Magnetic gradiometer and ground-penetrating radar (GPR) over 2.4ha grid in 2016. Baker's Flat total area =60ha
Excavation	Two field seasons, 2016 and 2017 8 trenches, excavating more than 120 m^2
Lab work	Cataloguing and analysis of almost 20,000 artefacts CERAMICS = 1,186 GLASS = 2,153 METAL = 15,911 BUTTONS = 264
Archives	South Australian newspapers - 23 publications, 1,273 articles, >200,000 words State government records - court cases Genealogical data - BDM, Catholic Church records, family histories, family notices → 145 different families, >65,000 words Data from National Folklore Collection, Ireland → subject areas, >30,000 words

of metal and 264 buttons.

Archival research underpinned the archaeological results. This included a search of the South Australian newspapers for any references to Baker's Flat – we are very fortunate in Australia to have a system called Trove run by the National Library, which digitizes historic newspapers and makes them freely available. Other records included the *Forster et al. vs. Fisher* court case, which runs to nearly 1,000 pages, and genealogical data for details about specific families. I was able to identify data for 145 separate families on Baker's Flat, all of whom had lived there at some point over nearly a century.

I also used folklore data from the National Folklore Collection at University College Dublin (UCD) to investigate traditional building methods and materials, fireplaces and chimneys, floors and foundations, any information about how people traditionally built dwellings.

Through these methods, I was trying to cover every element of the community, the kinship and alliances, how the landscape was used, the type of vernacular architecture being built, the artefacts of everyday life. This was to try and determine the extent of its Irishness and how that identity had been maintained over many decades.

A LITTLE BIT MORE HISTORY

To give a bit more background about the

settlement, the Irish occupation of Baker's Flat, as I have hinted already, was not trouble free. The Irish were not popular in the broader community, aligning with colonial South Australia's poor attitude towards Irish Catholics generally. At Kapunda, the general feeling was that they drank too much, that they were dirty – noting that in nineteenth-century South Australia there was not a lot of water around, so pretty much everybody would have been dirty most of the time, not just the Irish! – that they were lawless and not managing their animals in the approved way. The animals were renowned for roaming freely without fences and Baker's Flat was described as 'a blot on the landscape' (Charlton 1971).

Later, as the mine was winding down and it was no longer convenient to have the Irish close by, the legal landowners decided that they wanted their land back. The Irish, however, had no intention of giving it up and this led to continuing conflict. Attempts at eviction began in the late 1870s coinciding with the closure of the mine. A town mural in Kapunda shows a group of spirited Irishwomen seeing off the bailiffs, using brooms and sticks and boiling water. Women being at the forefront of resistance was not unusual in Baker's Flat. It is reminiscent of the Land War that was happening back in Ireland at the same time. During the Land War in Ireland, women were essential to the protests and the agitation. They taunted bailiffs, they threw mud and stones at police, they blocked roadways with their bodies. Even when men were present, women took the lead in challenging the authorities. And the same thing was happening on Baker's Flat. These were deliberate strategies. The Irish Land War was well covered in the South Australian press and the Baker's Flat 'land war' was using the same tactics.

A dramatic story from 1880 describes how three men were sent by the legal landowners to erect a fence on Baker's Flat (*Kapunda*

Above: **Part of a mural (now in storage) in Kapunda depicting the town's history, showing the women of Baker's Flat chasing police officers and bailiffs off their land.**

Herald 1880a). This was a tactic that under the legislation would have helped to establish their ownership. The women were having none of it. Upwards of a hundred of them 'turned out to drive off the would-be despoilers of their hearths and homes' (*Kapunda Herald* 1880a). The hapless fencers managed to dig a single posthole but immediately one of the women leapt into it. She declared that any further excavation would have to be through her body and the entire group of women avowed that they would all shed blood to save their land. During this time, they stood in groups of 10, 20 and more, so that they could pass on messages about who the fencers were, where they were and what they were doing. At this point in the proceedings, the three fencers went into a huddle, had a discussion and wisely decided to retreat. They were sent on their way by the women using brooms, sticks and shovels.

In the court case that followed, the six ringleaders were named as Ann Slattery, Mary Callaghan, Mary Lacey, Mary Jose, Ann Hoare and Catherine Driscoll (*Kapunda Herald* 1880b). There are photos of two of these women. Ann Hoare was about 55 years old at the time of this particular conflict, her photo shows her in her younger years. The photo of Catherine Driscoll is from when she was a much older woman; she was about 36 at the time of the fencing dispute. Interestingly, all photographs of Catherine Driscoll in later life show her side on. The family folklore says that she was on her way home from Mass one day, got into an altercation with a young boy who threw a stone at her and in the fracas, she lost an eye. From then on, all photographs showed her from her good side.

These troubles at Baker's Flat continued for many years eventually coming to a head in the *Forster et al. vs. Fisher* court case, beginning in 1892 with the aim of selling off the land and getting rid of the Irish once and for all.

The records of this court case contain hints as to how the Baker's Flat land was being managed (*Forster et al. vs. Fisher* 1892). The landowners offered some of the occupiers the chance to buy some of the land and a series of affidavits highlight how the Irish were working together and the expectations of mutual obligation. A man called Thomas Jordan occupied a hut and one-and-a-half acres. He said that 'the occupiers had already held two meetings

Above left: **Ann Hoare, *c.*1870.**

Above right: **Catherine Driscoll, date unknown.**

Opposite page: **Network of marriages between families on Baker's Flat.**

to consider their position . . .' and 'unless they could run their cattle on the whole of the said section, they could not live there and until they were forced to leave, they had all determined to remain' (*Forster et al. vs. Fisher* 1892).

Michael O'Brien, who occupied a hut and one acre, appeared tempted but said, 'It is no use my buying the land, because if I did the others would go against me' and any person who did buy the land 'would not be allowed by the other occupants . . . to live there' (*Forster et al. vs. Fisher* 1892). These are hints that the clachan and rundale system was in operation, where the Irish were making group decisions together about how best to manage the land and cattle.

KINSHIP BONDS

In other court cases, it became clear that a man called Daniel Driscoll was the *de facto* leader for the community. He was described in the *Forster et al. vs. Fisher* court case as spokesman for the Irish and by one of the witnesses for the prosecution as the head robber,

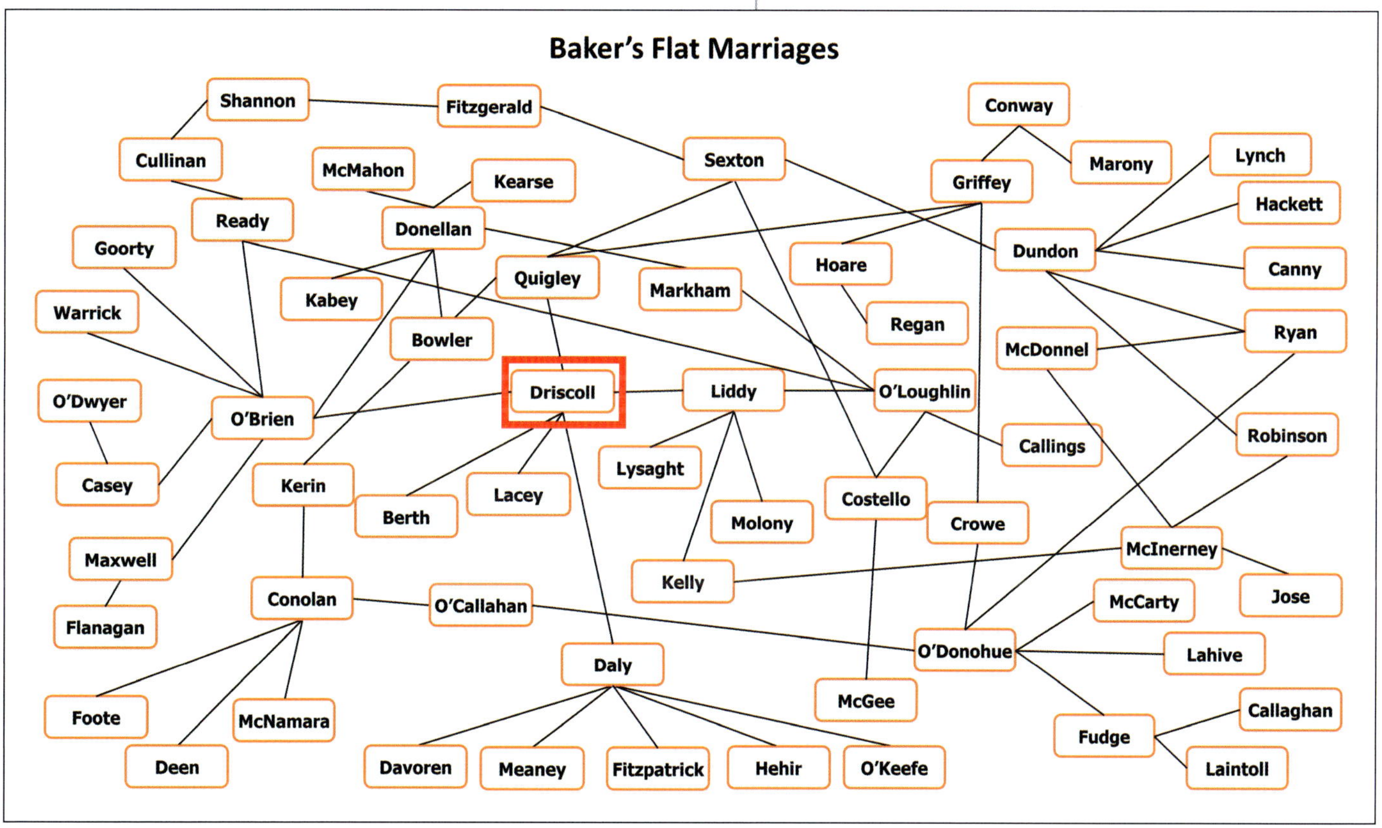

Barabbas (from the Gospel story of the thief who was chosen for release over Jesus Christ) (*Kapunda Herald* 1894). The Driscolls were probably the most influential family on Baker's Flat. Catherine Driscoll who had lost her eye (p88) was married to Daniel's cousin, Patrick. Catherine was also Mary Lacey's sister-in-law; Mary was one of the other female ringleaders and had been born a Driscoll.

These family connections are important because family and kinship are at the centre of clachan settlements. On Baker's Flat, many of the families came originally from County Clare, although they did not necessarily know each other when they were there. Sometimes they forged links on voyages to South Australia, or created bonds through marriage or friendships. A marriage between one family and another then created extra and additional connections over time. It was a web of interconnections, alliances and obligations and right at the heart were the Driscolls.

To recap, the family connections offer some insight into kinship bonds in Baker's Flat. The court records indicate how it was being run as rundale. The clusters of houses on the 1893 map hint that it was a clachan and the photographs show Irish-style houses. Using this data from the archival records, I thought it would be possible to gain a lot more information from the archaeology, such as evidence of the clusters of houses and Irish vernacular architecture.

GEOPHYSICAL SURVEY

For the geophysical survey, we concentrated on the northern part of the site, where many of the clusters of buildings were shown on

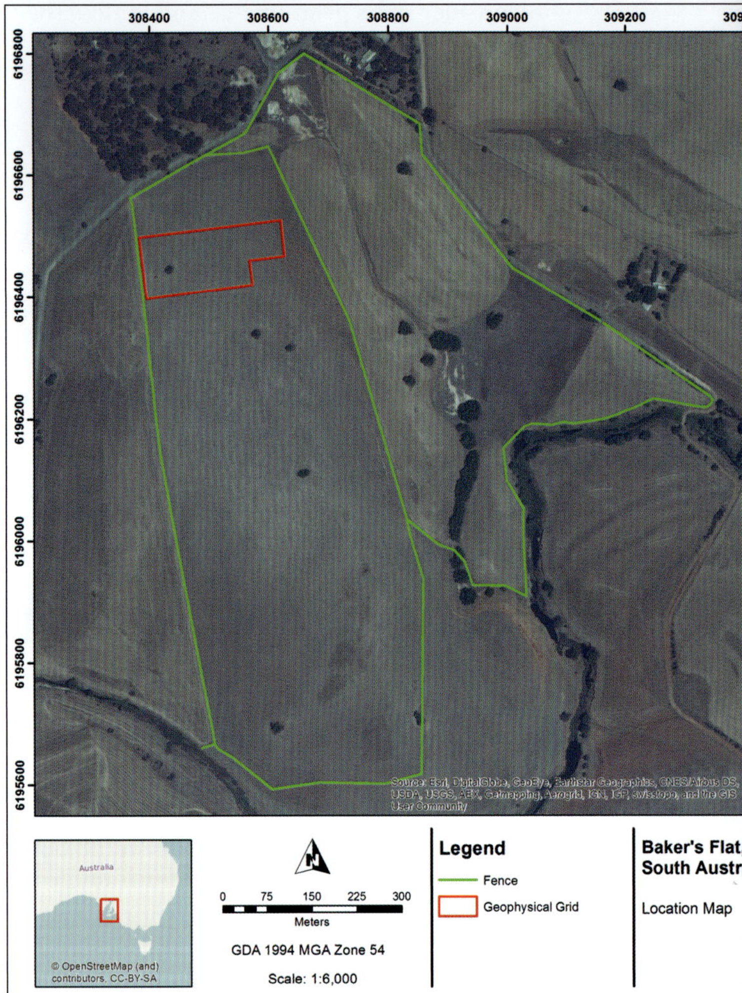

Above: **Geophysical grid outlined in red. Fence line in green showing Baker's Flat boundaries.**

Opposite page: **Team carrying out the geophysical survey using magnetic gradiometer, showing conditions on site.**

the 1893 map (p84). It was about 37 degrees Celsius when we were doing that work, so it was hot, dry and dusty. But, to our delight, we found several areas of interest. When the geophysical data was mapped and interpreted by a geophysical archaeologist, an array of inter-

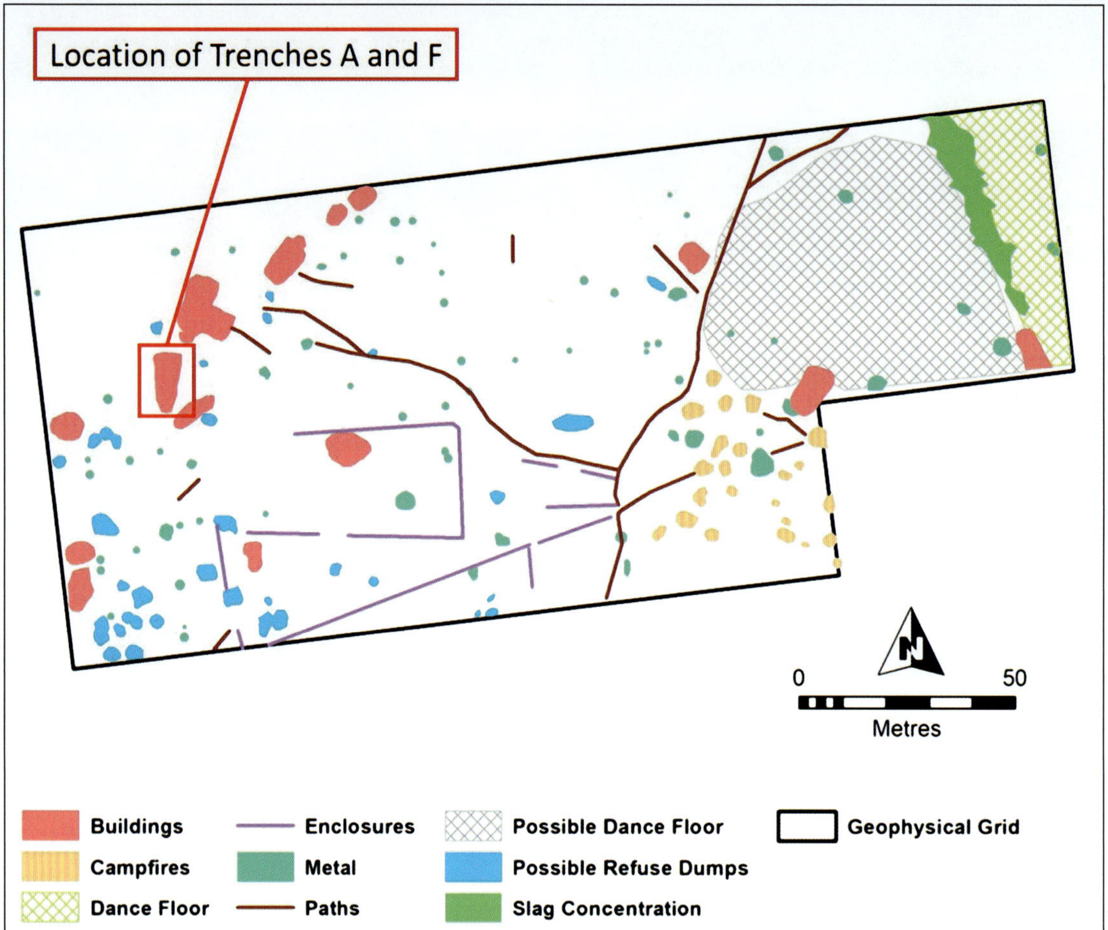

esting shapes and lines emerged. The diagram (above) shows a number of roughly rectangular-shaped red blobs interpreted as dwellings or other structures. The rectangular and triangular purple lines also generated a lot of interest because they resemble field enclosures – straight lines like these do not naturally occur in nature. Over to the east (on the right of the map), a mesh pattern indicates the dance floor area, which the landowner had told us was heavily compacted and had poor crop yields as a result. The geophysics confirmed that it was, indeed, highly compacted. A rough green line alongside the mesh area indicates a linear concentration of slag, sourced from the copper mine, that we think was used as an edging for the fires that would be lit to one side of the dancing area. The brown lines indicate possible rough paths, used to travel around the site.

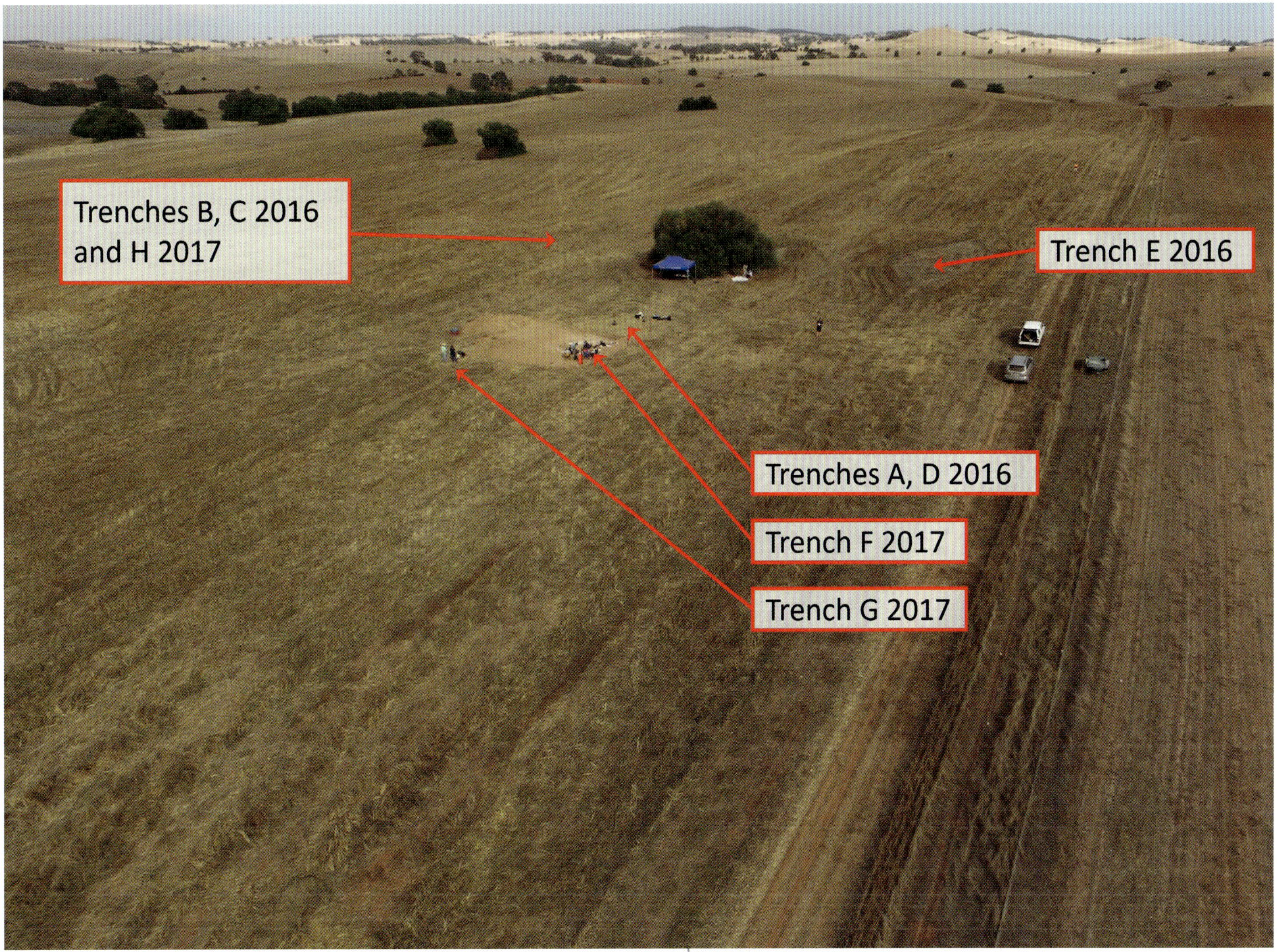

Above: **General location of trenches excavated in 2016 and 2017 field seasons.**

Opposite page: **Interpretation of Baker's Flat site based on the geophysical data. Note that areas marked as refuse dumps and campfires are extrapolated as such as they have not been tested by excavation.**

EXCAVATION

The geophysical results helped me to decide where to excavate – in a big field with no obvious structures remaining above the surface and just several large pepper trees that possibly indicated a nearby domestic

dwelling. On the image on page 93 the red arrows indicate the areas that were excavated over two field seasons. At trenches A and F, which covered both field seasons, we excavated the remains of a dwelling. During the first season, we excavated the southern end of that area, which I have interpreted as a dugout

Above: ***Burra Creek*****, 1851, attributed to William A. Cawthorne.**

Opposite page, above: **Overview of Trench A at completion of excavation, looking north.**

Opposite page, below: **Trench F at completion of excavation, looking north.**

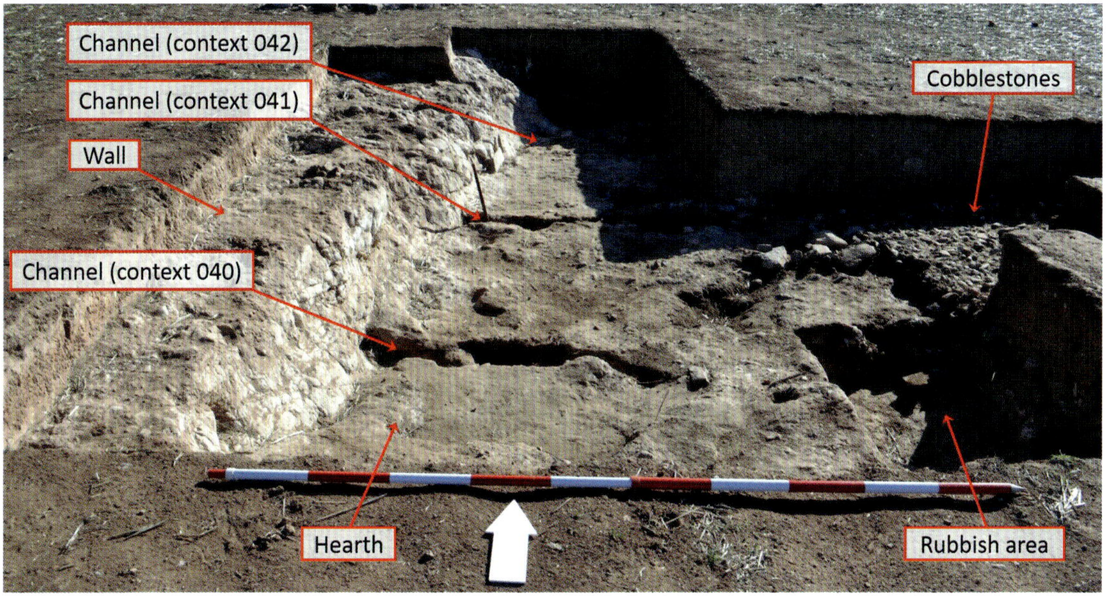
Channel (context 042)
Channel (context 041)
Wall
Cobblestones
Channel (context 040)
Hearth
Rubbish area

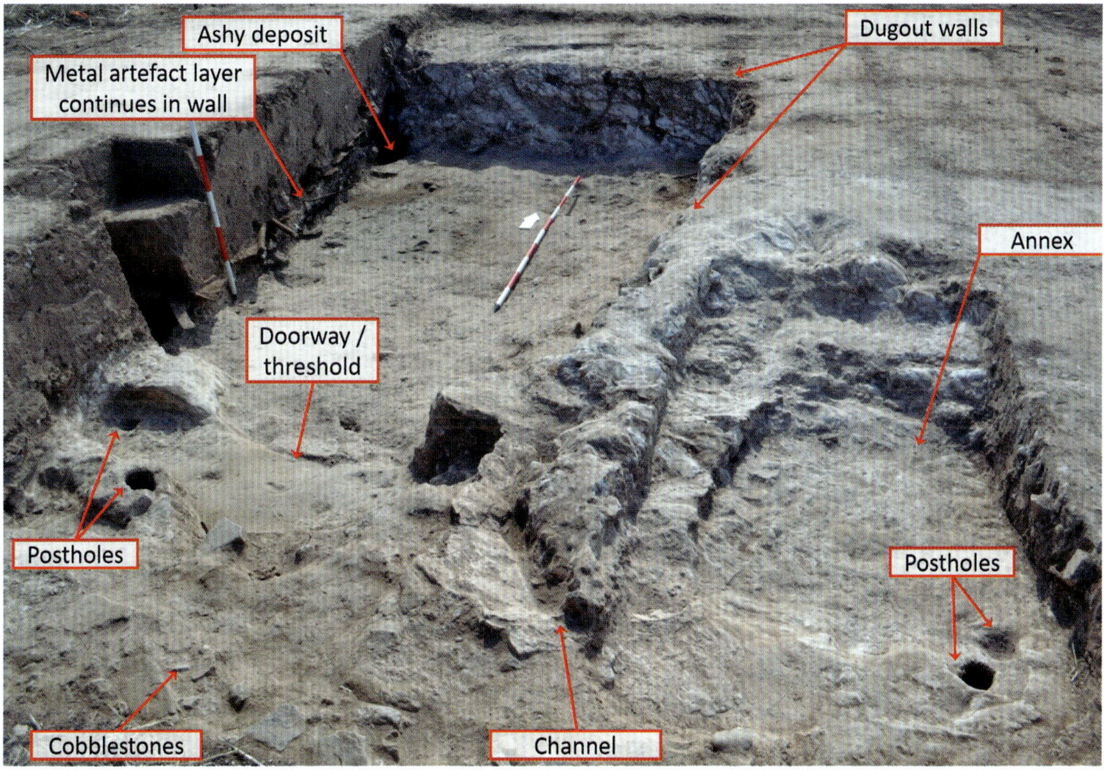
Ashy deposit
Metal artefact layer continues in wall
Dugout walls
Annex
Doorway / threshold
Postholes
Postholes
Cobblestones
Channel

dwelling. By this, I mean a structure that is dug into the slope of the land.

In nineteenth-century Ireland, poor people were familiar with the concept of digging into a slope or hillside to create a shelter or dwelling. Often, the gables and the front wall were made of sods of grass or turf. The hearth would be at a gable end at floor level, with the smoke escaping through a smoke hole in the roof. Chimneys were rare.

At the same time, the poor of South Australia were also living in dugouts but in these, the architecture was quite different. The homes shown on page 94 are dugout dwellings constructed at another copper mining town called Burra about 80 kilometres north of Baker's Flat. These were built by Cornish miners (Bell 1998, Mullen and Birt 2009). Here, the entirety of each house was dug into the steep banks of a creek. The drawing from 1851 illustrates how they nestled into the high sides of the creek almost like a terrace of houses, each with a front door, window and chimney stack. Every house had a chimney with a chimney stack on top, some even had verandahs. When people in South Australia think about dugouts, this is what they have in mind.

Back on Baker's Flat, the dugout wall that we excavated was very low and acted somewhat like a retaining wall (p95, above). On the long section of wall visible at the left-hand side (p95, above), there are regular cuts along the top surface. These probably held the supports for a wall and roof, the remains of which we found tumbled inside the structure. The cut is into calcrete, a type of limestone prevalent in South Australia. The floor surface, which has some channels dug into it, is also calcrete. There is a cobbled path to the east and this is almost certainly outside the structure because a rubbish dump was excavated close to and immediately south of the cobbles.

In the second field season, we excavated the remainder of the dugout structure (p95, below), starting from where we had finished the previous year and then continuing north. The retaining walls continued to the north and east, forming a rectangular shape. Next to these walls, we found the remains of flattened kerosene tins, sometimes covered in hessian. Kerosene tins were commonly used in South Australia as a form of walling, with the compressed tins acting as panels nailed or tied to wooden supports.

Interestingly, the doorway is not in the

Above: **Conjectural drawing of excavated house on Baker's Flat, elevations imagined.**

Opposite page: **Trench E at completion of excavation, looking south, which uncovered a small, round structure that was interpreted as a sweathouse.**

eastern wall where I would have expected to find it. Instead, it faces south, out of the prevailing wind. The cobblestones uncovered the previous year extend here. A small annex near the front door appears to have shelves or tiers to the rear. These tiers are slightly sloped and were possibly for roosting poultry.

Looking at the overall structure, it is essentially the remains of an Irish-style house dug into the slope of the land. The annex echoes an Irish custom of having a small space with a single opening for sheltering poultry or young animals. The house is a rectangular structure, one room deep, ten metres long and four metres wide. In the conjectural drawing (p96), based on the excavation results, we can see that it strongly resembles a typical Irish vernacular house. There is an extended frontage to accommodate the south-facing door, and a tiny annex. There were probably two windows, based on the scatters of window glass that we found at two locations. There was a thatched roof that would have been covered at some point by galvanized iron sheeting, which we also excavated from the middle of the trenches. Hessian that was found on the underside of the thatch would have been used as a lining to prevent bits of straw or reeds (and insects) falling into the house. In this particular house, there is no evidence that a chimney ever existed. The hearth was at the southern gable end and the smoke probably would have escaped slowly through one or two smoke holes in the roof.

Below: **Conjectural drawing of how the sweathouse on Baker's Flat may have appeared, elevations imagined.**

The house was one of three areas excavated on Baker's Flat. Over both field seasons, we also opened trenches B, C and H (see p93) over the rectangular and triangular shapes that had shown up in the geophysics and been interpreted as possible field enclosures. This area was about 60 metres long and about 40 metres wide. To begin with, we excavated using hand tools but reached the natural surface without finding anything that looked like an enclosure or a fence. Undeterred, we tried with a backhoe (mechanical digger). However, after the backhoe had successfully excavated seven metres of a planned 15-metre trench, the bucket arm snapped in the hard and unforgiving ground. It was unable to be repaired in time and it was impossible to go any further. An eight-metre length of the planned trench remains unexcavated but, given the clear magnetic signature in the geophysical results, it is possible that it does contain the remains of a wall or some type of enclosing feature, possibly built using slag from the mine, which was available in abundance and used elsewhere on the site. That slag is strongly magnetic and may be what was showing up in the geophysical results.

The excavation results over another area, trench E, south-west of the house (p93), were more fruitful. Digging in this area uncovered a small, round structure that did not align either with the typical shape of a domestic house or the form of an agricultural outhouse (p97). It was almost four metres wide, with walls built directly on the natural surface, i.e. no foundations. The internal floor was smooth and unstained, coated in a thin layer of white lime slurry and imprinted at one point by the base of a bucket. A stone entrance way (outlined in red, p97) was demarcated on the inside by the remains of two timber posts, set 82 centimetres apart, and on the outside by an edging of mixed stones, slag and brick. Immediately to the right on entering the building, a circular stone firepit contained ash remnants.

This was very puzzling but, after researching various forms of Irish vernacular buildings, the most likely explanation is that this was one of the most Irish features of all, a sweathouse. Like the clachan, these were ubiquitous in nineteenth-century Ireland but, as they fell into disuse, they also fell out of memory.

Based on the excavated evidence of the typical Irish sweathouse the drawing opposite shows what it might have looked like on Baker's Flat, nestled into the slope of the hill. The primary purpose of the Irish sweathouse was for health, to sweat out an illness or an ailment (Harte 2021, Richardson 1939, Whelan 2011). Most were built into banks or rising ground, maybe looking a little bit like a thimble, with low doorways that could be easily sealed. They were often covered with earth or sods of grass, most were circular in shape inside, some were D-shaped. Although they were often close to water for cooling off afterwards, this was not critical (Danaher and Lucas 1952, Price 1952, Richardson 1939, Weir 1989).

Prior to a sweathouse being used, a fire was maintained inside for at least two days. Once the walls and the floors were thoroughly heated, the ashes were raked out and the floors spread with green grass or straw to protect the users' feet (Danaher and Lucas 1952, Richardson 1939, Weir 1989). On Baker's Flat, the entrance gives no indication of how high the original doorway would have been but the doorposts are in the correct position to wedge a temporary door in place. The clean nature of the floor is consistent with it having been swept out numerous times and the ripples and the bucket imprint are further evidence of the floor having been regularly washed down. There is also the evidence of a fire pit just inside the door.

So, why would the Irish have built a sweathouse on Baker's Flat? The answer is most likely because it was what they had always done to manage health, in the same way as the clachan and rundale system was what they had always done to manage land. The sweathouse may have been another means, like the clachan, of giving that community every advantage, especially in terms of managing health in the early days when doctors and medicines were hard to come by.

ARTEFACT ANALYSIS

As well as the data that we were able to get from the geophysical survey and excavation, there are many excavated artefacts that can shed light on the lifeways of the Irish living on Baker's Flat. For example, the remains of 21 ceramic teacups and ten teapots found in the house point to the importance of tea drinking on the site. They also indicate how

Above: **Fragments from red-bodied teapot with enamelled gilt decoration.**

the consumption of tea in this small Irish house differed from other South Australian houses of the time.

A minimum number of ten teapots were

recovered from the house. The largest could have held up to 2.4 litres of tea, enough for about ten cups. Most are fairly utilitarian but there is one decorated teapot of higher quality with a beautiful, highly-vitrified black glaze and a gilt geometric pattern (opposite page). Ten teapots do seem like a lot, especially when it appears that by the end of the settlement there was only one elderly woman living in the house. By comparison, in other working-class households in South Australia, much smaller numbers of teapots have been excavated. In Burra, in a Cornish miner's dugout, just one teapot was excavated. In Port Adelaide, a working-class port suburb, two and zero teapots were excavated from neighbouring workers' cottages. At an Irish Catholic house in Melrose, much farther north in the Flinders Ranges, one teapot was found. These contrast markedly with the ten teapots from the Baker's Flat house.

There were also 21 teacups, none matching either each other or any of the saucers or creamers found during excavation. This is unusual on Australian sites, where matching cup and saucer pairs are common.

When we think about teapots and tea sets in the nineteenth century, we think of respectability, which the Irish were not really renowned for, and the ritual of afternoon tea. Even poor women of the nineteenth century could project respectability as they poured tea for their friends into paired teacups and saucers. I think that what was happening on Baker's Flat, however, was a deliberate nonconformity to respectability, because here the tea wares were not about manners or the tea ceremony. These women did not need to bond over a tea ceremony because their bond had already been forged through alliances and friendships and land and fences and activism. The larger ratio of teacups to saucers (3½:1) even suggests that there was no requirement for saucers except perhaps when the doctor or priest called in. This is the Irishness of it; community-focused, tea drinking in Baker's Flat was more about social togetherness and exploiting the familiarity of kin than the need for a staged performance of respectability and domestic bliss.

CONCLUSION

What do we know now about Irish identity in the South Australian settlement of Baker's Flat? First, Baker's Flat was a clachan, the first complete exemplar to be recognized so far outside of Ireland. For it to have survived for almost a century demands that the Baker's Flat Irish consciously and continually maintained this system, based on a robust sense of Irishness. They were living in a traditional, co-operative community that was perched on the edge of a capitalist economy driven by mining and farming. Here, they continued to build structures in the Irish vernacular style. They managed their land and stock co-operatively and maintained strong kin networks through their shared origins, astute marriages and longstanding friendships.

There was a continuation of vernacular architecture, with the residents building structures that aligned with their Irish vernacular traditions, houses that are evidenced through excavation and contemporary photographs, and also what is most likely a sweat-house to help meet the health needs of the community.

There were strong kin networks. In the absence of kin networks based on blood, new networks were formed, based on shared origins and journeys, on friendships and alliances that persisted across generations. One family, the Driscolls, emerged as community leaders, both the men and the women. The Baker's Flat community, over almost a century, stayed strong enough to resist incursions from outsiders, to preserve a shared architectural style and to engage in co-operative land management.

Women on the site played a central role. While the clachan was managed without visible boundaries or fences, the colony of South Australia was heading in a very different direction, with a clear English ascendancy and hierarchy, the enclosure of land and the comprehensive adoption of capitalism. At Baker's Flat, in a small colonial land war, the physical manifestation of this was fences. For the legal landowners, substantial boundary fences were required to assert ownership and control as well as to exclude the Irish. But when the fencers were sent in to build a fence in 1880, almost a hundred women, including three of the Driscoll clan, saw them off. Women remained at the frontline throughout the occupation of Baker's Flat. Women were the last people living on Baker's Flat as well, including the unknown elderly woman who liked her cups of tea. A recently unearthed photograph (above) does its bit to celebrate the work of women; this is the only photograph found so far of a woman on Baker's Flat inside a building. Dated 1907, she is milking her cow. Like the woman in the excavated house, she is unnamed.

The end result for the Baker's Flat Irish was that, no matter how hard the legal landowners tried to get their land back or how the broader community looked askance at the troublesome Irish and their tiresome settlement, those Irish would continue managing the land and stock as they were used to, declaring their Irishness through vernacular houses and drinking tea without saucers, and looking out for each other, until they were either ready to move on or no longer in need of the land. They continued their traditions and maintained their Irish identity under this different and faraway southern sky.

Above: ***Milking Time*****, Baker's Flat, near Kapunda, South Australia. Photograph by John Kauffmann, 1907.**

Acknowledgements

In Australia, it is common and respectful practice to acknowledge the traditional owners of the lands where we live and where our research takes place. I want to acknowledge that the lands where I carried out my research and wrote my PhD thesis, in what is now known as South Australia, are the traditional lands of the Ngadjuri and Kaurna peoples. I honour their Elders, past, present and future, and extend that respect to all Aboriginal and Torres Strait Islander people. I would also like to thank Professor Heather Burke and Associate Professor Alice Gorman who were supervisors for my PhD research; they pushed me to think deeply and supported me always.

BIBLIOGRAPHY

Adelaide Observer 1877. A shocking case. 15 December, p11.

Bell, P. 1998. The fabric and structure of Australian mining settlements *IN*: Herbert, E.W., Knapp, A.B. and Pigott, V.C. (eds) *Social Approaches to an Industrial Past: The Archaeology and Anthropology of Mining*. London: Routledge. pp27–38.

Charlton, R. 1971. *The History of Kapunda*. Melbourne: The Hawthorn Press. pp18–24.

Danaher, K. and Lucas, A.T. 1952. Sweathouse, Co. Tyrone. *The Journal of the Royal Society of Antiquaries of Ireland*. 82 (2), pp179–180.

Davitt, M. 1898. *Life and Progress in Australasia*. London: Methuen and Co. p62.

Forster et al. vs. Fisher. 1892. Records of the Supreme Court of South Australia, GRG 36/54 File 47/1892. Adelaide: State Records of South Australia.

Harte, A. 2021. Leitrim Sweathouse Project: Project Report 2021. Unpublished report prepared for Leitrim County Council. p6.

Kapunda Herald 1880a. A scene on Baker's Flat. 7 May, p2.

Kapunda Herald 1880b. Preliminary investigation. 4 June, p4.

Kapunda Herald 1894. Baker's Flat case–dismissed. 3 April, p3.

Kapunda Herald 1902. Baker's Flat cases. Supreme Court–civil sittings. 12 September, p3.

Kapunda Herald and Northern Intelligencer 1864. Magisterial cases. 26 November, p3.

Kapunda Herald and Northern Intelligencer 1866. Burglary. 23 February, p3.

Kapunda Herald and Northern Intelligencer 1874. Municipal Council. 7 August, p3.

Maloney, T.J. 1936a. Early days and ways in Kapunda: Baker's Flat, no man's land–a nursery of Catholicism in Australia. *Southern Cross*. 6 November, pp29–30.

Mullen, D. and Birt, P. 2009. Modernity and tradition: Considerations of Cornish identity in the archaeological record of a Burra dugout. *Australian Archaeology*. 69, pp59–67.

Nicol, R. 1983. Racial minorities and the settlement of Kapunda, part 1. *Historical Society of South Australia Newsletter*. 48, pp13–16.

Pike, D. 1967. *Paradise of Dissent: South Australia 1829–1857*. Carlton: Melbourne University Press. pp145–146.

Price, L. 1952. Sweathouse, Co. Wicklow. *The Journal of the Royal Society of Antiquaries of Ireland*. 82 (2), pp180–181.

Richardson, P. 1939. Sweathouses between Blacklion and Dowra, County Cavan. *Ulster Journal of Archaeology*. 2, pp32–35.

Sendziuk, P. and Foster, R. 2018. *A History of South Australia*. Cambridge: Cambridge University Press. ppxi.

South Australian Register 1860. Sanitary condition of Kapunda. 2 June, p3.

Tilbrook, L.N. (ed.) 1929. *Memories of Kapunda and District by A Circle of Friends*. Kapunda: Kapunda Herald Print.

Weir, A. 1989. Sweathouses: Puzzling and disappearing. *Archaeology Ireland*. 3 (1), pp10–13.

Whelan, K. 2011. The joy of small things *IN*: Aalen, F.H.A., Whelan, K. and Stout, M. (eds) *Atlas of the Irish Rural Landscape*. Cork: Cork University Press. pp246–255.

CHAPTER 6

English Peasant Settlement in Anglo-Norman Ireland

DR KIERAN O'CONOR

Kieran O'Conor is a Senior Lecturer in the School of Geography, Archaeology and Irish Studies at the University of Galway. His research interests include castles, medieval rural settlement and the archaeology of Gaelic-dominated parts of Ireland during the Anglo-Norman period. In this paper he examines the phenomenon and pattern of English peasant migration into Ireland in the one and a half centuries or so after the arrival of the Anglo-Normans to Ireland in 1169.

The arrival of the Anglo-Normans to Ireland in 1169 is often viewed – for good or for bad, depending on one's point of view and background – as the opening act of 800 years of domination by England. However, we must remember, too, that the Anglo-Norman knights, who spoke Norman French, in the decades after 1169 up to even the mid-thirteenth century encouraged mainly Middle English-speaking peasants, but also some Flemings and Welsh, to settle on their newly acquired lands and manors in Ireland (Bliss and Long 1987; Murphy and Potterton 2010, 181–4, 189–92, 207). Archaeologists in particular often see the Anglo-Normans as being a single group of invaders but the people who came to Ireland in the wake of this partial conquest were clearly from different ethnic and social backgrounds. They were not a homogenous group of people and this point is sometimes forgotten, with the newcomers often being described under the one heading of 'Anglo-Norman'.

MIGRATION IN EUROPE

To put this in its context, the period from *c.* AD 1000 to *c.* AD 1300, which coincided with the Medieval Warm Period in climatic terms, when average yearly temperatures were a little higher than in later centuries, was a time of major economic and population growth across Europe. Overpopulation in core areas of Western Europe led, firstly, to peasants and lords settling on peripheral parts of the lands that they lived on, land that either had been forested or had hitherto been regarded as unsuitable for agriculture. Secondly, due to this overpopulation, men and women of all social ranks began to migrate to and colonize quite distant lands. Between the tenth and late fourteenth centuries but particularly during the twelfth and thirteenth centuries, for example, hundreds of thousands of German

peasants, encouraged by their lords, moved eastwards and colonized large parts of what is now eastern Germany, Poland, the Baltic States and the edges of Czechia, with some going as far as present-day Estonia (Bartlett 1994; Higounet 2001; Duffy 1997, 84–5; O'Conor 1998, 41–2). German scholars believe that anything between one million and one and a half million Germans moved eastwards during this entire period but largely between 1100 and 1300 – a massive number indeed. For example, a site known as Alt-Wartenburg at Barczewko, in the north-east of modern Poland, was founded by a German lord in 1326. Although surrounded by an earthen bank topped by a palisade, it did not survive long. It was completely destroyed by the Lithuanians at some stage over the winter of 1353–54 and then permanently abandoned (Biermann, Hermann and Koperkiewicz 2016). This site is currently being excavated by a joint German-Polish team of archaeologists who have strong links to the pan-European Chateau Gaillard and Ruralia research organizations (https://colloquechateaugaillard.eu; https://ruralia2.ff.cuni.cz). The site at Alt-Wartenburg is an indication of how far east German colonization went during this period.

Different movements of not only members of the lordly class but also peasants took place in other parts of Europe and further afield at this time. For example, Christian Spain was expanding southwards at this time. Again, thousands of peasants and the younger sons of the lordly class migrated to the Holy Land during the Crusades of the twelfth century, in search of a better life. Closer to home, it is

Left: **Map depicting German migration eastwards during the *Ostsiedlung* (East settlement). The pink areas were settled in the twelfth century while the orange parts of the map represent areas colonized in the thirteenth century.**

Opposite page: **Luttrell Psalter: peasants working in a field.**

clear that there were also considerable movements of English and Flemish peasants into coastal south Wales, particularly south Pembrokeshire and the very south-west of Carmarthenshire, and even into Scotland, both before and after 1169 (Duffy 1997, 83–5). South Pembrokeshire to this day is still nicknamed by some as 'Little England Beyond Wales' (https://en.wikipedia.org/wiki/Little_England_beyond_Wales).

Therefore, Ireland's experience of widespread English peasant colonization, encouraged by Anglo-Norman lords, in the decades after 1169 and well into the thirteenth century, was not unique. Population increase in particular meant that peasants of various ethnicities were on the move right across Europe during this whole period but especially during the twelfth and thirteenth centuries.

ENGLISH PEASANT IMMIGRATION TO IRELAND

What do we know about the level of English peasant immigration into Ireland during the Anglo-Norman period? Detailed socio-economic documentation relating to Anglo-Norman society and economy dates mainly from the late thirteenth century. Far less detailed historical evidence survives for the early period of Anglo-Norman settlement in Ireland during the late twelfth and early- to mid-thirteenth centuries – the timeframe when this peasant immigration seems to have mainly taken place (Down 1987, 455; O'Conor 1998, 29). However, I think many historians have failed to realize the potential of archaeology, particularly archaeological excavation, to contribute to our understanding of this early period of Anglo-Norman and English peasant settlement. Sometimes archaeologists, historians, historical geographers and scholars who study medieval literature in its various forms work in different, separate silos and do not truly appreciate what other disciplines can bring to the study of the medieval period (O'Keeffe 2017, 161–3). In fact, an interdisciplinary approach, using evidence from a variety of disciplines and methods, has been proved time and time again to be the best way to understand aspects of the medieval period (O'Conor 2023a, 181).

Surviving detailed socio-economic documents indicate that by the late thirteenth century many of the manors in areas conquered and settled by the Anglo-Normans

since 1169 contained large numbers of peasants of mainly English origin living in close proximity to ordinary Irish tenants (Otway-Ruthven 1965, 77–83; 1968, 113–15; Down 1987, 443–8; Glasscock 1987, 213–21; Bartlett 1993, 144–8; O'Conor 1998, 41–2; 2004, 239–40; O'Keeffe 2000, 59–61; Murphy and Potterton 2010, 181–92, 207). A manorial extent was a survey of a landed estate or manor detailing the lord's demesne and the rents and services owed by his mainly peasant tenants to him. For example, a manorial extent of the manor of Cloncurry, County Kildare, which dates to 1304, indicated that over half of the peasant tenants on that manor in that year appeared to have been of English origin. The rest of the tenants on that manor were Irish (*Red Book of*

Above: **Cloncurry motte, County Kildare. This motte marks the *caput* of the manor of Cloncurry.**

Opposite page: **Aerial photograph of the deserted medieval town of Alt-Wartenburg / Barczewko in north-eastern Poland.**

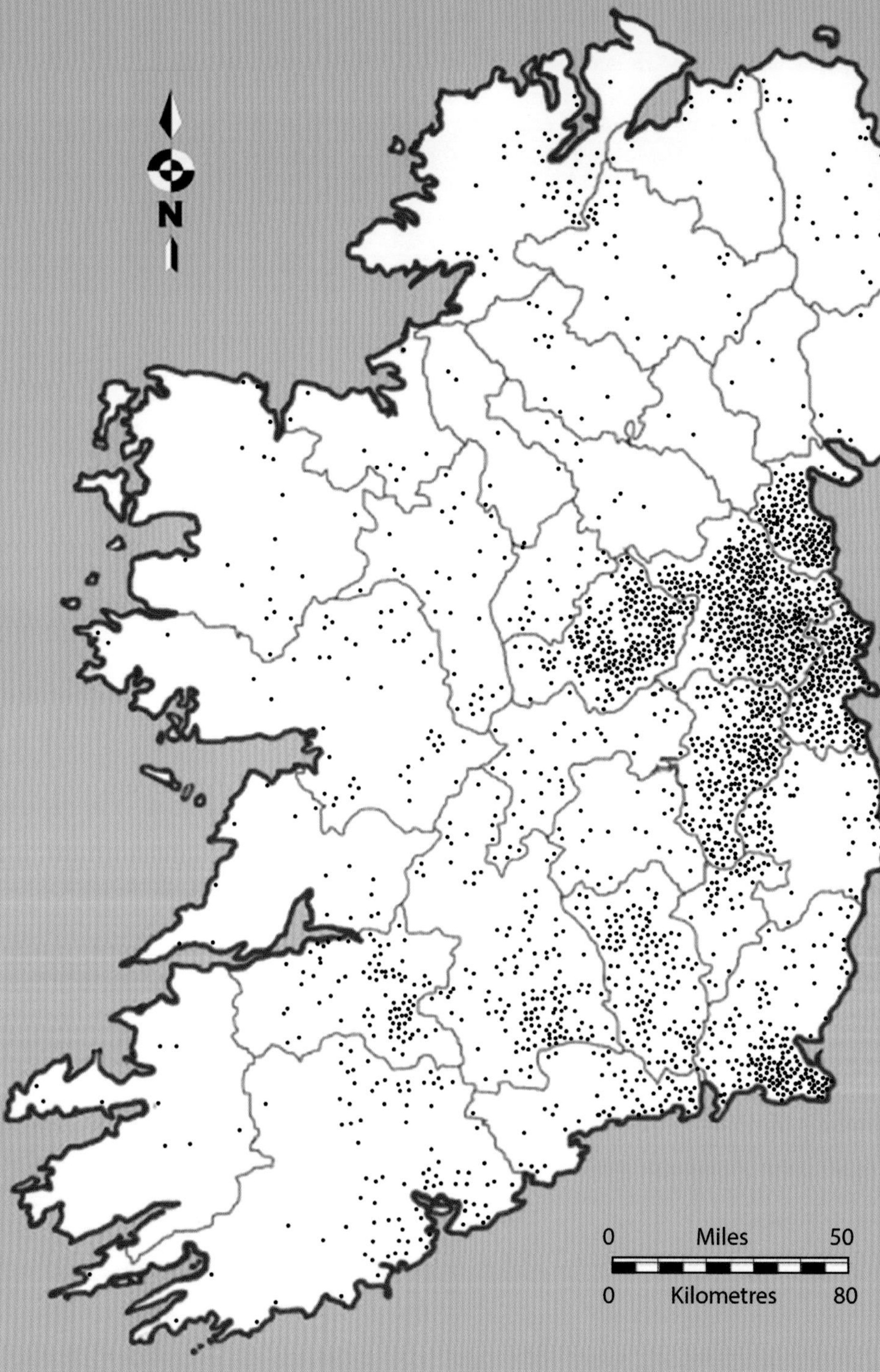

N
0 Miles 50
0 Kilometres 80

Ormond, 27–34). Again, the peasant population on the manor of Moyaliff in what is now south Tipperary seems to have been overwhelmingly of English origin in 1305 (ibid. 64–7).

Overall, it seems that a relatively wide range of manors throughout eastern and south-eastern Ireland had large numbers of peasants of English ethnicity living on them by the late thirteenth century. In fact, it has been argued that by 1300 or so anything up to 50 per cent of the manorial population in some agriculturally fertile lowland areas of eastern and south-eastern Ireland were the descendants of mostly English peasant colonists who had arrived into Ireland in the late twelfth and early thirteenth centuries (Otway-Ruthven 1965, 79–83; 1968, 115; O'Conor 1998, 41).

MIGRATION AND CONQUEST

On the other hand, other areas conquered by the Anglo-Normans saw little English peasant settlement. Tom McNeill, for example, in his 1980 book *Anglo-Norman Ulster,* indicated that the great majority of manorial tenants in the Anglo-Norman earldom of Ulster (effectively lowland areas of modern Counties Antrim and Down) were native Irishmen with little in the way of English peasant immigration (McNeill 1980, 88; O'Conor 1998, 45). This example from east Ulster shows that the geographical extent of English peasant settlement and that of Anglo-Norman conquest in medieval Ireland were not one and the same thing. In some areas, the conquest only saw the removal of the Gaelic elite and their replacement by Anglo-Norman lords (O'Conor 1998, 45; 2023b, 19–21). Tenantry and labour on the manors created in such areas remained mostly Irish. Indeed, in many areas but particularly in more western ones, such as in the de Burgh lordship of Connacht, even the Gaelic elite remained in place and continued to live on some of their old lands but now paying rent, tribute and military service to their Anglo-Norman overlords, instead of to Irish provincial kings (O'Conor 1998, 88; 2023b, 20–2).

So, if areas of Anglo-Norman military and political control and English peasant settlement do not always correlate, where then did the latter settle in numbers? Historians looking at the evidence from surviving manorial extents and from Inquisitions Post Mortem, which were records of important deceased tenants' estates, have argued that in general these peasant colonists settled in numbers across eastern and south-eastern Ireland in a swathe of the country from east Cork and east Limerick up to what is now the modern Ulster border with Leinster (Otway-Ruthven 1965, 77; 1968, 113–15; Glasscock 1987, 221; O'Conor 1998, 41; Murphy and Potterton 2010, 181–4, 189–92, 207). However, it is possible to be even more specific as to where English peasants settled in great numbers if place name evidence is used and then combined with the surviving historical evidence – a methodology recommended as long ago as 1970 by the historical geographer Tom Jones-Hughes (1970, 247) and then by the TCD historian J.A. Watt (1987, 311) at a somewhat later date.

Opposite: **English-language townland names ending with the suffix 'town'.**

Figure 5 is a distribution map of all townlands in Ireland ending with the English word 'town', such as Luttrellstown or Piperstown. Some of these place names are clearly associated with the Plantations of the late sixteenth and seventeenth centuries. However, most of these place names seem to date to earlier periods and where they cluster, they have been seen as indicating areas of heavy English-peasant settlement during the Anglo-Norman period (Jones-Hughes 1970, 247). The areas where these English place names occur most include south Wexford, Dublin, Meath, the eastern half of Westmeath, the southern two-thirds of Louth, a lot of east Kildare, the area around Carlow town and east Waterford (Watt 1987, 311). There also seems to have been a good scattering of English settlement across Kilkenny, south Tipperary, east Limerick, around Cork city, and the area between Cork and Youghal (ibid.). Again, the point must be made that the areas of Anglo-Norman political and military control and those of actual English peasant settlement are not always the same, based on the evidence for the distribution of place names ending in 'town'.

So, there is a difference between Anglo-Norman military control, political control and settlement and actual English peasant settlement on the ground. In fact, English peasant settlement was so strong and dense in places like south-east Wexford, particularly in the baronies of Forth and Bargy, that a dialect derived from Middle English, Yola, survived as a spoken language there into the nineteenth century (Browne 1927). A very similar language called Fingallian, also derived from Middle English, survived as well in rural north County Dublin and probably in adjacent parts of Meath too, also until the nineteenth century (https://en.wikipedia.org/wiki/Fingallian). Fingallian and Yola are thought to be the later surviving echoes of the language spoken by English peasant settlers across thirteenth-century eastern and south-eastern Ireland.

ATTRACTING LABOUR

Anglo-Norman lords needed labour to work their new lands – particularly men with the knowledge to work the great open fields that produced grain in great quantities – during this period, as there seems not to have been enough native Irish labour available to do this (Otway-Ruthven 1968, 115; O'Conor 1998, 42). Evidence suggests that at least the majority of these peasants came from England's West Country and the Anglo-Norman settlements in south Wales (Bliss and Long 1987, 709; Eagar 1988; Graham 1993, 73). The availability of land and the potential for employment in Ireland must have been major enticements for these English peasants to move to Ireland (O'Conor 1998, 42).

However, more might have been needed at times to encourage these people to move to what was often a troubled and turbulent frontier, at least in the early years of the colony. The experiences of Alan of Buildwas, a Cistercian lay brother and so of probable peasant stock, in the mid-1170s suggests that early colonists of all social ranks and ethnicities faced dangers even in places like south Wexford from the ferocity of the inhabitants (Stalley 1987, 10, 35–6). An anthropologist will tell you that rare is the cultural or ethnic group who have calmly let their lands be taken without some form of armed resistance. Presumably, even in heavily-settled areas, there must have been danger from small bands of dispossessed members of the local Irish elite, particularly in the earlier part of the colonization process during the late twelfth and early thirteenth centuries, the periods for which we have little surviving detailed socio-economic documentation.

Certainly, other enticements were used to woo peasants over to populate the manors of large parts of eastern Ireland. Anglo-Norman lords offered these peasants a chance to raise their social status to that of free tenant or burgess even in rural settings (Otway-Ruthven 1968, 116–18; Glasscock 1987, 223; Barry 1987, 73; 1996, 135; Duffy 1997, 83–4; O'Conor 1998, 42). Another major enticement for peasants to migrate to Ireland from the neighbouring island was the fact that labour services were far lighter on Anglo-Norman manors in Ireland than on manors in England or in south Wales (Otway-Ruthven 1951, 9–10; 1968, 110, 118).

Below: **Depiction of the *Lokator* in the Heidelberger Sachsenspiegal. The *Lokator* is depicted wearing a hat.**

COLONIZATION PROCESS

Such facts help to explain why peasants would come to Ireland, despite the real or perceived dangers. In comparison to the colonization of large parts of eastern Europe, little is known about how these mainly Middle English-speaking peasants were recruited and chosen, as well as the organization behind how they came to settle on particular manors. We know far more about arguably similar processes in German lands. There, most princes and magnates transferred the specific recruitment of settlers, the distribution of the land and the establishment of the settlements to so-called *Lokators* (allocators of land). These men, who usually came from the minor lordly or urban merchant classes, organized the equipment needed by the colonists and the wagon trains that brought them to their new lands. The *Lokators* also oversaw land clearance and the building of these new settlements.

Most German peasants seem to have willingly gone east in search of a better life. However, there are quite a few references surviving to peasants being offered an unpalatable choice, with criminals being effectively asked to choose between moving east or being imprisoned or even executed. Examples exist of German lords pardoning criminals and sending them east to settle on the new lands there (Frey 2012, 194). Perhaps some English peasants came to Ireland under these dubious circumstances as well. Whether it was eastern Europe or the new colonies in Ireland, such men were tough and even ruthless, qualities that may have been useful in the colonization process in both territories.

Some illustrations in the early fourteenth-century illuminated manuscript known as the *Heidelberger Sachsenspiegel* (the Heidelberg Saxon Mirror) depict aspects of the colonization process in Germany and eastern Europe in the thirteenth century. One illustration shows the *Lokator* being granted the right to clear forest for farmland and to build a village (https://digi.ub.uni.heidelberg.de/diglit/cpg164/0066). He is also shown recruiting peasants who are depicted clearing forest and building timber-framed houses. Another image shows the *Lokator* acting as a judge and sitting on a bench in front of the new settlement's church (ibid.). Yet another image depicts a robber being sent eastward apparently because he was a brave man and so ready for war. Medieval German manuscripts and illustrations like this are useful for Ireland and may suggest or hint at how the movement of English peasants to this island was achieved.

ENGLISH PEASANT OR IRISH *BETAGH*

While the historical place names and even much later linguistic evidence suggest there was considerable English peasant immigration and colonization across quite large parts of eastern and south-eastern Ireland, it can be difficult in these areas to distinguish English peasant settlement from low-status Irish or *betagh* settlement by excavation and fieldwork

Below: **A peasant, accompanied by his dog, sowing corn, depicted in the Luttrell Psalter.**

alone (Gardiner and O'Conor 2017, 147). In a general sense, the evidence from the documentary sources, such as it is, suggests that Irish tenants on Anglo-Norman manors, mostly but not all *betaghs,* lived in relatively small, unplanned kin-based house clusters in townlands located at varying distances away from the *capita* or centres of these manors, where Anglo-Norman lords resided (Otway-Ruthven 1951, 3, 12; 1965, 76; 1968, 110–12; O'Conor 1998, 44; see, also, Murphy and Potterton 2010, 184–9). The problem here is that, certainly from the mid-thirteenth century onwards if not before, there is evidence for individual peasants of English origin living out in the townlands that made up manors also at a distance from the manorial centres (Gardiner and O'Conor 2017, 136–46).

The difficulty, as just stated above, lies in deciding what is the archaeological signature for farmsteads and small settlements inhabited by English-speaking peasants as opposed to ones occupied by Irishmen of the same status. It is hard in many cases to draw definite conclusions about the ethnicity of a site's occupants based on settlement morphology and material culture alone, at least in eastern and south-eastern Ireland. This is partly because many medieval peasant farming sites across Ireland, Britain and Europe that were occupied for even long periods of time do not produce much in the way of finds when excavated, regardless of ethnicity. This lack of finds on rural sites seems to be because household rubbish was often collected, dumped into manure heaps and then spread out as fertiliser on surrounding fields (Wrathmell 1989, 31–3; O'Conor 1998, 65). This scarcity of finds from many rural excavations may also be an indication that many of the everyday objects used on medieval farms were made of organic materials and so do not survive to be uncovered by excavation (O'Conor 1998, 65).

MATERIAL CULTURE

Irish and English tenants, therefore, lived in relatively close proximity on many manors in eastern Ireland. Processes like acculturation, even intermarriage, and similar responses to local, physical conditions may also have lessened the differences in material culture between the two ethnic groups. Despite these problems and general observations, scholars at times have attempted to identify the ethnicity of the occupants of a lower-status, rural settlement by material culture. For example, the excavator of Attyflin, County Limerick, James Eogan (2009) noted that this small nucleated settlement of thirteenth- and fourteenth-century date was located in a peripheral part of a manorial estate, well away from its *caput*. He also pointed out that finds of sherds of cooking ware from the site were rare. In this respect, there is some evidence to suggest that the native Irish, over the southern two-thirds of the country, tended not to use pottery for the preparation of food during the whole Later Medieval period (O'Conor 2021, 44–45). For example, Michelle Comber's long-term research excavation of Caherconnell cashel in the Burren, a site associated with the O'Loghlen sept during Later Medieval times, has not produced one sherd of pottery of any kind, despite the richness of the artefact assemblage from the site and its closeness to the Anglo-Norman trading towns of Galway and Athenry (Michelle Comber, pers. comm.).

In all, given the lack of cooking ware from the site and its peripheral location well away from the *caput* of the manor in which it was located, Eogan (2009, 75–77) argued that the site at Attyflin may have been a settlement inhabited by Irish tenants, possibly *betaghs* but who may, perhaps, have been of a higher status than this, based on the evidence of some of the finds. However, on many manors betaghs were more prosperous or had the potential to be more prosperous than the lower grades of English tenants (Down 1987, 458; O'Keeffe 2000, 60). The thirteenth century was a very wealthy period in Ireland and, in my opinion, all levels of society, regardless of status or ethnicity, would have benefited from this prosperity.

Above: **Aerial photograph of the site of the rural borough at Newtown Jerpoint, County Kilkenny.**

Opposite page: **Reconstruction of an excavated house at Bourchier's Castle, County Limerick. It has been argued that the house itself consisted of two rooms, with a barn attached onto its rear.**

SETTLEMENT PROFILE

On the subject of further differences in material culture between the Irish and English and, for that matter, the Anglo-Normans, it has been suggested, again based on a mix of historical, later pictorial and a little excavated evidence, that the continued use of post-and-wattle buildings as residences (as opposed to their use as agricultural buildings, which was seen across the island) was really a Gaelic Irish cultural trait, regardless of status, and that timber-framed buildings were to be seen in Anglo-Norman and English peasant rural contexts (O'Conor 2003).

There has been some attempt, therefore, to try and solve this problem of identifying low-status Irish sites from English peasant ones by recognizing differences, even slight ones, in material culture and house types. Arguably, much more could be done to answer this question. How can this relatively small amount of work be built upon? The historical background and siting of low-status settlements are important in helping to understand the lifeways of English peasant settlers and their immediate descendants in thirteenth-century Ireland and, if possible, to aid building up a roadmap as to how archaeologists carrying out future excavations could distinguish between the settlement sites of the different ethnicities.

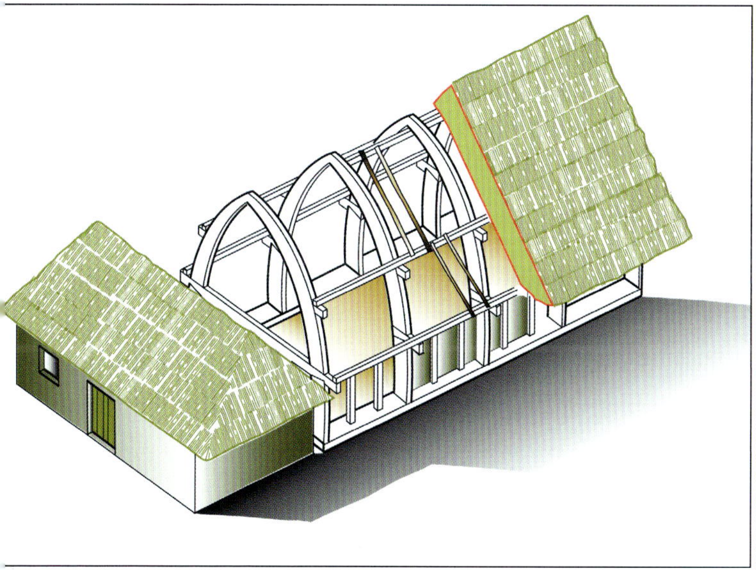

In this regard, the historical evidence does suggest that the inhabitants of the rural boroughs, effectively agricultural villages with market functions, and the nucleated villages at manorial centres were invariably of English rather than Irish origin. This seems to have been particularly true of those large parts of eastern and south-eastern Ireland mentioned above where the historical and place name evidence suggests heavy English immigration took place during the late twelfth and thirteenth centuries. At the very least, for example, the excavated evidence from such sites as the rural borough of Dunmanogue (Sleeman and Hurley 1987) or the medieval village at Mullaghmast (Bolger 2017), both in County Kildare, or future excavations at sites like the deserted rural boroughs at Newtown Jerpoint, County Kilkenny, (Oxford Archaeology 2007) or Castlemore, County Carlow, provide or will provide, particularly from their earlier layers, much needed information on the lifeways of ordinary English immigrants and their immediate descendants. The next step would be to carefully combine this information from rural sites with excavated evidence from the towns and cities, which again the surviving historical records indicate were mostly inhabited by Englishmen or their progeny by the very early thirteenth century (Eagar 1988), to build up a better profile of the typical material culture and house types found on

English settlement sites of the Anglo-Norman period. In fact, using a very similar methodology, I argued back in 1998 that the excavated evidence from rural boroughs and villages that the historical sources suggest were inhabited by English peasants indicated that two-roomed houses, divided into living and sleeping quarters (with the central hearth in the former area), regardless of whether they were built of cob, stone or were timber framed, were a popular form of dwelling in such settlements (O'Conor 1998, 56–7). Such house plans are known from peasant contexts in villages in England of the same date. This discussion also demonstrates very clearly that the historical context of a site will be an important tool in identifying further settlement sites occupied by English peasants for excavation and building up a better profile of their material culture. Furthermore, future DNA and isotope analysis of the skeletal remains from burial grounds associated with known English peasant settlements will also provide information as to the origins of these people and the lifeways of their descendants in the thirteenth and early fourteenth centuries.

Below: **Reconstruction of the farmstead excavated at Boyerstown, County Meath.**

Opposite page: **Aerial photograph of a moated site in the Irish countryside today.**

Building up a profile of how to identify dispersed English peasant settlement sites living out beyond the manorial centres from ones inhabited by the ordinary Irish, across the landscapes of Anglo-Norman manors, is a more difficult task. Again, using the approach outlined above (which, as noted, will hopefully be improved upon by the results of future excavations at known nucleated English peasant settlements), such as examining the amount of cooking ware or the types of houses excavated on any given site, combining this with the available historical and place name evidence, such as it is, it may be possible to distinguish the ethnicity of the people dwelling in such dispersed locations away from manorial centres.

MOATED SITES

On analogy with England, it is also highly likely that many of the moated sites built across eastern, but particularly south-eastern, Ireland were built by prosperous peasants of English origin and descent in the period from the mid-thirteenth century into the early fourteenth century, maybe a bit later. Invariably, in south-eastern Ireland, moated sites are located away from manorial centres

in more peripheral parts of the manor. Certainly, the finds from many of these sites are linked to farming and, whilst suggesting prosperity, are not particularly high status in character (O'Conor 2023b, 20–1, 24, 27–30).

The results of the excavations carried out on National Roads Authority / Transport Infrastructure Ireland road schemes and other developments over the last 20 or 30 years have dramatically increased our knowledge of rural settlement during the Anglo-Norman period particularly in lowland parts of eastern and south-eastern Ireland, where English peasant settlement was dense (Gardiner and O'Conor

Above: **The motte at Castlemore, County Carlow.**

Opposite page: **Reconstruction image of the rural borough at Castlemore, County Carlow, as it would have appeared in the thirteenth century.**

2017). One surprise to me was the amount of undefended, isolated farmsteads of thirteenth- to fourteenth-century date, along with the number of hitherto unidentified moated sites, which were identified and excavated during the course of these infrastructural develop-

ments, just one example of which was the farmstead at Boyerstown, County Meath, which was excavated by Kevin Martin for Archaeological Consultancy Services in 2006 (Martin 2009; Gardiner and O'Conor 2017, 141–4). The picture that emerges from these excavations, if it is combined with evidence from the surviving historical sources, is that the rural landscape of eastern and south-eastern Ireland of the thirteenth and earlier fourteenth centuries was a more managed, populated and wealthier place than was once believed (Gardiner and O'Conor 2017, 150).

Tenants on Anglo-Norman manors in eastern and south-eastern Ireland, whether English or Irish, seem to have achieved prosperity during this economic boom of the thirteenth century, which seems to have continued into the early fourteenth century (ibid.). The combined evidence, I would feel, also suggests that in certain areas of eastern Ireland this prosperity continued in certain core areas of the colony into Late Medieval times and beyond, despite the speed bumps of various famines, the Bruce War (1315–18), the Gaelic Resurgence (*c.*1300-*c.*1500) and the Black

Death (1348) along the way.

A peasant living on a manor around the year 1290 in places like Meath, north Dublin, east Kildare, south Wexford and in the environs of Cork, living, for example, at the nucleated settlement beside Castlemore village or borough in County Carlow, or living in a moated site like Ballinvinny near Cork city (see Cotter 2009), speaking by now a distinct Irish dialect of Middle English, must have believed that the decision of either his or her great-grandfather or grandfather from England or the English colonies in south Wales to migrate across the Irish Sea to Ireland had been the right choice. He or she must have felt that their immediate antecedents had created, or at least colonized, parts of a land that was not unlike 'Cokayne', the mythical land of plenty in the medieval mind.

Acknowledgements

The writer would like to thank Dr Niall Brady, Dr Christian Frey, Dr Felix Biermann, Dr John O'Keeffe of the Discovery Programme and Frank 'Jay' Hall for their help in carrying out the research for this article.

BIBLIOGRAPHY

Edited Primary Sources

Red Book of Ormond. White, N.B. (ed.) 1932. *The Red Book of Ormond*. Dublin.

Secondary Sources

Bartlett, R. 1994. *The making of Europe: conquest, colonisation and cultural change, 950–1350*, London.

Barry, T.B. 1987. *The archaeology of medieval Ireland*. London and New York: Methuen.

Barry, T.B. 1993. Rural settlement in Ireland in the Middle Ages; an overview. *Ruralia*. 1, pp134–41.

Biermann, F., Hermann, C. and Koperkiewicz, A. 2016. Alt-Wartenburg / Barczewko – Interdisziplinäre Erforschung einer spätmittelalterlichen Stadtwüstung in Ermland (Nordestpolen). *Zeitschrift fur Archäologie des Mittelalters*. 44, pp115–48.

Bliss, A. and Long, J. 1987. Literature in Norman French and English to 1534 *IN*: Cosgrove, A. (ed.) *A new history of Ireland, Volume II. Medieval Ireland, 1169-1534*. Oxford. pp708–36.

Bolger, T. 2017. *Colonising a royal landscape: the history and archaeology of a medieval village at Mullamast, County Kildare*. Dublin: Transport Infrastructure Ireland.

Browne, K.A. 1927. The ancient dialect of the baronies of Forth and Bargy, County Wexford. *Journal of the Royal Society of Antiquaries of Ireland*. 17, pp127–37.

Cleary, R. 2018. *The archaeology of Lough Gur*. Dublin: Wordwell.

Cotter, K. 2009. The medieval moated site at Ballyinvinny South, Co. Cork *IN*: Corlett, C. and Potterton, M. (eds.) *Rural settlement in medieval Ireland in the light of recent archaeological excavations*. Dublin: Wordwell. pp49–58.

Down, K. 1987. Colonial society and economy in the High Middle Ages *IN*: Cosgrove, A. (ed.) *A new history of Ireland, Volume II. Medieval Ireland, 1169–1534*. Oxford. pp439–91.

Duffy, S. 1997. *Ireland in the Middle Ages*. Dublin: Macmillan. pp83–85.

Eagar, B. 1988. The Cambro-Normans and the lordship of Leinster *IN*: Bradley, J. (ed.) *Settlement and society in medieval Ireland*. Kilkenny: Boethius Press. pp193–206.

Eogan, J. 2009. A betagh settlement at Attyflin, Co. Limerick *IN*: Corlett, C. and Potterton, M. (eds.) *Rural settlement in medieval Ireland in the light of recent archaeological excavation*. Dublin: Wordwell. pp67–77.

Frey, G. 2014. The Burgward organisation in the Eastern Marches of the German realm – frontier mentality and inculturation *IN*: Ettel, P., Flambard-Héricher, A-M and O'Conor, K. (eds.) *Château Gaillard 26: château et frontière*. Caen: Presses Universitaires de Caen. pp 193–8.

Gardiner, M. and O'Conor, K. 2017. The later medieval countryside lying beneath *IN*: Stanley, M., Swan, R. and O'Sullivan, A. (eds.) *Stories of*

Ireland's past: knowledge gained from NRA roads archaeology. Dublin: Transport Infrastructure Ireland. pp133–52.

Glasscock, R.E. 1987. Land and people, *c*.1300 *IN*: Cosgrove, A. (ed.) *A new history of Ireland, Volume II. Medieval Ireland, 1169–1534*. Oxford. pp203–39.

Graham, B.J. 1993. The High Middle Ages: *c*.1100–*c*.1350 *IN*: Graham, B.J. and Proudfoot, L.J. (eds.) *A historical geography of Ireland*. London: Academic Press. pp 58–98.

Higounet, C. 2001. *Die deutsche Ostsiedlung im Mittelalter*. Berlin.

Jones-Hughes, T. 1970. Town and baile in Irish place names *IN*: Stephens, N. and Glasscock, R.E. (eds.) *Irish Geographical Studies*. pp244–58.

Martin, K. 2009. Boyerstown: a rediscovered medieval farmstead *IN*: Deevy, M. and Murphy, D. (eds.) *Places along the way: first findings on the M3*, NRA Scheme Monographs 5. Dublin: National Roads Authority. pp135–51.

McNeill, T. 1980. *Anglo-Norman Ulster: The history and archaeology of an Irish barony, 1177–1400*. Belfast: J. Donald for Institute of Irish Studies.

Murphy, M. and Potterton, M. 2010. *The Dublin region in the Middle Ages: settlement, land-use and economy*. Dublin, Four Courts Press.

O'Conor, K. 1998. *The archaeology of medieval rural settlement in Ireland*, Discovery Programme Monograph 3. Dublin.

O'Conor, K. 2003. Housing in later medieval Gaelic Ireland. *Ruralia*. 4, pp201–10.

O'Conor, K. 2004. Medieval Rural Settlement in Munster *IN*: Ludlow, J. and Jameson, N. (eds.) *Medieval Ireland: the Barryscourt Lectures I-X*. Kinsale: Gandon Editions. pp225–56.

O'Conor, K. 2021. Settlement in Gaelic Ireland, 1100–1350. *Eolas*. 13, pp43–71.

O'Conor, K. 2023a. Moygara Castle through time *IN*: O'Conor, K. (ed.) *Moygara Castle, County Sligo, and the O'Garas of Coolavin*. Dublin: Four Courts Press. pp181–208.

O'Conor, K. 2023b. Moated sites in Ireland: the current state of knowledge *IN*: McAlister, V.L. and Shine, L. (eds.) *Rethinking medieval Ireland and beyond: lifecycles, landscapes and settlements*. Leiden and Boston; Brill. pp9–55.

O'Keeffe, T. 2000. *Medieval Ireland: an archaeology*. Stroud, England: Tempus.

O'Keeffe, T. 2017. Routes across the familiar past: reflections on NRA-funded excavations and the challenge facing the 'post-medieval' archaeology of rural Ireland *IN*: Stanley, M., Swan, R. and O'Sullivan, A. (eds.) *Stories of Ireland's past: knowledge gained from NRA roads archaeology*. Dublin: Transport Infrastructure Ireland. pp153–64.

Otway-Ruthven, A.J. 1951. The Organization of Anglo-Irish Agriculture in the Middle Ages. *Journal of the Royal Society of Antiquaries of Ireland*. 81, pp1–13.

Otway-Ruthven, A.J. 1965. The character of Norman settlement in Ireland. *Historical Studies*. 5, pp75–84.

Otway-Ruthven, A.J. 1968. *A history of medieval Ireland*. London.

Oxford Archaeology. 2007. *Newtown Jerpoint – Heritage Conservation Plan*. Kilkenny: The Heritage Council.

Sleeman, M.J. and Hurley, M.F. 1987. Blackcastle, Co. Kildare *IN*: Cleary, R.M., Hurley, M.F. and Twohig, E.A. (eds.) *Archaeological excavations on the Cork–Dublin gas pipeline (1981–82)*, Cork Archaeological Reports 1. Cork: Department of Archaeology. pp101–5.

Stalley, R. 1987. *The Cistercian monasteries of Ireland*. London and New Haven: Yale University Press.

Watt, J.A. 1987. Approaches to the history of 14th-century Ireland *IN*: Cosgrove, A. (ed.) *A new history of Ireland, Volume II. Medieval Ireland, 1169–1534*. Oxford. pp303–13.

Wrathmell, S. 1989. *Domestic settlement 2: medieval peasant farmsteads*. York: University of York.

ONLINE SOURCES

https://colloquechateaugaillard.eu

https://digi.ub.uni.heidelberg.de/diglit/cpg164/0066

https://en.wikipedia.org/wiki/Fingallian

https://en.wikipedia.org/wiki/Little_England_beyond_Wales

https://ruralia2.ff.cuni.cz

CHAPTER 7

The Buildings of Dublin's Historic Immigrant Communities

PAUL DUFFY

Paul Duffy is an archaeologist, historian and author specializing in medieval and urban archaeology. He has directed numerous excavations in Dublin, has led projects in the UK, France and Australia and is a project manager with IAC Archaeology. Duffy is currently completing a PhD with Leicester University on the lost medieval architecture of Dublin. He describes here a number of excavations that reflect the immigrant influence on buildings in historic Dublin.

In discussing this topic, I aim to give the reader not so much a holistic overview of the medieval and early modern buildings of Dublin per se but to lead them more on a personal journey through a range of excavations that I have been lucky enough to have been involved in that have brought me face to face with the buildings of immigrant communities in the city. I will introduce you to some of the buildings, dwellings and other structures that I and my colleagues have come across or excavated, some of which have not yet been published, which also makes this a perfect opportunity to present them to the public. These are shown in the map (right) and, as is apparent, they all fall outside of the circuit of the medieval walled town, with seven sites south of the Liffey and the city walls, and two north of the river.

In considering the subject of this paper and also the theme of the conference, Migration and Ireland through Time, we should appreciate these structures and acknowledge the people that built them, setting aside for now some of the potentially problematic labels that may come to mind, such as raiders, pirates, invaders, colonists, Ascendancy and so on.

Before looking at the sites themselves, I want to give some context as to what urban archaeology looks like. In advance of digging these sites within the built urban environment, there has to be an element of demolition, for example, large concrete slabs or modern building features must be removed. Indeed, there is a whole planning process that must happen even before that point is reached. When we actually get to the ground level, we can be working in a whole different range of conditions, generally in close proximity to heavy construction plant and machinery. The rewards that come from working in these sometimes challenging environments, however, can be all the richer for the stratified levels that can be preserved in urban contexts.

VIKING DUBLIN

In examining Dublin's immigrant building structures, I want to start off a little way outside of Dublin, at a location between the coastal suburbs of Baldoyle and Portmarnock in north County Dublin. An aerial photograph taken as part of an Irish Air Corps survey in 1932 showed a very dramatic-looking earthwork at the confluence of the Mayne River

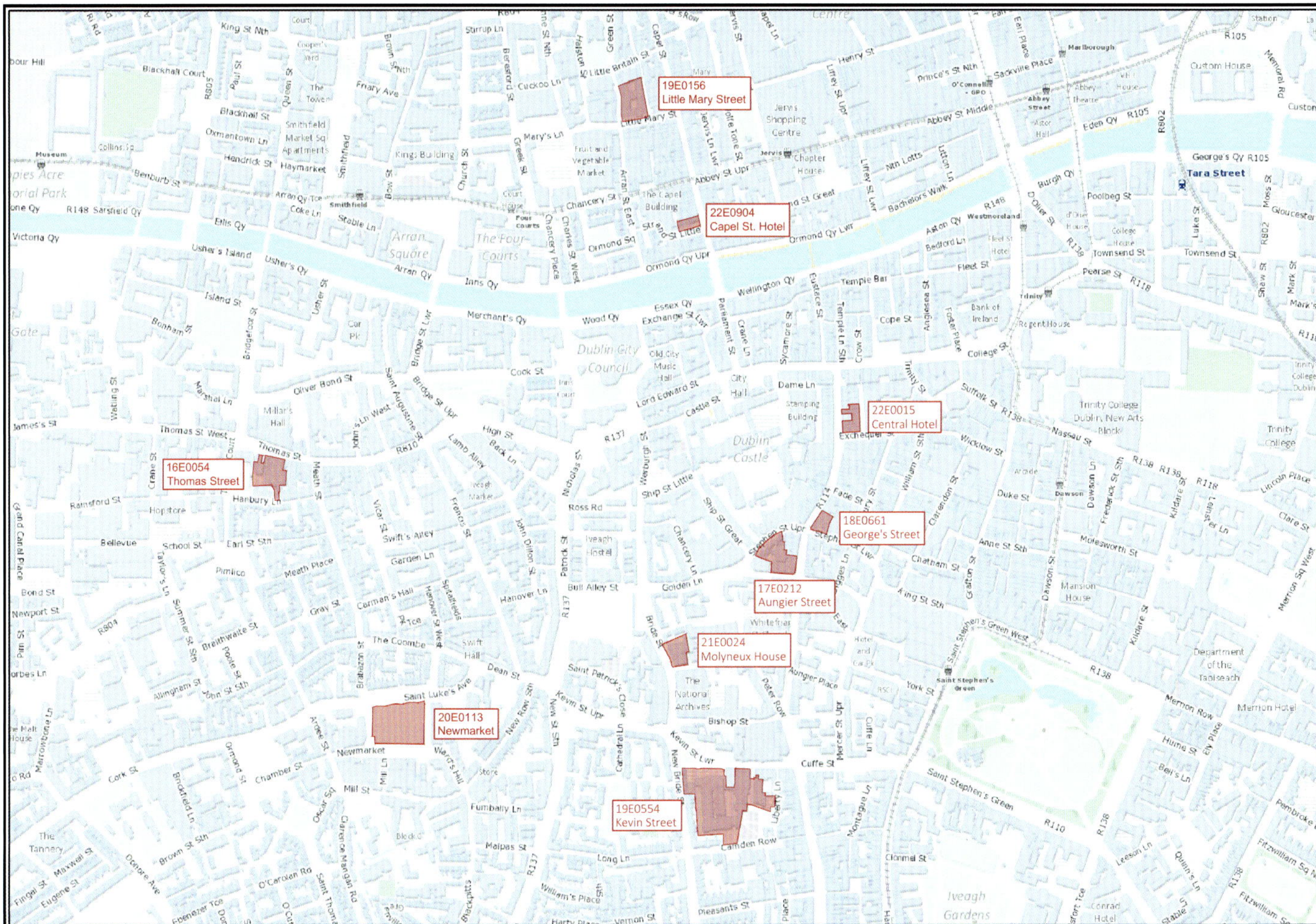

Above: **Map showing sites discussed in the text.**

where it is joined from the south by a smaller river, just before the combined river flows into Baldoyle estuary. In the medieval period, Baldoyle estuary was much deeper and navigable than it is today (before heavy silting caused by the construction of Howth Harbour in 1813) and Baldoyle is an area that is very much associated with Scandinavian place names.

I start here because Dublin itself – urban Dublin – owes its genesis to Scandinavian people. When they arrived, Dublin was not a built-up or urbanized area. The very first structures at Dublin, discounting the Gaelic Irish monastic site that we think may have

been located beside the tidal pool on the river Poddle, may have looked something quite like the earthworks at Maynetown (DUO15-152) on the Baldoyle estuary. Visible in the image is a raised D-shaped area defined by a deep ditch that connects to the river. These earthworks conform to the criteria of a *longphort* or Viking shore camp and ship enclosure (Duffy et al. 2024).

A reader standing at Dublin Castle now would be very much in the heart of the landscape of that early settlement. From the lower gate into Dublin Castle, one can see the ground rise up towards the main Georgian buildings in the Upper Castle Yard, which we believe was where the original *dún* area or Viking *longphort* would have been located and where the medieval castle was later built. If you can imagine superimposing the Maynetown D-shaped structure onto Upper Castle Yard, overlooking the Liffey to the north and the Poddle and Black Pool to the south, this is probably a close approximation of what the original *dún* or *longphort* of Dublin would have looked like. This can be a contentious subject and archaeological excavations and new research are constantly refining our understanding but it is important to start off the story of Dublin's buildings with the Scandinavians.

Some 240 metres to the south-west of Dublin Castle is the site of the Aungier Street excavation that we undertook throughout most of 2018 and into 2019. It is bounded on the north by Stephen Street Upper and by Longford Street to the south. The site is on a

Below: **Aerial image showing the Aungier Street excavations in progress.**

Opposite page: **Earthworks at Maynetown with Baldoyle estuary to right and Maine River visible.**

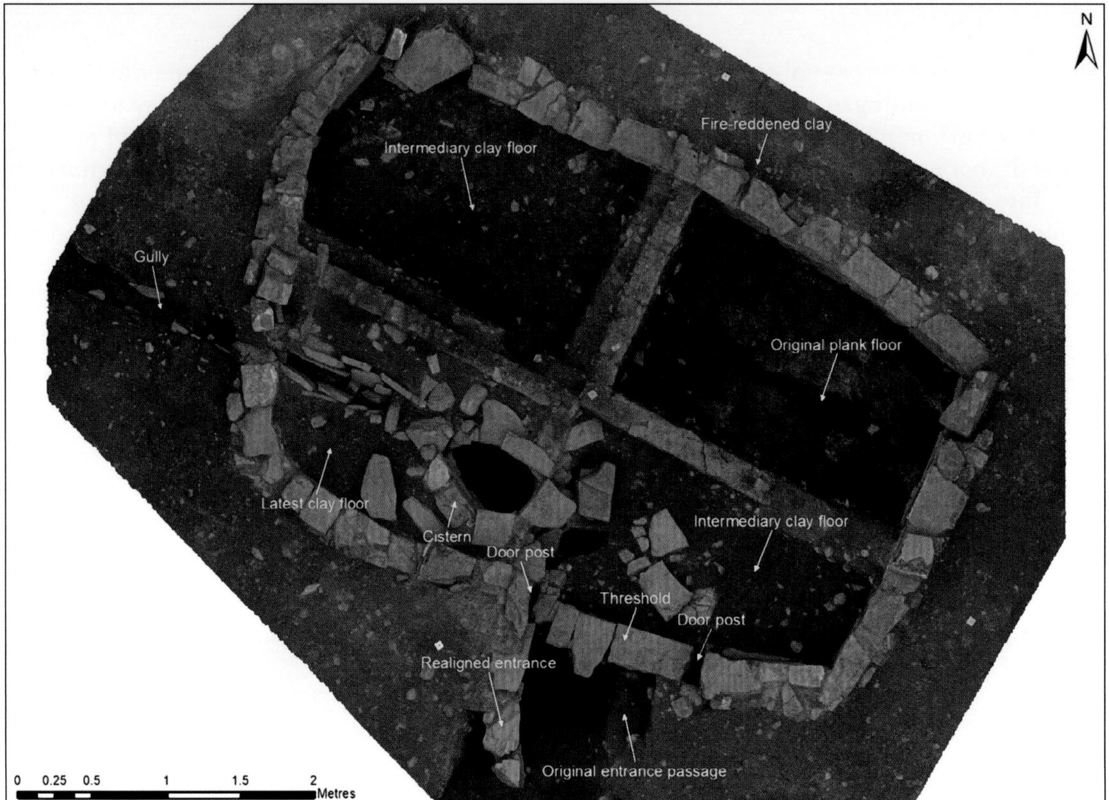

rise that originally would have overlooked the *dubh linn* or 'black pool', which is the tidal pool at the confluence of the Liffey and Poddle from which Dublin gets its modern name. The pool of the *dubh linn* extended around the south of the *dún* and, although the rise is less obvious in the modern, built-up landscape, you can still feel the pull of the hill if you walk up Ship Street at the back of the castle, walking from the now infilled pool up to the top of the slope at Stephen Street. A thousand years ago, this would have been a rise or hill that would have overlooked the pool and the *dún*.

Excavating this very large site at the top of that rise, we were hoping to find traces of the church of St Peter's on the Hill as it was named in medieval sources. Whilst we did find the church (discussed below), quite unexpectedly

Above: **High-definition orthomosaic image of the sunken-floored structure at the Aungier Street site.**

Opposite page, above: **Entrance passageway and finds from around the doorway of the sunken-floored structure, Aungier Street, Dublin 8.**

Opposite page, below: **Reconstruction drawing of the sunken-floored structure at the Aungier Street site.**

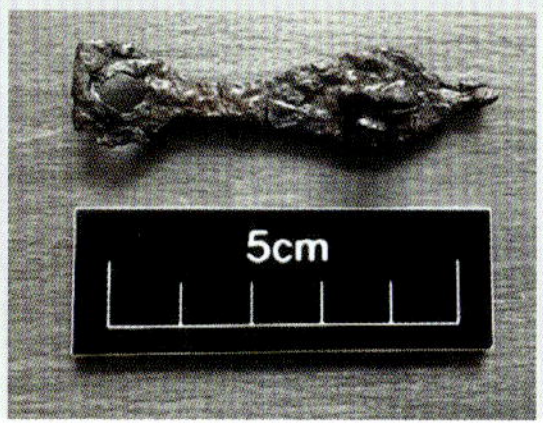

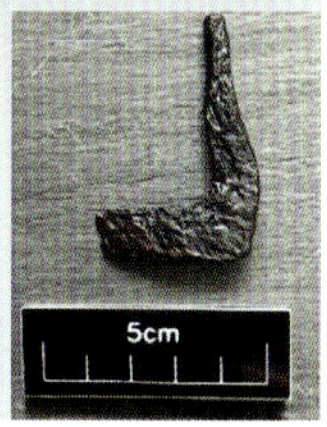

we also found a unique sunken-floored structure dated to AD 1025–1154 at the centre of the site.

Within this structure at Aungier Street we identified an original wattle floor and a later stone-lined cistern cutting through the floor, fed by a slate-lined gulley. This structure had been subject to a catastrophic fire at some stage around 1100 and was subsequently rebuilt and renovated a number of times. The fire had burned so hot that the stone lining transferred heat to the surrounding subsoil resulting in a ring of fire-reddened clay around the structure.

We did not fully excavate the structure as it was proposed to put it on public display. The structure is now under quite a large and impressive glass floor viewing space within the Lidl shop on Aungier Street.

What has survived at Aungier Street is the bottom 50 centimetres of the sunken-floored structure. The whole centre of the site was scarped out in the 1950s, so the context of this structure has been lost. It almost certainly would have been located within a busy suburb that had plots, houses and associated fences and roadways. It appears that none of these other structures had sunken floors or cellars and therefore have not survived. We did find a number of cesspits and storage pits that allow the rough shape of these plots to be suggested. It is unlikely that this is a primary residence but it is likely to have stood to the rear of a main house akin to a Viking Dublin type one house that would have fronted the road.

Leading down to the structure there was a sloping entrance passageway. This had been infilled during a later phase of activity and a stone threshold, flanked by two door jambs, had been installed. Inside the door we found a beautiful iron key, as well as a hinge and a latch, possibly all associated with the timber door.

Taking all of this information, in addition to the environmental information from soil sampling, our goal was to try to imagine what the structure had looked like, accepting the fact that no above-ground structure was left and that the whole floor level and the surrounding natural ground had been reduced.

What we did know was that the structure had a stone-lined sunken element. The stones were not structural in the sense that they were not carrying a wall. They were battered inwards very slightly and were laid edge on edge. We can only surmise that the upper part of the structure had been made of timber or wattle with a thatch roof. The sloping entrance passage was lined with stone and planked and there was a wattle screen floor inside. We can picture a woman of the house inside spinning wool with the spindle whorl that we found and with, perhaps, the key on her belt. We found one sherd of pottery and a bucket handle from within the cistern. All of that material helped us to propose a reconstruction of what had been going on in the structure but we do not know for sure what it was being used for.

While we did find an area of burning it is uncertain whether it was a hearth or not. Sunken-floored structures found in Dublin previous to this are characterized by not having a hearth, so potentially something else was happening here.

Structures with sunken floors are ultimately derived from a Germanic tradition and are known from Anglo-Saxon England and from Viking Age Scandinavia. Sunken floors have been found in Hiberno-Norse buildings in the Scandinavian-founded towns of Waterford and Limerick, though these are somewhat different to the Aungier Street example. Archaeologist Linzi Simpson, in earlier excavations at Temple Bar West (Simpson 2011), found sunken-floored structures, with rounded corners and sub-floor drains similar to the Aungier Street example, but these were made purely from wattling and dated to *c.*250 years earlier. The fact that a sunken-floored structure was constructed at Aungier Street many generations later gives us a sense that there was an enduring Scandinavian character and identity being expressed in buildings in Dublin. At the same time, the differences in the structures and the location of the Aungier Street example outside of the walled Scandinavian town shows us that these people were adapting and changing, becoming intermeshed with the surrounding 'indigenous' populations.

MEDIEVAL CHURCHES

Although we do not always associate the construction of churches with Scandinavians in Dublin, we are finding increasing evidence for a very lively episode of church building in the city from the middle of the eleventh century. Reminding ourselves that we approached the excavation of the Aungier Street site with a hope of finding the church of St Peter's on the Hill, mentioned in documentary sources as early as *c.* AD 1115, the site did provide us with a very important piece of information to this end – a large limekiln, the scale and location of which can only have been for a large structure such as a church. An early date of AD 1028–1155 was retrieved from the primary fill of the kiln. Unfortunately, nothing of the fabric of the earlier church, other than the limekiln, survived. It was all

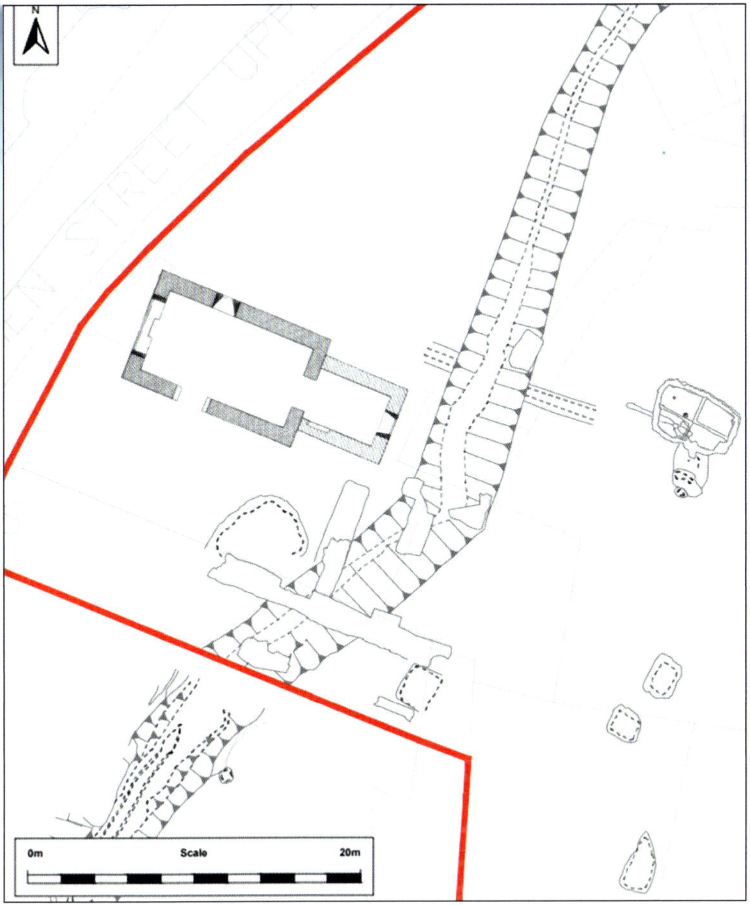

cannibalized, presumably, for the later church that was constructed over the limekiln.

Above: **Excavation plan showing the curving boundary ditch, sunken-floored structure (to right), limekiln and later St Peter's church with the plan of Palmerstown church inserted in the suspected location of the early church.**

The location of the church was separated from the area of the sunken structure by a curving ditch dating to the eleventh century. At the very bottom of the ditch, we recovered a curved, red earthenware roof tile. This kind of roof tile is known from the excavations at Wood Quay and they are believed to have been a part of the original eleventh century roofing of Christ Church cathedral. These were imported roof tiles from England, possibly from Chester or York, where they are known to have been used in this period. A red tiled roof is something we do not imagine so much for Irish churches at this time. However, this find is an indication that Dubliners were influencing the built environment with imported building materials.

In trying to visualize what this church looked like, the closest parallel we can find for a church in the Dublin area for a date of *c.*1100, if not earlier, is Palmerstown church in west Dublin. Taking the floor plan of the Palmerstown church and placing it onto the Aungier Street site plan, it was found that it fit quite snugly into a space formed by a kink in the boundary ditch that divided the ecclesiastical land of the church on the left from the suburban area of the sunken structure (Duffy 2023a). The church was rebuilt and extended eastward, probably in 1380, and it is the foundations for this phase of building that were found onsite.

Nearly 700 metres due south of the Aungier Street site, at the former Dublin Institute of Technology campus on Kevin Street, we excavated adjacent to the site of St Kevin's church and park for over a year. The church, which is off Camden Row, sits within a public park that was formerly the graveyard. For a long

time, there has been a question mark over the origins and dating of the church. St Kevin's appears in records from the later twelfth century but there has always been a suspicion that it may be older and had some connection with the ecclesiastical and pilgrimage centre of Glendalough, especially in light of its name (Clarke 2002).

Above: **Excavations in an urban context at a site on Kevin Street, Dublin 8.**

Opposite page: **View north-east of St Kevin's church.**

Our excavations uncovered a rectilinear enclosure, resembling a moated site in some ways, that wraps around St Kevin's church. Within that enclosure, we found a large limekiln with a date range of AD 990–1150, which compares very well with the St Peter's church limekiln. A limekiln of that size beside a church presents strong evidence that the original stone church of St Kevin was built at roughly the same time as St Peter's. It is possible that elements of the current St Kevin's church may be medieval in date. However, this is difficult to ascertain without excavation due to extensive rebuilding in the seventeenth and eighteenth centuries. Further analysis and targeted excavation at this structure might reveal that some standing elements at the lower courses date to the time of the original church.

What did these churches that were built during the time of Hiberno-Scandinavian hegemony in Dublin look like? We have the example of St Michael le Pole with its round tower, which was located between Chancery Lane and Ship Street. Its name meant St Michael of the Pool, because it overlooked the black pool, *dubh linn*. St Michael le Pole also had a limekiln, which was excavated by Edmond O'Donovan in 2007–08 (O'Donovan 2008), and the radiocarbon date range (AD 1022-1164) accords very neatly with the kilns at St Peter's and St Kevin's, further pointing to a boom in church construction at this time.

EARLY ROMANESQUE

This boom in church building, evidenced by the limekilns discussed above, straddles the advent of new forms and styles in ecclesiastical architecture. It is generally accepted by scholars writing about Romanesque architecture in Ireland that Dublin – an outward-facing trading port with wide-reaching trade links – was the point of entry for the arrival of this new style into the country (O'Keeffe 2015, Ó Carragáin 2010). Dublin has also been recognized as a place where innovative church forms were developed during this time – forms that are believed to have influenced the churches at Glendalough, which are early nave and chancel buildings with various engaged round towers (ibid). The magnitude of this boom in church building is best expressed by the fact that archaeologists and historians cannot definitively prove there was a single church standing in Dublin prior to AD 1000[1] but by about AD 1100 Dublin had over 20 ecclesiastical buildings, by far the largest concentration of church structures anywhere in the country. Clearly there was a significant transformation happening here as the descendants of Scandinavian settlers embraced Christianity. It is likely that the construction of Christ Church cathedral, which followed the pilgrimage of the Hiberno-Norse king of Dublin, Sitric Silkenbeard, to Rome in 1028, launched this boom in church building in Dublin.

[1] There were almost certainly some but we lack evidence for these structures that may have been made of wood.

It has been recognized in recent years that the diversity of church designs found at Glendalough, including nave-and-chancel churches, true arches and engaged round towers, was effectively an attempt to replicate what had been built by the Hiberno-Norse in Dublin. What we see in the standing remains at Glendalough allows us to hold a mirror up to the innovative Dublin churches that no longer exist. As at Glendalough, the Dublin churches seem to have embraced the round tower, as with the engaged round tower that

Above left: **Early limekiln (eleventh / twelfth century) on left beneath the reconstructed St Peter's church *c.*1380.**

Above right: **Red earthenware rooftile from near the church site, an example of imported building materials.**

Left: **St Mary's Abbey gatehouse with diagonal buttresses visible (centre front and upper left).**

Opposite page: **St Canice's church, Finglas, with string course and early gable highlighted and elevation of St Mary's, Glendalough, superimposed for comparison.**

once rose from the chancel of Kilmacnessan church on Ireland's Eye, off the coast at Howth. A round tower once stood at the church of St Michael le Pole and there are also barrel-vaulted churches surviving within what was once the Scandinavian-controlled hinterland, stretching up to Skerries in north County Dublin (St Doulagh's in Kinsealy, St Patrick's off Skerries and Kilmacnessan on Ireland's Eye). The links with Glendalough are further seen in several features found in the eleventh-century church of St Canice in the Dublin suburb of Finglas – the site of the famous female Viking burial. These include a string course along the eastern wall of the nave, a feature seen at St Kevin's and St Mary's churches in Glendalough, dating from the years around 1100. The line of the orig-

inal west gable at St Canice's can be seen among later fabric and indicates that the building once had a higher pitch, similar to early churches at Glendalough. There is also a batter to the nave walls, a feature seen at the early churches of Palmerstown and Glendalough. These architectural features help us to visualize what the churches constructed by late eleventh- and early twelfth-century Hiberno-Norse Dubliners may have looked like (Duffy 2023b).

ANGLO-NORMAN CONSTRUCTION

The next incomers to Dublin were the Anglo-Normans – a catch-all phrase to cover the various Bristolians, Welsh, Flemish, Cambro-Normans, English and other ethnicities who came to Dublin in number following the grant of the city to the 'men of Bristol' by Henry II in 1171. Over the following decades, this community re-shaped the city, engaging in large defensive building works, establishing religious foundations and constructing many administrative buildings. In addition to importing new building styles and forms, the Anglo-Normans also imported specific building material that served to enhance the decorative elements of their architecture whilst also signalling their cultural identity. Dundry stone is a type of limestone from the Bristol area and it was used extensively by the Anglo-Normans in Ireland, in particular in the construction of high-status buildings. Its distinctive creamy/yellow colour and its suitability for carving makes it an ideal stone for decorative elements such as reveals around windows and moulding around doors.

Our excavations encountered evidence for

Above: **Carved Dundry architectural fragments recovered from excavations across Dublin.**

Opposite page: **The court of the Irish Exchequer in the reign of Henry IV.**

both this new administrative architecture and the use of Dundry stone at the site of the Royal Exchequer in 2023. The Exchequer was where all of the crown revenues were gathered in Ireland and it was a very pivotal part of the colonial infrastructure. The Exchequer itself got its name from the use of a chequerboard arrangement of striped silk laid out on a table to make up a chequerboard and then counters were placed on the silk as a way of keeping tally of the various accounts owed.

Though the location of the early

Exchequer is unknown, it is likely it would have been based first in Dublin Castle, the centre of English administration. By the early thirteenth century the Exchequer had moved outside the city walls into the surrounding suburbs and it had been assumed that the Exchequer had been located on the corner of George's Street and Exchequer Street.

During the excavation we identified a substantial medieval wall with characteristic cream-coloured lime mortar, constructed of local calp limestone. Although the site was quite small, it was very rich archaeologically speaking. As well as the medieval wall running along the southern boundary of the site, there were two circular stone bases or pads that would have formed a base for timber uprights to sit on. One post pad had been heavily disturbed by a seventeenth-century well.

When trying to establish what this building was and how it related to the Houses of the Exchequer, we were lucky in that a lot of the Exchequer records survive, because they were audited quite frequently from England. Looking at what was happening in the Exchequer building around that time, there are references to a 'John the Mason' carrying out quite substantial works for £4 13s 0d around 1292. In the following year, there is reference to Peter the Smith making a window and then, later again, there is reference to building materials including lime and timber being stored in the courtyard (Connolly 1998, O'Brien 2013). We recovered a penny from the reign of England's King Edward I from the level of the circular bases, which gave us a date range of 1272–1307 for

these structures, suggesting they were constructed at the time that John the Mason was engaged on work to the Exchequer.

In and around the stone bases we uncovered a floor surface covered with small fragments of chipped Dundry stone. Having retrieved many carved Dundry fragments from other excavations around the city, I have never come across this kind of compacted layer of crushed Dundry before. Areas of lime surface were also found suggestive of mortar being mixed on the ground. The fragments of Dundry totalled 43 kilogrammes in all, of which the biggest were fist sized. Of the 43 kilogrammes of fragments, 35 per cent had tooling marks but just rough chiselling on the outside faces as opposed to fine tooling or decorative work. This suggests that the Dundry was coming to the site as rough blocks, presumably shaped in the quarry prior to transport by sea. Of that 35 per cent with tooling, 17 per cent had tooling on three faces; 49 per cent had tooling on two faces and 33 per cent had tooling on a single face. This is good evidence that roughly squared blocks were being worked into finer shapes onsite, with the rough external faces being chipped away to create door jambs, window tracery, quoins, corbels or other decorative features. It is very likely that this layer represents the remains of John the Mason's work in the 1290s as he carved roughed-out blocks with all of the chips of Dundry accumulating on the ground as he worked.

We know from Exchequer records that between 1292 and 1294, the king ordered a new house be built in the courtyard of the Exchequer (Connolly 1998, O'Brien 2013). I suggest that our site was within the courtyard itself, located outside of the Exchequer precinct and that the medieval wall we identified represents the precinct boundary. The two post pads are likely, therefore, to represent the remains of a lean-to building where Dundry stone was being worked while lime was being mixed in the yard around the structure. The findings at the Exchequer provide a very rare glimpse of a mason's workspace and go some way to answering the longstanding question as to whether the beautifully carved objects in Dundry stone that are found in Dublin were arriving on the quay pre-carved or were the artistic output of immigrant masons. In light of the information from the Exchequer, we can propose the latter and suggest that the beautifully carved pieces of Dundry that we have come across on Dublin sites over the last number of years were carved here by immigrant masons. These include medieval examples like the carved column base from Kevin Street, a finely undercut foliate piece from St Thomas' Abbey on Thomas Street (among the finest carvings in the country), or an unusual circular column base from Bride Street.

To come back to Aungier Street and the ecclesiastical architecture of these Anglo-Norman immigrants, we know that St Peter's church had been rebuilt over the early limekiln discussed above. The foundations we uncovered onsite that are preserved beneath the development relate to the church that was rebuilt, *c.*1380. During the excavations we retrieved some impressive fragments of building materials that give us an idea of what that church looked like, with decorated floor tiles and fragments of cut-stone column bases, window fragments and many fragments of painted plaster from around the chancel area. In St Peter's church, the stone is mainly sandstone, the high point of Dundry use in the city having passed by 1380, and more local stone was being sourced from Dublin and Meath. To visualize the design and appearance of this later church, we used the medieval church of Newcastle

Above: **Reconstruction drawing of St Peter's church, *c.*1450.**

Opposite page: **Reconstruction drawing of the mason's yard at the Central Hotel (Exchequer) site.**

Lyons in south-west County Dublin as a model as we know the two churches were built around the same time and both were prebendal churches of St Patrick's cathedral. When the outline of the Newcastle Lyons church was overlaid onto what we had uncovered at Aungier Street, the dimensions were a very close match. Using all of the above information, we were able to create a conjectural reconstruction drawing of St Peter's on the Hill as it would have looked around 1450, with a central tower (suggested by the arrangement of the foundations), painted plaster and decorative features.

This structure is preserved *in situ* and we provide Heritage Week tours of the church once a year, though it is beneath steel doors in the loading bay of the Lidl shop and is not easy to access.

Moving now to the north of the Liffey, we can look at the continental orders of monks who flourished under the English administration. During excavations within the former precinct of the Cistercian St Mary's Abbey, at the junction of modern-day Abbey Street and Capel Street, we identified the abbey gatehouse dating from around 1350 during excavations in 2019. In terms of architectural styles that had been brought into the country, we found very distinctive diagonal buttresses at the corners of this structure, which is a very rare feature in Ireland, though common in England and France at this time. The gatehouse itself had been significantly remodelled over the years and was almost entirely rebuilt in the seventeenth century, although medieval elements survived at foundation level.

Again, we recovered some architectural fragments (including Dundry) and floor tiles from around the structure and these helped us to construct a picture of what the gatehouse may have looked like. We also have John Speed's map of the area in 1610, which shows an outer gate in the northern precinct wall from which a laneway leads south to a building that was the inner gate into what had been the cloistral range of the abbey. Drawing on this information and looking at surviving monastic gatehouses, we were able to create a conjectural reconstruction of the gatehouse to the abbey as it might have looked around 1450, with diagonal corner buttresses and square buttresses framing the entrance archway. As in other medieval buildings, Dundry stone had been used to enhance windows and the archway. This surviving section of the structure has been preserved for public display beneath a glass floor at the Staycity aparthotel on Little Mary Street. We arrange guided tours of the feature during Heritage Week and interpretive signs are on permanent display. It is interesting to note that the only other example currently known of a diagonal buttress in Ireland is from the Cistercian grange of Beaubec – a foundation constructed by French monks (see Stout p154).

TUDOR AND JACOBEAN DEVELOPMENTS

Moving on to the Tudor period, between 1485 and 1603, and the influx of the 'New English' during the upheavals of the Reformation, in my own experience excavating in the city, very little structural material from this period of occupation has been found. One site that did produce the remains of a Tudor-

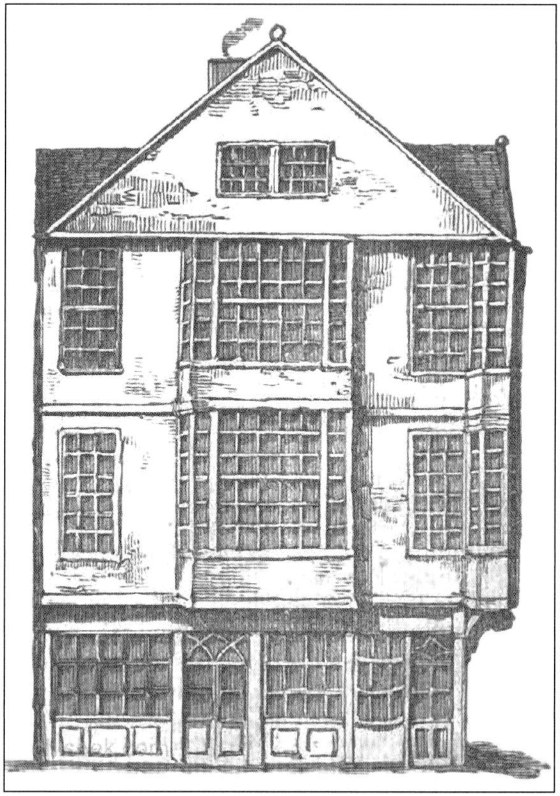

period structure was located about 170 metres south-east of Dublin Castle, at a site on the corner of South Great George's Street and Longford Street. Excavations uncovered a boundary along the southern limit of the site that had been maintained over hundreds of years and dug and re-dug with many intercutting ditches and evidence for timber palisades (Duffy 2023a).

Above: **Depiction of the last cagework house in Dublin prior to its demolition in 1813.**

At one point around the year AD 1500, the ditches were all filled in. The foundations for a structure, consisting of a lot of stakes that would have acted as piles in the soft ground, would have supported either timber beams for a cagework house or, alternatively, would have supported a stone foundation. One of the stakes was radiocarbon dated to between AD 1431 and AD 1620. This structure does not appear to have stood for long as it was soon cut through by a renewal of the boundary ditch. This sequence brings to mind the description of George's Lane penned by the Dublin-born historian and diplomat Richard Stanyhurst in 1577, in which he recorded that the inhabitants of George's Lane (now George's Street), 'being dailie and hourlie molested and praied by their prolling mountain neighbours, were forced to suffer their buildings fall into decie and embraised themselves within the city walls' (CARD vol 2, Appendix V). Difficult though it might be to understand today that just 170 metres from Dublin Castle, people could not secure their residences and had to fall back within the city walls, the archaeology seems to corroborate Stanyhurst's record. The foundations of a structure in the period Stanyhurst wrote of would appear to have been constructed over an infilled defensive boundary before being abandoned soon after to allow the boundary to be re-dug.

Coming on to the Augustinian abbey of St Thomas, which was located just south of Thomas Street and later became Thomas Court, we carried out a large excavation there in 2016 and discovered part of the cemetery of the abbey as well as a stretch of the precinct wall. Following the dissolution of the

monasteries in 1536, the abbey lands and buildings were granted to the Brabazon family. A sketch by John Smyth, which was made in 1634 for a legal dispute between the Earl of Meath and his tenants, shows terraces of structures that had been built just on the edge of the excavation area fronting what is now Catherine's Lane. The excavation revealed a spine wall running parallel to the lane and which corresponds to these structures. Several corner fireplaces survived within these structures. We know that the structures were built around 1612, in the Jacobean period (1603–1625). Generally, corner fireplaces are considered to be later seventeenth century features so these examples could be insertions. However, the possibility remains that they are original, particularly given that the position of the chimney stacks as depicted in the sketch would not preclude corner fireplaces. The Smyth sketch shows the façade of the terrace with a series of doors, leaded windows and small dormers in each house. A parallel for this arrangement is found in a grand Tudor building that features dormer windows – the much more lavish mansion of Thomas Butler, tenth Earl of Ormonde, at Carrick-on-Suir, County Tipperary, built sometime after 1565.

A depiction survives of the nearby Newgate prison in 1608 and on it can be seen the same sort of leaded windows and similar dormer and oculus window as those shown by Smyth. Located at the top of Cornmarket near Christ Church cathedral, it was one of the city's gates up to 1485 at which point it became the city prison.

One very pleasing detail from Smyth's sketch shows a terrace of three houses that have a little picket fence defining a garden in front of each house. John Smyth's deposition for the court case describes this picket fence as a 'pall of boards' and he has depicted it on his map with a gate corresponding to each house, with a hinge visible on each. This kind of suburban domesticity is not something we usually think about when we think about Dublin in the early modern period and may be seen as an innovation that came to Ireland with the influx of 'New English'. The contrast between this image of Dublin's suburbs contrasts very starkly with Stanyhurst's description of Irish marauders

Above: **Extract from John Smyth's sketch of Thomas Court.**

Opposite page: **Structural timbers re-used as foundations for mid eighteenth-century fireplace.**

ravaging to the gates of the city only 39 years beforehand.

We have not come across cagework or 'Tudor-style' houses in our excavations in Dublin but it is possible that we are finding their locations but that these types of structures are not immediately obvious in the archaeological record. For example, some patches of cobbles associated with post pads or column bases were uncovered during excavations along a former laneway on the Kevin Street site. The position of these esoteric remains is where you might expect to find houses but the remains were not complete enough to be conclusive about their function. We will have to look more closely at these and other, similar findings as there is potential that the fabric of the cagework houses was entirely recycled in the past.

The last standing cagework house in Dublin was at the corner of Werburgh Street and Castle Street and was demolished in 1813. We know that the house itself was sold for £40 for the timber to be re-used. We have recently captured a similar event in the archaeological record during excavations at Capel Street, with timbers used in the foundations of corner fireplaces of mid-eighteenth century date in an area of reclaimed land on the north side of the city. This shows us that the timber from earlier buildings was still valued as building material and structures were being dismantled and taken off site, potentially explaining why we are not finding much evidence of cagework houses in situ during our excavations.

SEVENTEENTH-CENTURY EXPANSION

Moving back again to Aungier Street, we have another interesting building – a seventeenth-century house with a small cobbled cellar. I would be interested to know if anybody has found a parallel for this because, although the finds are all very solidly seventeenth century and we should be getting into the period of the famous Dutch Billy gabled-fronted houses in Dublin, this structure is something different. The cobbled cellar takes up only a corner of the house footprint and there are cesspits and wells in the plot to the rear. An early eighteenth-century deed records that prior to the redevelopment of this plot in the later 1600s 'old ruinous houses were then standing' (Keenehan 2024).

This record may suggest that the stone foundations and cellar actually belong to an early, possibly sixteenth-century structure that, unlike the other house plots along Stephen Street, was refurbished and re-used into the eighteenth century.

Both the evidence for recycling of timbers from domestic structures and the presence of partial cellars beneath post-medieval houses may shed some light on several large storage pits that we uncovered at Bride Street. These large pits were dated to the fourteenth century and were located within a clearly urban context, though no evidence for houses was uncovered. Considering the evidence above, it may be possible that these pits were once crude cellars within sill beam or cagework structures, the timbers of which were subsequently removed from the site leaving no trace in the archaeological record. In this case, the large storage pits/cellars at Bride Street would form a bridge between the sunken-floored structure at Aungier Street and the seventeenth century, partially cellared structure fronting Stephen Street, representing a continuity of a tradition across several different immigrant communities.

The final immigrant communities to discuss are those that are traditionally associated with a building style that swept through and reconfigured the city from the later seventeenth century and dominated for 60 years. The phenomenon of the Dutch Billy – redbrick, gable-fronted houses, generally constructed around a massive square chimney stack set at 45 degrees, to provide corner fireplaces to two adjacent houses (McCullough 2007) – arrived at a time when the first planned developments in Dublin were being established in the suburbs of the city, generally on former monastic lands. The immigrant communities associated with this style of architecture were, initially, the Huguenots from 1685, Protestant French who fled persecution to Ireland bringing their skills as artisans in weaving, lace-making and many other trades. These continentals were followed shortly by an influx of Dutch and Flemish Protestants in the wake of the Battle of the Boyne in 1690. The term Dutch Billy apparently comes from this event and was a colloquial homage to William of Orange, the new king, while the spread of these buildings is often explained as an ostentatious act of loyalty to the new order.

Below: **Gable-fronted buildings and corner fireplaces along Stephen Street (Aungier Street excavations).**

Opposite page: **House foundation and rear plot fronting Stephen Street (part of the Aungier Street excavations) dating from the sixteenth / seventeenth century.**

At the Aungier Street site, we identified extensive evidence for the proliferation of this process. Development at the Aungier estate, also on former monastic lands, represents the first planned housing development in Dublin, dating from the 1660s. Our excavations uncovered the cellars of a row of houses fronting onto Stephen Street, which were gable-fronted, Dutch Billy in style with corner fireplaces. The project of development was driven by Francis Aungier, likely a first-generation Dubliner and grandson of an English commissioner for the plantation of Ulster in 1616 and holding the title of Lord Longford. Aungier laid out the street that now bears his name and granted leases of various plots to developers who built townhouses fronting the new streetscape. The

houses in the Aungier estate were originally built for Dublin's upper classes, though, as the Georgian period arrived bringing new architectural tastes, these houses became more mercantile in character. The houses in the Liberties, however, an area strongly associated with Huguenot and Dutch/Flemish artisans, were built for and by artisans and merchants from the outset.

In the heart of The Liberties, during a large excavation fronting Newmarket Square, we uncovered over 40 house plots dating from the 1690s when the square was formally laid out and plots were leased for development. The big story of Newmarket Square was the timber water pipe system established in the 1680s that connected all of these houses with water from the Abbey stream. This was the first large-scale planned domestic water system in the city and hollowed out, timber pipes joined with copper fittings ran beneath the houses into the rear yards where they filled underground timber or brick-lined cisterns that were then used by households for their domestic needs. Matt Whyte's tavern on the corner of the Newmarket Square development was the only house in the whole area that had a cellar as well as the ubiquitous corner fireplace. This tavern would have served a mixed community of first- and second-generation Dubliners of Huguenot, Dutch, Flemish and English heritage. This grand building with pedimented gable was torn down in the 1890s and a Victorian pub was built on the site. This building was, in turn, removed during the redevelopment of the site but the location of Matt Whyte's tavern has been reinstituted as a pub as part of the modern redevelopment of the area and a new thoroughfare has been opened, where there is heritage information for those who want to learn about the history of the site.

Above: **Matt Whyte's Tavern, located on the corner of Newmarket, drawn prior to its demolition in the 1890s.**

While the architectural innovations and trends that we uncover during our excavations in Dublin do not neatly stop in the eighteenth century, the influx of people into the city in the nineteenth and twentieth centuries was overwhelmingly from rural Ireland. These people contributed in many ways to the changing fabric of the city; however, that story is beyond our scope here.

I will finish by making the point that extricating the story of Dublin's immigrant communities from the story of Dublin itself is an impossible task in a city where the arrival of, reaction to and absorption of different peoples has shaped the urban character for centuries. Historic Dublin, from its outset, was a hybrid of cultures, at times set apart from the surrounding Irish identity, at times central to it. In speaking of 'the' Vikings and 'them' Huguenots and 'those' English planters we are talking about us – modern Dubliners, cultural and genetic inheritors of this mix of peoples. This is, of course, an ongoing process as people arrive daily from all continents choosing to come here for fellowship, for protection, for experience or for love. By applying a bit of hindsight, it is possible to imagine in them the 'us' of the near future. I, for one, am excited to see what they do with the place.

Acknowledgements

I would like to acknowledge all the help and support I have received, in particular from the various site crew and staff on the sites discussed; IAC Archaeology's post-excavation team; Enda Lydon, Chris Coffey and Bob Burns of IAC Archaeology for their assistance with the photogrammetry and images; both Linzi Simpson and Peter Keenahan for their generosity with their knowledge; Dublin City Council Archaeology; the National Monuments Service, and the Wordwell Group.

BIBLIOGRAPHY

CARD (Calendar of ancient records of Dublin in the possession of the municipal corporation of that city) volume 2 Gilbert, J.T. (ed). 1891. London: Joseph Dollard.

Clarke, H. 2002. *Irish Historic Towns Atlas no. 11 Dublin, part I, to 1610*. Dublin: Royal Irish Academy.

Connolly, P. 1998. *Irish Exchequer Payments: 1270–1446*. Dublin: Irish Manuscripts Commission.

Duffy, P., Giblin, A. and Mongey, M., 2024. Maynetown Earthworks – The Port Mannan Longphort? *Archaeology Ireland*. 38 (2) Issue 148.

Duffy, P. 2023a. Structures of Import: St Peter's church, a unique sunken-floored structure and Dublin's southern suburb *IN*: Duffy, S. (ed.) *Medieval Dublin XIX*. Dublin: Four Courts Press.

Duffy. P. 2023b. St Canice's Church, Finglas and the Hiberno-Norse churches of Dublin. *Archaeology Ireland*. 37 (3) Issue 145.

Duffy, P. 2021. Saints and skinners: excavations along the northern precinct of the abbey of Saint Thomas the Martyr, Dublin *IN*: Duffy, S. (ed.) *Medieval Dublin XVIII*. Dublin: Four Courts Press.

Keenehan, P. 2024. *Report on the historical and documentary sources for the redevelopment site at Aungier Street/Longford Street/Stephen's Street, Dublin*. Unpublished report for IAC Archaeology.

McCullough, N. 2007. *Dublin, an urban history*. Dublin: Anne Street Press.

O'Brien, N. The building, fixtures and fittings of the medieval Irish Exchequer [online]. Available from: https://celtic2realms-medievalnews.blogspot.com/2013/11/the-building-fixtures-and-fittings-of_30.html [accessed 5.12.23].

Ó Carragáin, T. 2010. *Churches in Early Medieval Ireland. Architecture, Ritual and Memory*. New Haven and London: Yale University Press.

O'Donovan, E. 2008. The Irish, the Vikings, and the English: new archaeological evidence from excavations at Golden Lane, Dublin *IN*: Duffy, S. (ed.) *Medieval Dublin VIII*. Dublin: Four Courts Press.

O'Keeffe, T. 2015. *Medieval Irish Buildings, 1100–1600*. Dublin: Four Courts Press.

Simpson, L. 2011. Fifty years a-digging: a synthesis of medieval and archaeological investigations in Dublin city and suburbs *IN*: Duffy, S. (ed.) *Medieval Dublin XI*, 9–112. Four Courts Press: Dublin.

CHAPTER 8

Beaubec: An alien cell in the Boyne Valley

DR GERALDINE STOUT

Dr Geraldine Stout is a retired archaeologist from the National Monuments Service. She is a recognized authority on the archaeology of the Boyne Valley, having been involved in excavations and research in the region for over 30 years. She describes here what excavations revealed about an 'alien' monastic farm at Beaubec, County Meath, which was an offshoot of a Cistercian abbey in Normandy.

Beaubec is a medieval monastic farm established at Bey More townland, County Meath, by a small community of French monks from the de Bello Becco Cistercian monastery near Rouen in Normandy. This is a story about this community of monks. They were granted lands by the Norman Lord of Meath, Hugh de Lacy, in the 1170s. This was one of just a series of very strategic grants that Hugh de Lacy made in east Meath to religious houses from his homelands in Wales, England and Normandy. These religious communities were very effective in managing landed estates and they were hugely significant in the whole Norman colonization process. Religious orders like the Augustinians from Llanthony in Wales got lands at Duleek and Colp, and the Cistercians at Furness Abbey in Cumbria were given part of Mornington, while a foundation of the same order at de Bello Becco in Normandy were granted land at Bey More, where they established Beaubec. These orders developed Drogheda as a town and they established the port of Drogheda as an entrepôt for the east coast of Ireland.

At the time that Beaubec was founded,

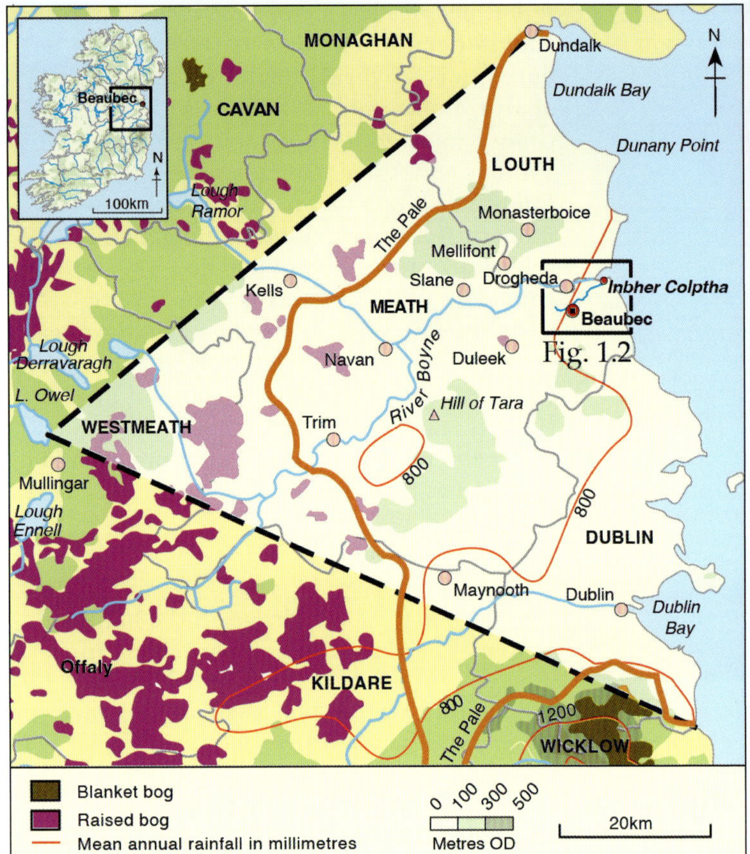

Above and opposite page: **Location map of Beaubec in the Boyne Valley.**

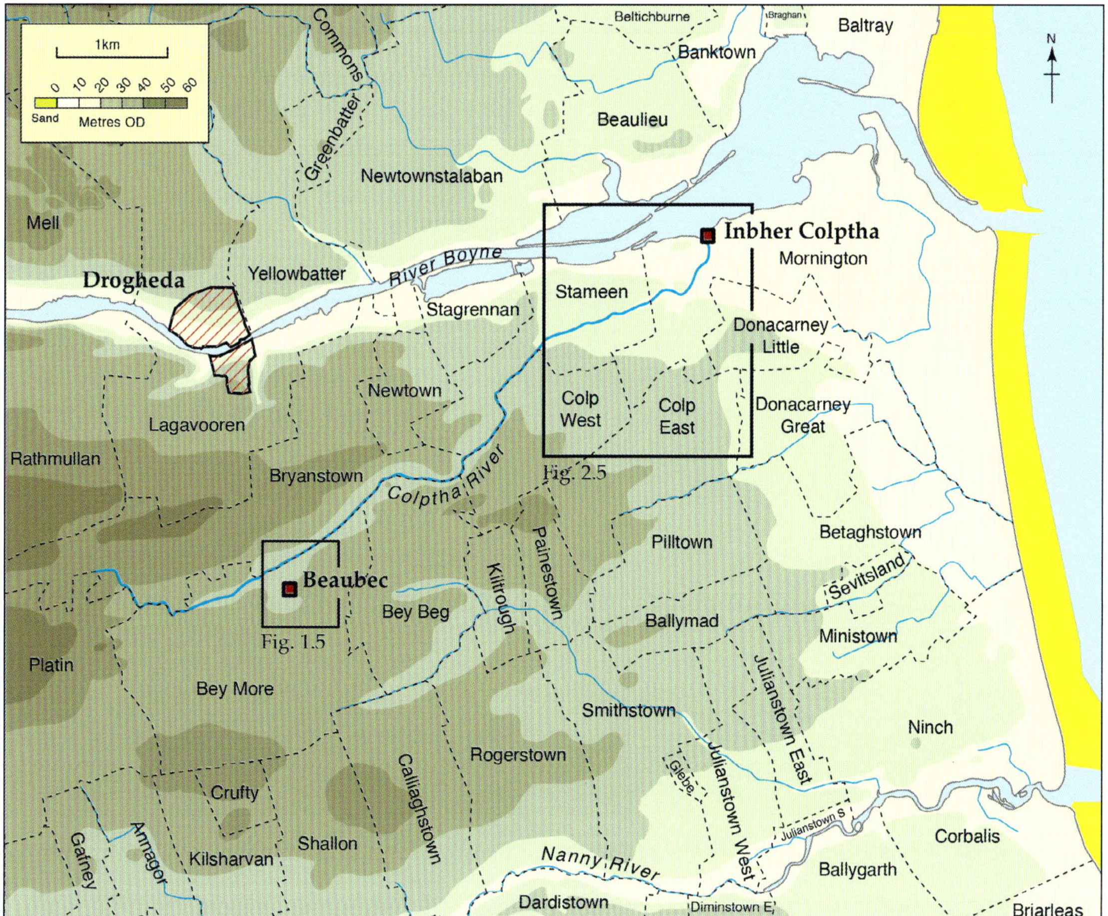

Normandy was still part of the French possessions of the Angevin kings of England. These were Henry II and his two sons, Richard and John, who ruled between AD 1154 and AD 1216. At this time, we see a very distinct territory comprising the east of Ireland, England and Normandy forming an area that is referred to as the 'Angevin Empire' (Norgate 1887). What we see also is how important the seas were and the geographic links they provided. The creation of this 'empire' really encouraged movement of people and produce across the sea.

ALIEN CELLS

Beaubec was quite exceptional in that it was a French holding on Irish soil. There were only two other French-owned medieval religious properties in Ireland, that at Fore Priory in

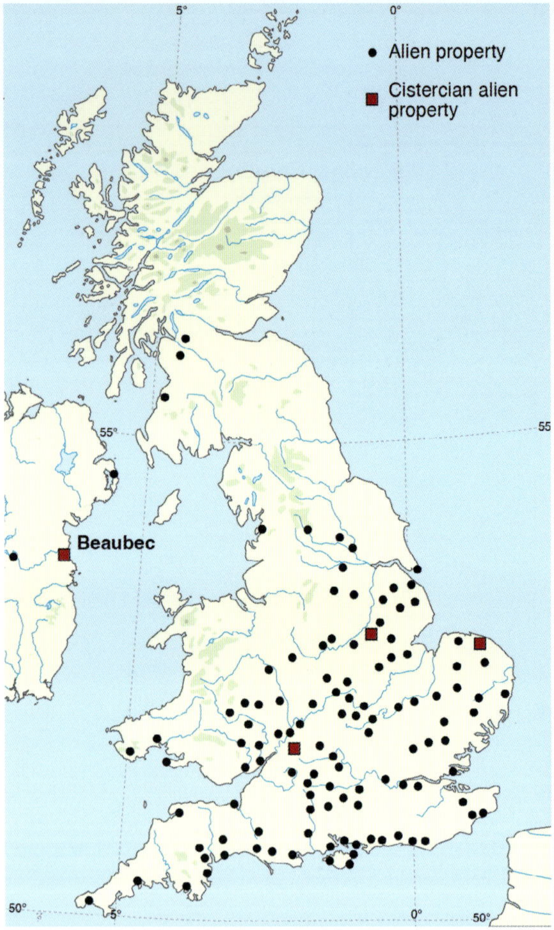

County Westmeath, a cell of the abbey of Évreux, and the Black Priory of St Andrews of the Ards in County Down, affiliated to Lonlay-L'Abbaye in Normandy, both Benedictine. They are unique in that they were directly answerable to France. They did not have a motherhouse in Ireland directing how and what they would be doing. Such foundations are called 'alien cells' or 'alien priories'. In England, there was a huge number of such

Left: **Distribution map of alien priories in Ireland and Britain.**

Below: **De Bello Becco chapel, Normandy.**

Opposite page: **View of de Bello Becco Abbey, Normandy *c.*1750.**

alien priories. There appears to have been only a very small portion in Ireland, which makes the site at Beaubec important.

The problem with the status of these alien priories was that, when England started war with France in the late thirteenth and fourteenth centuries, the seas became a battleground, and this resulted in the demise of these alien cells and priories. They could not trade or send money and surplus goods over to France, which was their mission. That is the broader context for the foundation of Beaubec.

The French monks came from de Bello Becco Abbey in northern Normandy. Today, the abbey of de Bello Becco is in a small *commune* with a population of about 200 in a village called Beaubec-la-Rosière just northeast of Rouen. Unfortunately, de Bello Becco, like many religious sites in France, was badly affected by the Anglo-French wars in the fourteenth century and also by the French Revolution (1789–1799), so very little of the actual abbey remains to be seen. Fortunately, the impressive thirteenth-century chapel just at the entrance gate of the precinct of the abbey has still survived. This chapel alone indicates the scale of the abbey in its day. Geophysical work has been done there and the footprint of the abbey has been identified.

LAND MANAGEMENT

It is particularly interesting to see how the Cistercians managed their lands. In de Bello Becco itself, when one realizes that their estate extended over 15,000 hectares, it had a huge impact on the landscape around it. In the 1970s, Susan Deck mapped the estate of de Bello Becco (Deck 1974) and she was able to show that there were 14 outfarms or granges

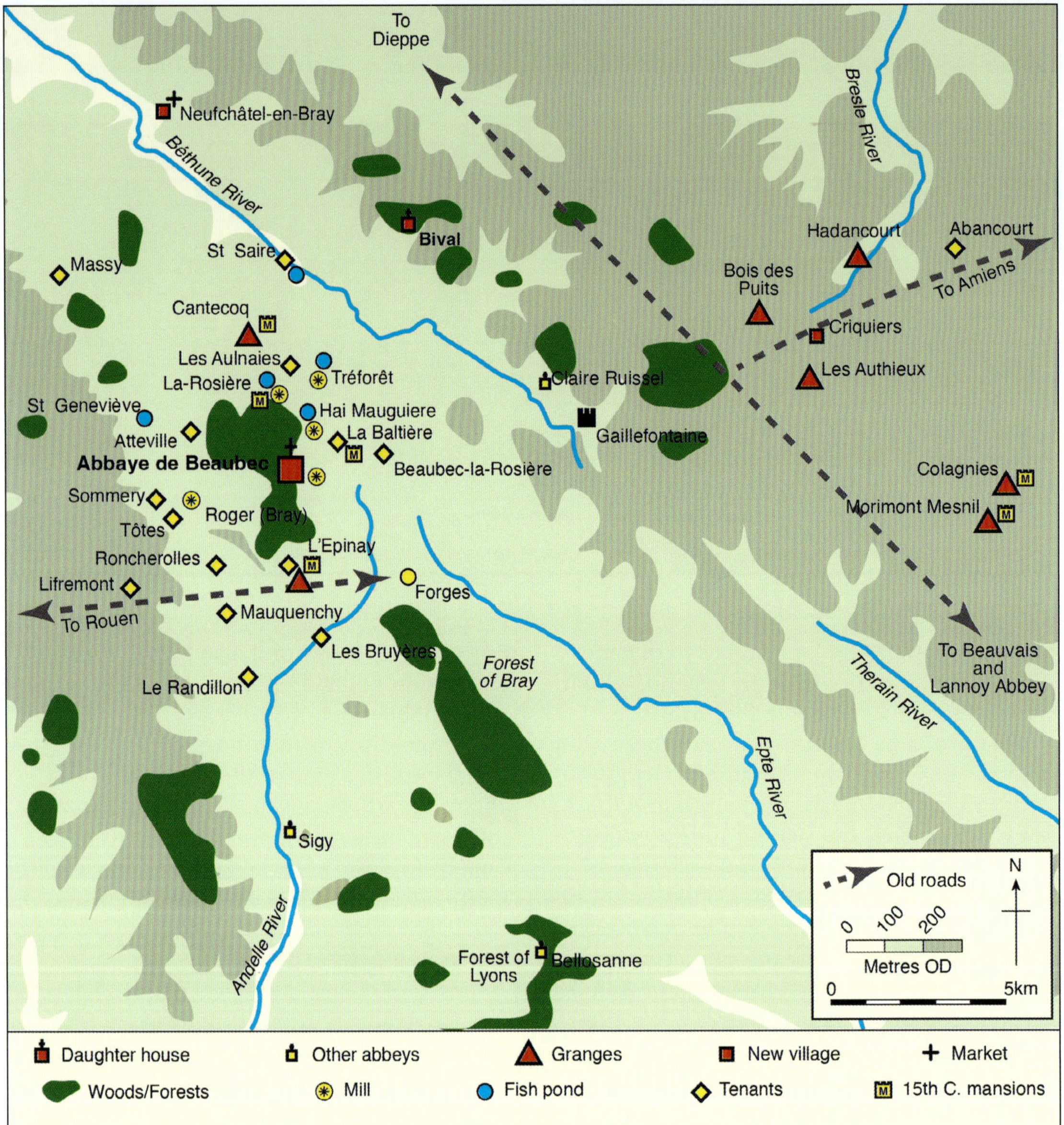

on the estate all around the abbey. They actually developed a new town called Criquiers, which is about 50 kilometres south-east of Dieppe. They were involved in the

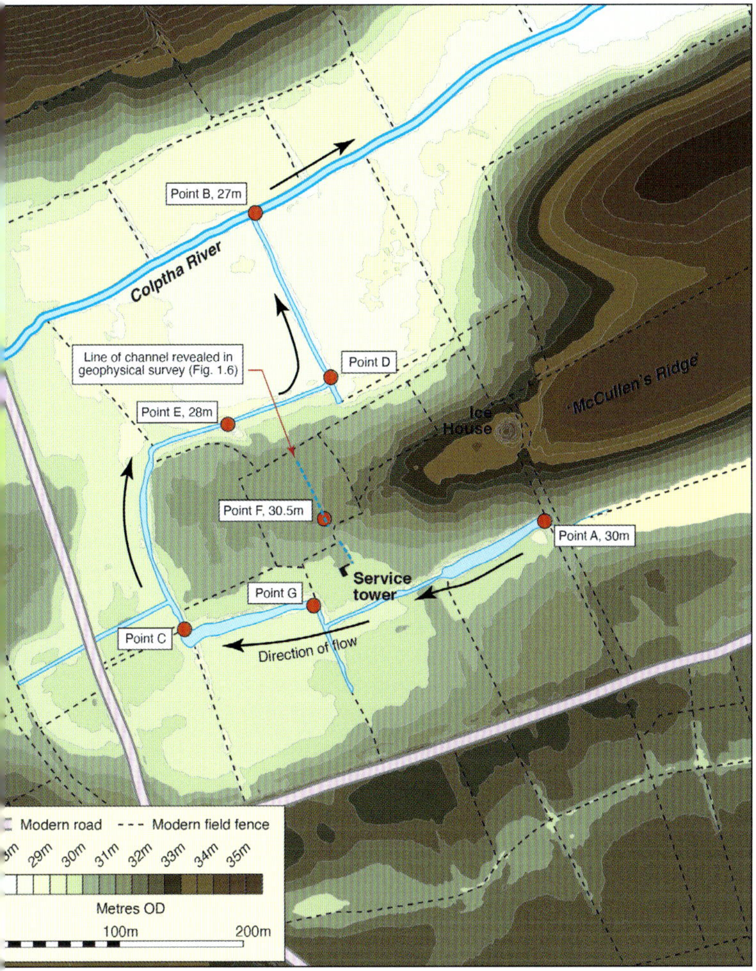

Above: **Medieval drainage system at Beaubec, County Meath.**

Opposite page: **Map of de Bello Becco Abbey and its monastic estate based on Deck 1974.**

development of a walled town in Neufchatel, north of the abbey, where they had property. They also were involved in the development of the port of Dieppe, where the Normans had earlier built a harbour. The monks were making a significant impact on the landscape around them. There was a huge forest and a lot of marshlands in the area and the monks there drained and cleared a lot of this land. These were the kind of highly skilled, experienced land managers who came to Bey More and they brought their expertise with them.

We have evidence from a confirmation charter that the monks were in residence on the site by 1215. The grant itself goes back to the 1170s. The earliest evidence that we found on the site for medieval presence in Bey More was evidence for cultivation and drainage of the land. When we excavated, we found a series of cultivation furrows that completely criss-cross the site. Cultivation furrows are a type of cultivation that is associated with grain production. The environmental archaeologist on the excavation, Dr Penny Johnston, identified wheat, oats and weeds associated with arable production in the fill of these furrows. We also identified a lot of structural ironwork, such as hinges, staples and nails, which indicates that there might have been some timber buildings on the site.

The Cistercians are famous for their expertise in land drainage. Geographer Aidan Giblin, who was part of the excavation team, has done a wonderful study of the water management on the Beaubec site. He has been able to show that they used a combination of natural and artificial channels, including drains and culverts, to manage the water system around the site (Giblin 2023). The Bey

More site is located in a natural basin right at the end of a ridge. The rainwater coming off the ridge at this point was flowing west around the farm site and then, by gravity, it was falling into the Colptha River to the north of the site. So, water was circulating around the site. Then, a whole series of drains was created to use that water for flushing latrines and for drainage of the land. The Colptha River runs to the north of the site and into the Boyne estuary at Mornington, where Beaubec monks also had properties and a fishery.

The monks constructed a moated enclosure next. Because my colleagues and I excavated only a small part of the site, we just found the south-east corner of this moat that ran around and through the buildings. The moat is about five metres wide. When we excavated it, water started to emerge from it and the moat still functioned when we dug it. It is quite spectacular how it became a moat again once it had been excavated. A huge amount of environmental evidence came from that moat because it was still waterlogged, even though this is a dryland rural site. Because of the dampness on the site, we were able to retrieve huge amounts of waterlogged organic material. We found evidence for worked timber and we were able to get environmental evidence for blackberries and elders, and even for insects that are associated with the dung from cattle. We know there were stables on the site. Carbon 14 analysis gave us a date range of 1275–1313. A little bit in from the moat there was a berm and then a revetted wall, so there was some kind of earthwork inside of the moat enclosure.

MONKS' RESIDENCE

We found that the moat turned around and then ran under the service tower section of the upstanding building that is on the site, which we have interpreted as the monks' residence. When we excavated the interior, the excavation levels started to go down quite deep at the end and we eventually exposed the remains of a really impressive, plank-centred, arched, intra-mural culvert running through the walls of the service tower building. The planks still can be seen in the culvert today. Dendrochronological analysis puts the date at around AD 1356. A series of holes that were uncovered in the gable would have held a wooden superstructure for a latrine that would have sat on that wall in the tower. From the cess material in the latrine, we found cherry and plum stones. Even more exciting, we found evidence for figs and grapes, fruits that would have been very valuable at the time. They would suggests the monks had a high standard of nutrition and that they were bringing in produce from abroad.

The service tower with the moat running in underneath it was attached to a two-storey building that may have been the monks' residence and chapel, based on a documentary reference from 1224 that stated: 'the said prior and canons have granted to us to have there the chapel of the monks in which the monks who reside there will minister' (Hogan 2008). There was supporting evidence for a chapel at Bey More. In addition to the reference, we found grisaille glass, which is a term for monochrome painting on stained glass or other media. It is a type of glass that has been found in places like Duiske Abbey, in Kilkenny, and the Cistercian abbeys in Ireland. Also, there was quite a lot of carved stone in the building. So, we think there was probably a chapel here.

All that stands in the field today is the south elevation of that building. There was a diagonal buttress at one corner of the building, which is an unusual feature of which there

Above: **Plank centring in the western culvert.**

Left: **An eighteenth-century avenue runs through the medieval walls.**

Opposite page: **Excavation of moat with berm and revetment wall.**

are very few examples (Duffy and McIlreavy 2002). Medieval archaeologist Con Manning, formerly of the National Monuments Service, has suggested that this type of buttress might reflect French influence and that it is often referred to as a 'French buttress' (pers. comms.) (see Duffy p138). English archaeologist Glenn Coppock gave me quite a number of examples of this type of buttress occurring in thirteenth-century buildings in England, including one at a site called Skendleby, Lincolnshire, that has been dated to the thirteenth century (see Clay 2006).

One of the things that we wanted to do on the site was to try and get the footprint of the monks residence but unfortunately an eighteenth-century avenue levelled much of the building. The place where we opened cuttings to excavate the services tower was on the route of this eighteenth-century roadway and the builders cleared away a lot of the buildings there. We did find some evidence for the foundations of a wall, so we were able to do some reconstruction of the building,

Below: **Reconstruction drawing of monks' residence after Elizabeth Gardner.**

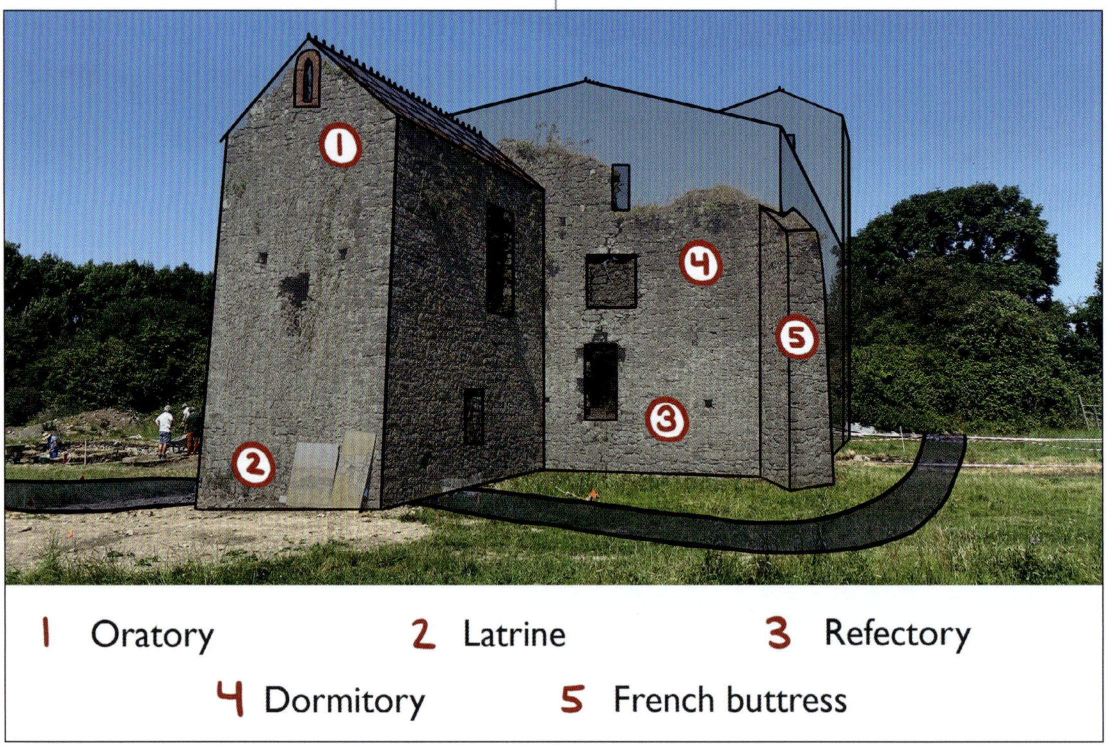

Opposite page: **Medieval louvre from Beaubec.**

which we are interpreting as the monks' residence. A reconstruction drawing by archaeological illustrator Elizabeth Gardner gives some idea of what that building would have looked like.

One of the more unusual finds on the site was a ceramic piece that was a louvre or a ventilator that would have sat on the roof ridge of the building. Originally, we thought it was a funerary pot but it was a louvre that would have sat into a collar-shaped ridge tile on the roof. I will discuss later some parallels for this feature.

We found a lot of evidence for worked timber and Cathy Moore and Ellen O Carroll, experts in archaeological wood and wooden artefacts, examined both our worked wood and our bulk samples and identified all the species of wood that were being used in the building of this monks' residence. They had used oak, ash and hazel as well as smaller amounts of yew, alder and willow. Some of the structural timberwork were pegs, a dowel and a reworked piece of planking that would have been used in the construction of the site. We know from examining buildings in Normandy, where the home abbey was located, that there was a large amount of timberwork in those structures, and we think that a lot of timber was used in the structure of this Beaubec building.

ARCHITECTURAL PARALLELS

What was the architectural tradition of these migrant monks? Did they bring their plans in their heads from France or did they look at what was around them? We tried to identify where the influences for this type of architecture might have come from. When I started looking, the closest parallels for the structure of the monks' residence at Bey More seemed to be with hall houses. These are two-storey rectangular buildings built around a hall or large room, and there are many examples dating from the thirteenth century. The entrance is on the first floor and the ground floor is defensive. They are single structures, usually not part of a wider building complex.

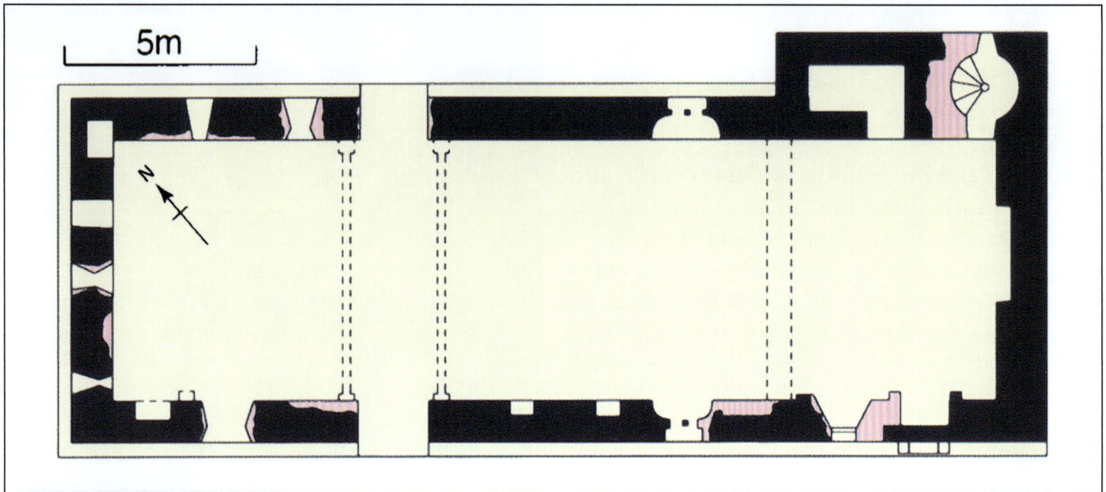
5m
N

The late archaeologist David Sweetman has written a lot about them (Sweetman 1998). I also consulted the Archaeological Survey of Ireland, a database managed by the National Monuments Service that is a fantastic resource, and I identified a number of hall houses that were ecclesiastical holdings.

One of the sites that were similar to Bey More was Rathumney Castle, County Wexford, which was the residence of lay brothers who would have worked lands on an outfarm or grange of the Tintern Abbey estate located on the Hook peninsula. This was founded in 1200 by William Marshal, who had inherited Strongbow's Irish lands through marriage. It is interesting to see that there was a link here with the Cistercian Order, because Cistercian monks came to Rathumney from Tintern Abbey in Monmouthshire, Wales. Although called Rathumney Castle, it is more accurately a hall house. It is a two-storey building and it has a garderobe and a lot of features that are quite similar to Bey More.

In the case of another building, in Clonshire in County Limerick, which was owned by the Bishop of Limerick, when I put the plans of Bey More side by side with those of Clonshire, you could see that the layout of both sites was quite similar. This similarity in building design suggests that some of the architectural influences of Beaubec's French monks may have been from Ireland rather than France.

I then started to examine alien priory sites in England and I found very close parallels for the building that is in Bey More. One such site was the 'alien' priory of Grovebury, also called La Grava, in Bedfordshire, whose mother house, Fontevraud Priory in Anjou, France, was endowed by the Angevin / Plantagenet kings. A large excavation of Grovebury Priory's grange took place between 1973 and 1985,

Above: **Comparative drawing of Clonshire, County Limerick (right) and Beaubec, County Meath.**

Opposite page: **Hall-house at Rathumney, County Wexford, after Colfer.**

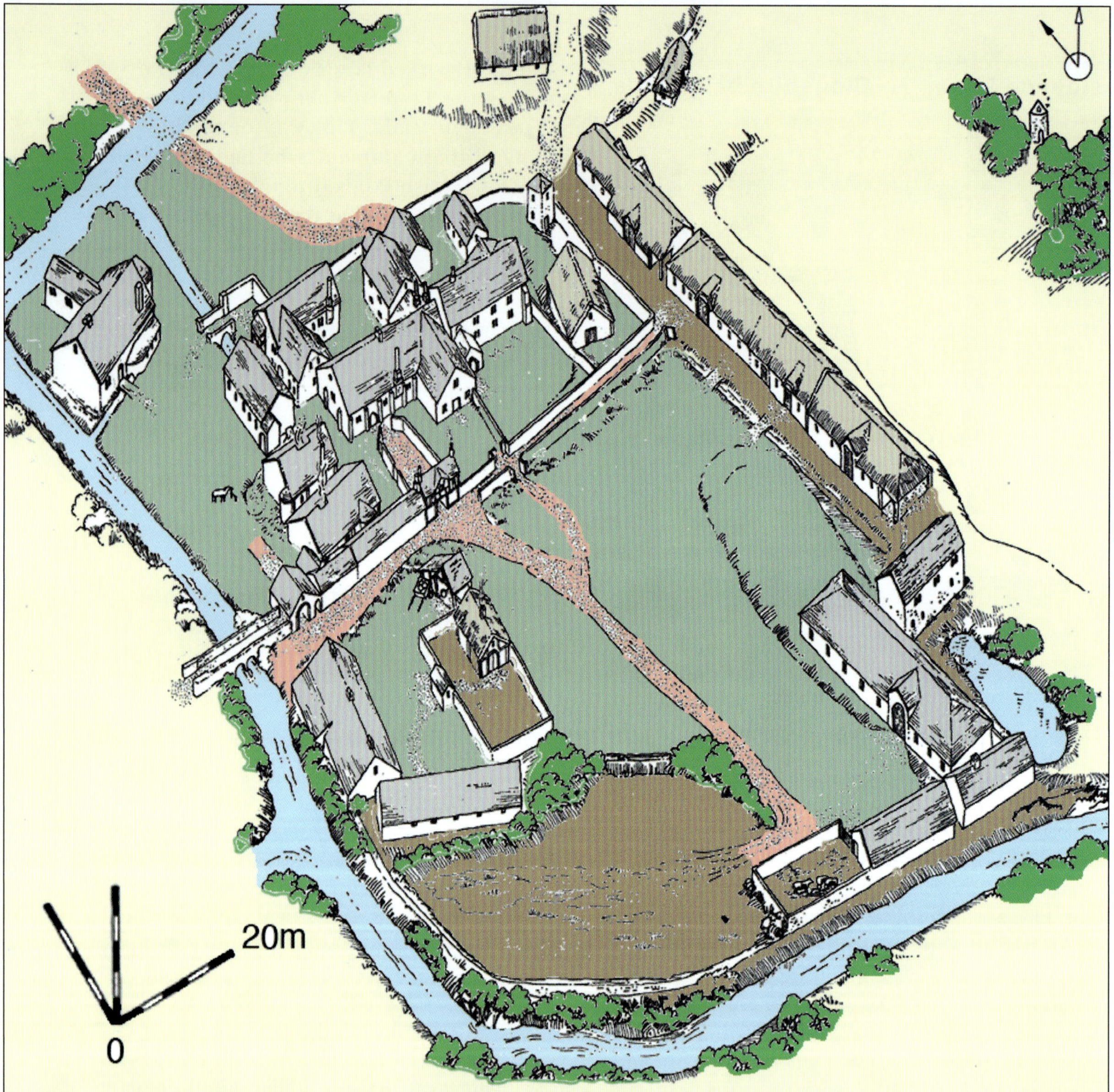

which has proven to be a great resource for medieval archaeologists (Baker 2013). One of the buildings excavated is referred to as the prior's lodging; it is thirteenth and fourteenth

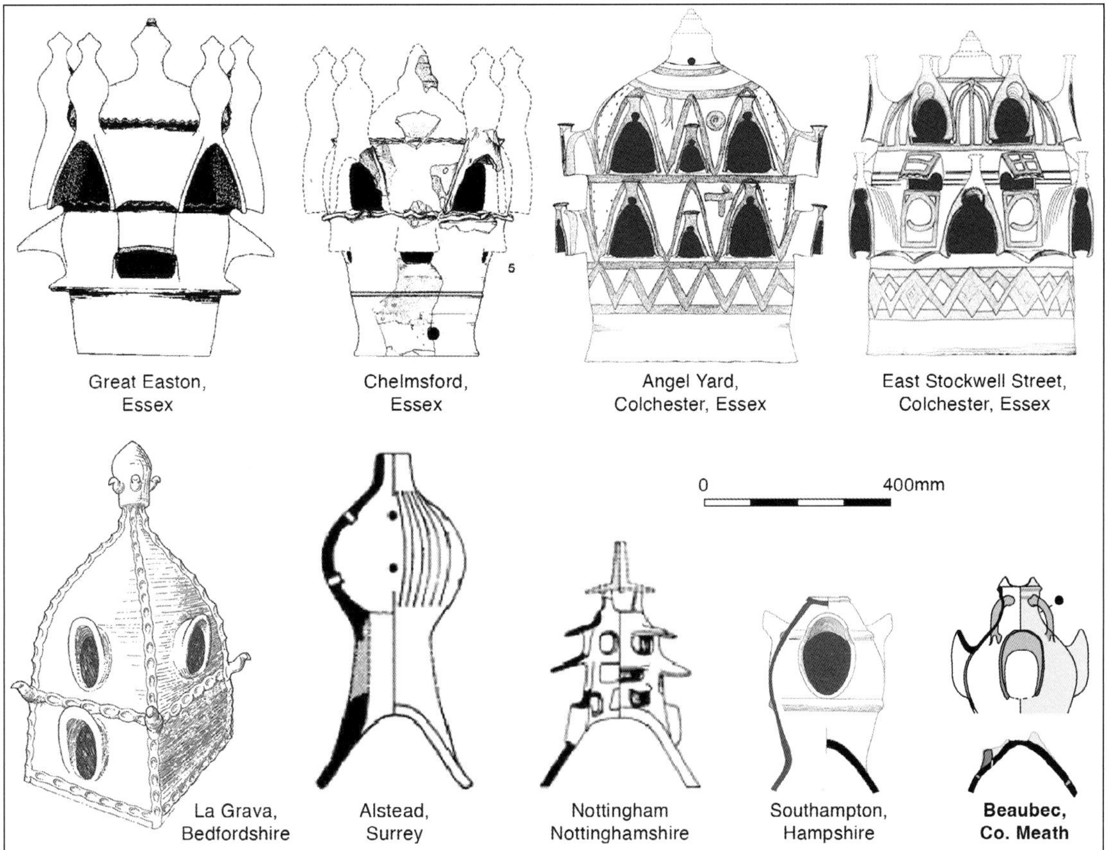

century and it was built to an L-shaped design that is quite similar to the building in Bey More. The archaeologist suggested that this was used both as a refectory and a dormitory, and there might have been a prior's lodging at the top of the building.

Another example of a latrine block was excavated at La Grava and again the system of drainage was quite similar to the monks' residence building in Bey More, including the way the water fed into the moat. Again, the louvre on the top of the roof of the prior's lodging at Grovebury was very similar to the one from Bey More. The accompanying illustration shows just some of the parallels we found for the louvre structure – the one that came from La Grava and there are several other examples of louvres found on priory sites in England.

Above: **Comparative drawings of louvres from other medieval sites.**

Opposite page: **La Grava buildings (Baker 2013).**

BARN BUILDING

When we excavated west of the monks' residence, we found the footprint of quite a huge building. It is about 24 metres long by seven metres wide. There are walls that are over 1.4m in width – that is wide enough for a castle. It is a very impressive rectangular building, with an entrance to the north. Inside, there is a whole series of features that I will describe in more detail below.

On a ground plan of that building one can see at the south section of the wall a series of undulations. These are hollows for holding up the timber uprights that would have supported a massive timber roof (Dr Niall Brady pers. comms.).

We found an entrance in the north that was about four metres wide. The entrance was recessed, suggesting that there might have been a barn door on that side. There was a kiln at one end and we found a flagstone area with the remains of a circular setting that we have interpreted as a setting for a cooking pot. We also found a series of drains. The circular setting in the middle was part of what would have been a circular upstanding structure with an opening on one side. In that same area, we found a very dense concentration of peas, beans and grains. Archaeologist Con Manning (pers. comms.) referred me to an example of a similar site from the thirteenth-century Templar Preceptory site in Lincolnshire (UK), which was of similar size and also had kilns and cooking sites very like Beaubec (Mayes 2002).

We also found a circular kiln, the remains of a bowl with a flue to one side, and Penny Johnston (Johnston 2023), the excavation's environmental archaeologist, identified huge amounts of grain still in position on the site as well as some peas and beans. Kilns in buildings are a very dangerous combination and we know that the Bective Abbey barn burnt down because of the kiln, which resulted in serious damage to the lay brothers' quarters, so the risks were there, but the kiln is definitely *in situ* within the barn at Beaubec.

The drain was a typical Cistercian drain, very well built. In the side of it, Aidan Giblin found a groat of *c.*1360 date, the reign of Edward III, which was a great aid to dating this feature. The presence of the drain sug-

Below: **General view of barn foundations under excavation.**

Opposite page: **Plan of Beaubec barn.**

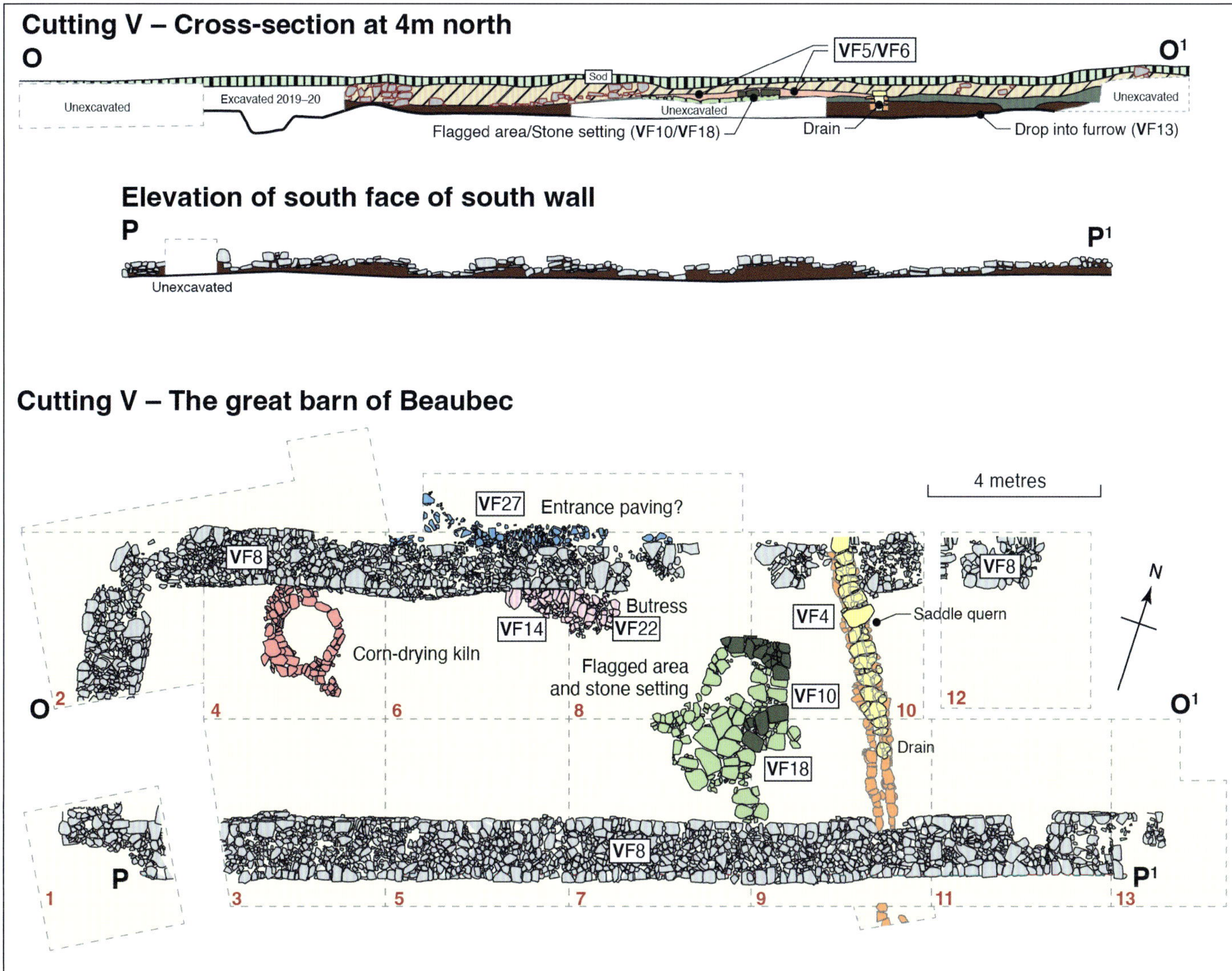

gests that there would have been farm animals in this end of the building. In summary, we found evidence for a whole range of activities going on in this building. We made a reconstruction drawing of the interior of the building showing the different activities that were going on.

I want to emphasize that this was a massive building for such a small community. We looked for parallels or comparative sites and we found a similar barn at Bective Abbey but it had been at a much smaller scale than that of Beaubec. If we compare the building with tithe barns in England, Beaubec comes in as being around middle size, which gives some sense of the scale of the building.

FARMING ACTIVITY

The mission for monks in alien priories like Beaubec was to manage the land and send the income and produce back to their homeland. The monks focused on grain and grain production, which was a very strategic thing to do because wheat production was really important in the greater Drogheda and Boyne Valley area. The monks obviously had adapted, they knew that it was the most valuable crop. We know from the environmental evidence also that wheat was what was being processed and stored and exported from this site. We even have a reference from 1295 to grain being sent from Bey More to Scotland (Sweetman 1881).

In terms of the farm stock, when zooarchaeologist Fiona Beglane looked at the evidence, she was able to show that a lot of the results we got were very similar to what was found on other Cistercian sites and that sheep husbandry was very important. Sheep were being kept for over three years for their wool. They also kept pigs for prime meat and the cattle were being kept mostly for traction and transport on site. There is a reference from 1271 that said:

> Roger, the proctor of the abbot of de Bello Becco, took fourteen sacks of wool and two sacks of sheep skins to be used in the clothing of the monastic community in the mother house in Normandy (Maxwell Lyte 1891–1916 vol. 6, 595).

As part of their diet, we found evidence for fish of every kind including herring, cod, ling, hake, gadidae – cod-type fish such as haddock and pollock – and gurnard. There was evidence for hens that were laying, geese, ducks, partridge and, of course, oysters. One of the interesting facts that Fiona Beglane (2023, 148) discovered was that the monks were not cooking the oysters; when you heat an oyster, it will open. They were opening up the oysters and there were marks on their shells where they had opened the oysters. These French monks were very fond of their fresh oysters. Beglane has stressed that the evidence suggests that their diet consisted of a lot of shellfish, fish and birds and less of meat. We know this contrasts with Bective

Abbey where they were very fond of their beef. When we excavated there (2009–2012), we were surprised at how much evidence we found for beef. One of the remarkable facts that Fiona Beglane discovered at Beaubec was the amount of cat bones present. There were more cat bones than cow bones. That, of course, tied in very well with the whole emphasis on grain production. Cats were part

Below left: **Monk fishing, from Nuremburg House Books**

Below right: **Monk with hoe, from Nuremburg House Books.**

Right: **Detail of image Türmer (Tower keeper) showing a cat catching a rat, from Nuremburg House Books.**

Opposite page: **Bective barn.**

of pest control on the site and, particularly where you had grain, the cats were very important.

ABANDONMENT

We know that the site was abandoned in the mid- to late-fourteenth century. When we thought about this initially, we assumed that the community of French monks had been affected by the plague or Black Death, which arrived in 1348. Drogheda and the surrounding area were very severely affected by this. However, when the medieval historian David Thornton started to look at the history of the site, a lot of his observations made us totally reinterpret the abandonment of this site (Thornton 2023). It was abandoned because of its alien status (see above) when in 1294 Edward I (1239–1307) started a war with France and started restricting trade with France. He also began to look at confiscating the lands of these alien priories. Suddenly in 1301, the abbot of Beaubec was asked to go to the justiciar, the king's representative in Dublin, in relation to a plea regarding his lands. The Crown was starting to think about taking the lands of Beaubec. Between 1301 and 1333, 17 lawyers, attorneys and proctors were sent from France to Ireland to deal with this issue. Thornton (ibid.) has identified the names of many of these. Most of them were French monks or laymen coming from the area very close to Beaubec itself, for example, from Hermanville, and other nearby locations.

The Crown was determined to take the lands so Beaubec decided to hand the abbey over to the Cistercian abbey of Furness, which had lands at nearby Mornington. So, in 1332 they started negotiating this handover to Furness. Then the king intruded on the whole exercise and there was a whole series of litigation again and we know that from 1356 Furness still did not have Beaubec (Maxwell Lyte 1891–1916, vol. 3, 224). Between the 1350s and 1390s, abbots were being sent over to Ireland from Furness in Cumbria to try and sort things out. I find it significant that one abbot from Furness came over four times to deal with the issue of the changeover of the lands at Beaubec, which suggests that this was considered a very valuable property that was worth fighting over. In the 1390s, Furness stopped sending over its abbot and concentrated on its rental properties in Drogheda. At that point we are seeing the death knell of Beaubec in the fourteenth century.

This is just one story about one small community of monks from Normandy. It does highlight the vulnerability of alien communities during times of warfare. However, the monks left a legacy in the form of a building on a farm in County Meath. They also left a legacy of a huge body of evidence that we have been able to extract from the excavation of the site. We are now able to tell their story today on the site.

Acknowledgements

I want to thank everybody who was involved in the Beaubec project notably the McCullen family and my former colleagues in the National Monuments Service and the OPW, who were very much involved in the restoration of the building. We had a huge community of volunteers and professional archaeologists working on the site and I cannot thank them enough. I am grateful to FBD Trust for financing the research excavation and the publication. I am indebted to the following for all the support we received: Kilsharvan Community Council, Meath County Council, Dublin City University, the Royal Irish Academy, ^{14}CHRONO Centre, Queens University Belfast, University of Notre Dame Dublin Global Gateway, Dundalk Institute of Technology, Lacey Solutions, Mythical Ireland and Droichead Arts Centre. These are just some of the organizations that were involved in trying to tell the story of this small community of French monks.

BIBLIOGRAPHY

Baker, E. (ed.) 2013. *La Grava: the archaeology and history of a royal Manor and Alien Priory of Fontevrault*. CBA Research Report 167, York: Council for British Archaeology.

Beglane, F. 2023. Faunal remains from Beaubec, Co. Meath *IN*: Stout, G. and Stout, M. (eds.) *Beaubec Co. Meath: a French Cistercian Grange in the Boyne Valley*. Chapel Press, pp132–157.

Clay, C. 2006. *The Park, Skendleby, Lincolnshire*. Unpublished excavation report for Lincolnshire County Council, Department of Planning and Conservation.

Deck, S. 1974. Le temporel de l'abbaye cistercienne de Beaubec. *Annales de Normandie*. 24, pp131–56.

Duffy, P. and McIlreavy, D. 2022. Discovery of the 'Cemetery Gate' at St Mary's Cistercian Abbey, Dublin *IN*: Gleeson, P. and Ó Carragáin, T. (eds.) Medieval Britain and Ireland – fieldwork highlights in 2021. *Medieval Archaeology*. 66 (2), pp468–89.

Giblin, A. 2023. Location and landscape *IN:* Stout, G. and Stout, M. (eds.) *Beaubec Co. Meath: a French Cistercian Grange in the Boyne Valley*. Chapel Press. pp1–7.

Hogan, A. 2008. *The priory of Llanthony Prima and Secunda in Ireland, 1172–1541: lands, patronage and politics*. Dublin: Four Courts Press.

Johnston, P. 2023. Plant macrofossils from Beaubec, Co. Meath *IN:* Stout, G. and Stout, M. (eds) *Beaubec Co. Meath: a French Cistercian Grange in the Boyne Valley*. Chapel Press. pp164–176.

Mayes, P. 2002. *Excavations at a Templar Preceptory: South Witham, Lincolnshire 1965–67*. The Society for Medieval Archaeology Monograph 19. Leeds: English Heritage.

Maxwell Lyte, H.C. 1891–1916. *Calendar of the Patent Rolls preserved in the Public Record Office*. Prepared under the superintendence of the Deputy Keeper of the Records. Edward III. 16 vols. London: H.M. Stationery Office. vol. 6, p595.

Maxwell Lyte, H.C. 1891–1916. *Calendar of the Patent Rolls preserved in the Public Record Office*. Prepared under the superintendence of the Deputy Keeper of the Records. Edward III. 16 vols. London: H.M. Stationery Office. vol. 3, p224.

Maxwell Lyte, H.C. 1895–1909. *Calendar of the Patent Rolls preserved in the Public Record Office*. Prepared under the superintendence of the Deputy Keeper of the Records. Richard II. AD 1388–1392. 6 vols and supplement. London: H.M. Stationery Office.

Norgate, K. 1887. *England under the Angevin Kings*. London: Macmillan and Co.

Stout, G. and Stout, M. 2021. Bey More, Meath 2021:537. Excavations.ie: Database of Irish Excavations Reports 2021:537 [Online]. Available from: https://excavations.ie/report/2021/Meath/031728a/ [Accessed 16.1.2024].

Stout, G. and Stout, M. 2020: Beaubec, Bey More, Meath 170. Excavations.ie: Database of Irish Excavations Reports [Online]. 170. Available from: https://excavations.ie/report/2020/Meath/0030016/. [Accessed 16.1.2024].

Stout, G. and Stout, M. 2019. Beaubec, Bey More Td, Co. Meath, Meath 2019: 668. Excavations.ie: Database of Irish Excavations Reports 2019. [Online]. 668. Available from: https://excavations.ie/report/2019/Meath/0029935/. [Accessed 16.1.2024].

Sweetman, P.D. 1998. The hall-house in Ireland. *Archaeology Ireland*. 12 (3), pp13–16.

Thornton, D. 2023. The monks and attorneys of Beaubec *iuxta* Drogheda, *c.*1300–1400 *IN*: Stout, G. and Stout, M. (eds.) *Beaubec Co. Meath: a French Cistercian Grange in the Boyne Valley*. Chapel Press. pp28–34.

Sweetman, H.S. (ed.) 1881. *Calendar of Documents relating to Ireland, 1293–1301*. London: Public Records Office London. pp110–11.

IMAGE CREDITS

COVER:

'While you were sleeping'. ©Hugh MacConville. www.hughmacconvillephotographer.com

CHAPTER 1:
The Irish DNA Atlas: Providing a map of Irish genetics in and out of Ireland

Pages 6–7
Map of regional clusters of shared Irish ancestry.
©Edmund Gilbert.

Scotland from Torr Head, County Antrim.
Creative Commons.
https://commons.wikimedia.org/wiki/File:Scotland_from_Torr_Head_-_panoramio.jpg. ©Keith Ruffles.

Page 9
Irish DNA Atlas of Surname Origins.
©Edmund Gilbert.

Page 11
Migration route of Neolithic farmers from Near East.
Creative Commons. Gronenborn, Detlef and Horejs, Barbara, Börner, Ober.
https://www.academia.edu/9424525/Map_Expansion_of_farming_in_western_Eurasia_9600_4000_cal_BC_update_vers_2021_1_.

Page 12
Flow of Yamnaya steppe pastoralists.
Narasimhan et al.
https://www.science.org/doi/10.1126/science.aat7487. *Science*.

Pages 14–15
Map of British Isles with genetic clusters.
Gilbert et al.
https://www.pnas.org/doi/10.1073/pnas.1904761116. *Journal of the Proceedings of the Natural Academy of Sciences in the USA (PNAS).*

Pages 16–17
Viking migration 800–950 CE.
Leslie, B. Winney, G. Hellenthal, G. Davison, D. Boumertit, A. Day, T. et al. 2015. The fine-scale genetic structure of the British populations. *Nature*. 519 (7543), pp309-314; Accession Number: 25788095 PMCID: PMC4632200 DOI: 10.1038/nature14230.

Irish-British gene flow into Scandinavia.
Rodríguez-Varela et al.
https://www.cell.com/cell/fulltext/S00928674(22)01468-4. *Cell Press*.

Pages 18–19
Source areas of Gaelic ancestry found in Iceland.
Gilbert et. al.
https://www.pnas.org/doi/full/10.1073/pnas.1904761116. *Journal of the Proceedings of the Natural Academy of Sciences in the USA (PNAS).*

Painting of Heliesun Harbour, southern Norway, 1800.
Public domain. Painting by John William Edy (1760–1820), *Boydell's picturesque scenery of Norway*, London, 1820. Plate no. 2.

Pages 20–21
Vestmannaeyjar Islands from Fljótshlið in Southern Region, Iceland.
Creative commons CC BY-SA 2.0 de.
https://commons.wikimedia.org/w/index.php?curid=4644149. ©Christian Bickel.

In Newfoundland Irish ancestry comes from the south-east of Ireland and British ancestry from the south-west of Britain.
Gilbert et al.
https://www.nature.com/articles/s42003-023-04844-9 *Communications Biology*

Pages 22–23
A bay in Newfoundland.
https://davehowellsphotos.com.

Newfoundland genetic map. Mainly Irish ancestry on South Coast and Avalon Peninsula.
Gilbert et al.
https://www.nature.com/articles/s42003-023-04844-9. *Communications Biology.*

Page 24
Luce Sands, near Stranraer, Scotland. Migration from Scotland into Ireland is believed to have been a 'constant flow' type.
Creative commons 2.0. https://commons.wikimedia.org/wiki/File:Looking_southwest_along_Luce_Sands_-_geograph.org.uk_-_3726152.jpg. https://www.geograph.org.uk/profile/7213. ©David Baird.

CHAPTER 2:
Raiders, Traders and Settlers in Late Iron Age and Early Medieval Ireland and Britain

Page 27
Aerial image of Lambay Island.
©Rob Sands, UCD School of Archaeology.

Pages 28–29
Useful Isotopes.
After Pike 2009.

Geological map of Ireland.
Public domain. After J.B. Whittow, 1975, *Geology and Scenery in Ireland*, Penguin. https://commons.wikimedia.org/wiki/File:Geological_Map_of_Ireland_Whittow.svg.

Page 31
Navan Fort, County Armagh.
Crown Copyright.

Pages 32–33
Lambay beaded torc.

©National Museum of Ireland. This image is reproduced with the kind permission of the National Museum of Ireland

Ornate terminal of the Attymon horse-bit; three-link Irish type in bronze, Raftery type E, found in County Galway.
©National Museum of Ireland. This image is reproduced with the kind permission of the National Museum of Ireland.

An orthoimage of the impressive promontory fort of Drumanagh at Loughshinny, County Dublin.
CYSL50409433 ©Tailte Éireann – Surveying.

Pages 34–35
Area 1A (Drumanagh) interpretative plan showing principal geophysical anomalies.
©Discovery Programme, Dublin.

The former copper mine known as 'Smuggler's Cave', Lane townland, Loughshinny, County Dublin.
©Discovery Programme, Dublin.

Pages 36–37
Small gold *(left)* torc end inscribed with punch dot or pontille SCBNS.MB and copper alloy leaf *(right)* lightly etched with ogham inscription, both from among second to fourth century AD Roman finds from Newgrange.
©National Museum of Ireland. This image is reproduced with the kind permission of the National Museum of Ireland.

African Red Slipware.
Creative commons 3.0.
https://commons.wikimedia.org/wiki/File:Roman_pottery_African_Red_Slip.jpg.
©AgTigress.

Pages 38–39
Barbarica conspiratio AD 367.
Charles Thomas, 1986, *Celtic Britain*.

St Patrick depicted in *Legenda aurea* manuscript (Jacobus de Voragine).
HM 3027. Huntington Library, San Marino, CA.

Page 40
The Stoneyford Roman glass burial urn.
©National Museum of Ireland. This image is reproduced with the kind permission of the National Museum of Ireland.

CHAPTER 3:
Encounters, Stories and Connections: Hunter-Gatherer Ireland

Page 44
Hunter-Gatherer Ireland.
©Sadhbh Warren.

Page 46
Microliths of the Knowles collection, Glenone, County Derry/Londonderry.
©National Museum of Ireland. This image is reproduced with the kind permission of the National Museum of Ireland.

Page 49
George Augustus Robinson.
Public domain.
https://commons.wikimedia.org/w/index.php?curid=17858497. Tasmanian State Library Image Archive: see http://images.statelibrary.tas.gov.au for more.

Page 51
Moynagh Point from Cloonaragh, County Roscommon.
©National Museum of Ireland. This image is reproduced with the kind permission of the National Museum of Ireland.

Page 52–53
Later Mesolithic chert pick from Lough Kinale, County Longford.
©National Museum of Ireland. This image is reproduced with the kind permission of the National Museum of Ireland.

Perforated Trivia arctica (cowrie shell) beads from Fanore More 2, County Clare.
©Michael Lynch.

(Top) Site map showing Later Mesolithic features at Newrath 34, County Waterford. (Bottom) Site drawing of Curraghprevin 3, County Cork, showing Later Mesolithic features.
(Top) Eogan, J. and Shee Twohig, E. (eds.) 2011. *Cois tSiúire: Nine Thousand Years of Human Activity in the Lower Suir Valley: Archaeological excavations on the route of the N25 Waterford City Bypass*. Dublin: NRA Scheme Monographs 8. Image by Headland Archaeology Ltd. Courtesy Transport Infrastructure Ireland. (Bottom) Hanley, K. and Hurley, M.F. (eds.) 2013. *Generations: the archaeology of five national road schemes in Cork. Volume 1: prehistoric sites*. Dublin: NRA Scheme Monographs 13. Image by ACS Ltd. Courtesy Transport Infrastructure Ireland.

Page 54
Reconstruction of Mount Sandel-type house at UCD Centre for Experimental Archaeology and Material Culture.
©Graeme Warren.

Page 57
Porphyritic andesite found at Belderrig, County Mayo, but probably from Antrim.
©Graeme Warren. Image ©johnsunderland.com.

Page 58
Excavation of a Later Mesolithic and Neolithic site, Belderrig, County Mayo, carried out by UCD School of Archaeology.
©johnsunderland.com.

CHAPTER 4:
Archaeological Remains of Coffee Plantations: A history of pre-Famine Irish migration to Cuba

Page 63

Map of Irish properties in Cuba, including the estimated area where the coffee plantations were located.
©Giselle González García.

Map of Irish coffee plantations in La Sierra Maestra.
©Giselle González García.

Pages 64–65

A view of nineteenth-century Santiago de Cuba by artist Winslow Homer.
Public domain.
https://commons.wikimedia.org/wiki/File:Winslow_Homer_-_Santiago_de_Cuba,_street_scene.jpg.

Morro Castle and entry to the Port-City of Santiago de Cuba (1855).
Creative commons. Lithograph collection by Pierre Toussaint Frederic Mialhe. Album Pintoresco de la Isla de Cuba. B. May y Ca. Oilprinting Storch & Kramer, Berlin. David Rumsey Historical Map Collection, David Rumsey Map Center, Stanford Libraries. https://www.davidrumsey.com/luna/servlet/detail/RUMSEY~8~1~288626~90060279.

Page 66

Irish 'Wild Geese' migratory routes to Cuba.
©Giselle González García.

Migratory routes of second group of Irish immigrants to Cuba.
©Giselle González García.

Pages 68–69

Signature in 1818 of Sebastián Kindelán O'Regan (1757–1826).
Public domain. ImageZP3NPUN3.jpg.
https://commons.wikimedia.org/w/index.php?curid=43285226.

Letter written by James J. Wright, Santiago de Cuba, to Martha Wright, Dublin (February 28, 1834).
Originals held at the Historical Library of the Society of Friends (Dublin), Portfolio 35X, Letter No.3. Digital copies courtesy of the Cuba-Ireland Digital Archive (CIDA), at https://exhibitions.library.universityofgalway.ie/s/cuba-ireland/page/wright.

Page 71

Land plots and jurisdictional divisions in La Sierra Maestra. Based on the 1832 map of the terrains bought by Prudencio Casamayor in the zone between Guantánamo and Juraguá.
Drawn by the author to highlight Irish properties. Original at the Archivo General de Indias, MP-Santo Domingo, 811. ©Giselle González García.

Page 72

***Cafetal La Ermita en las lomas del Cusco* [La Ermita coffee plantation in the hills of Cusco].**
Creative commons. Lithograph by Pierre Toussaint Frederic Mialhe. *Album Pintoresco de la Isla de Cuba.* B. May y Ca. Oilprinting Storch & Kramer, Berlin. Creative Commons License: https://creativecommons.org/licenses/by/2.0/. Cuba Extra Images rights and acknowledgements.
https://www.flickr.com/photos/bibliodyssey/5195359736/sizes/o/

Pages 74–75

Santiago de Cuba street scene. Watercolour by American artist Winslow Homer.
Public domain.
https://commons.wikimedia.org/wiki/File:Winslow_Homer_-_Santiago_de_Cuba,_street_scene.jpg.

La Isabelica coffee plantation museum today.
©Giselle Gonzaléz García.

Pages 76–77

Estates owned by the Kindelán-Mozo de la Torre-Garvey family.
Source: Compiled by the author from the Collection *Protocolos Notariales* (1814, 1819) at the Archivo Provincial de Santiago de Cuba. ©Giselle González García.

Remains of slave barracks at the archaeological site of coffee plantation La Gran Sofía, identified by Dr Yaumara López Segrera and her team *c.*2010.
©Yaumara López Segrera.

The main house at the archaeological site of coffee plantation La Gran Sofía, identified by Dr Yaumara López Segrera and her team *c.*2010.
©Yaumara López Segrera.

CHAPTER 5:
Under a Southern Sky: The Irish settlement of Baker's Flat in colonial South Australia

Pages 80–81

Location of Baker's Flat in the south-east corner of the Mid North region, South Australia.
Map ©Vanessa Keast-Pizzino.

Baker's Flat landscape, the distant tree line defines the course of the river Light. (Right, above) Pepper tree with thorny bush at its right; (below) blue-and-green banded ceramic shard, found on surface.
©Susan Arthure.

Pages 82–83

Baker's Flat houses in 1906, depicted in a series of photographs taken by John Kauffmann, published in the *Christmas Observer*, 13 December 1906, Adelaide.
Courtesy of Kapunda Historical Society Museum.

Records of the *Forster et al. vs. Fisher* court case.
©Susan Arthure.

Page 84
Survey plan of Baker's Flat, Section 7598, drawn in 1893 in preparation for a sale.
Source: State Records of South Australia GRG 36/54/1892/47.

Pages 86–87
Summary of archaeological fieldwork and research methods used in the Baker's Flat project.
©Susan Arthure.

Part of a mural (now in storage) in Kapunda depicting the town's history, showing the women of Baker's Flat chasing police officers and bailiffs off their land.
Photograph of mural ©Susan Arthure.

Pages 88–89
Ann Hoare, *c.*1870.
Courtesy of Hoare descendants.

Catherine Driscoll, date unknown.
Courtesy of Driscoll descendants.

Network of marriages between families on Baker's Flat.
©Susan Arthure.

Pages 90–91
Geophysical grid outlined in red. Fence line in green showing Baker's Flat boundaries.
Map courtesy of Kelsey Lowe.

Team carrying out the geophysical survey using magnetic gradiometer, showing conditions on site.
©Susan Arthure.

Pages 92–93
Interpretation of Baker's Flat site based on the geophysical data. Note that areas marked as refuse dumps and campfires are extrapolated as such as they have not been tested by excavation.
Map courtesy of Kelsey Lowe.

General location of trenches excavated in 2016 and 2017 field seasons.
Courtesy of Jason Lange.

Pages 94–95
***Burra Creek*, 1851, attributed to William A. Cawthorne.**
Courtesy of State Library of New South Wales, FL1033100.

Overview of Trench A at completion of excavation, looking north.
©Rachel Hagan.

Trench F at completion of excavation, looking north.
©Jarrad Kowlessar.

Pages 96–97
Conjectural drawing of excavated house on Baker's Flat, elevations imagined.
©Viv Szekeres.

Trench E at completion of excavation, looking south, which uncovered a small, round structure that was interpreted as a sweathouse.
©Susan Arthure.

Page 98
Conjectural drawing of how the sweathouse on Baker's Flat may have appeared, elevations imagined.
©Viv Szekeres.

Page 100
Fragments from red-bodied teapot with enamelled gilt decoration.
©Brendan Kearns.

Page 102
***Milking Time*, Baker's Flat, near Kapunda, South Australia. Photograph by John Kauffmann, 1907.**
Source: Michael Treloar Antiquarian Booksellers.

CHAPTER 6:
English Peasant Settlement in Anglo-Norman Ireland

Pages 104–105
Luttrell Psalter: peasants working in a field.
©British Library Archive.

Map depicting German migration eastwards during the *Ostsiedlung*. The pink areas were settled in the twelfth century while the orange parts of the map represent areas colonized in the thirteenth century.
Map based on the research of Walter Kuhn.

Pages 106–107
Aerial photograph of the deserted medieval town of Alt-Wartenburg / Barczewko in north-eastern Poland.
Image J. Mialdun, after Biermann, Herrman and Koperkiewicz 2016, 121.

Cloncurry motte, County Kildare. This motte marks the *caput* of the manor of Cloncurry.
©Joe Fenwick.

Page 108
English-language townland names ending with the suffix 'town'.
Based on a map by Jones-Hughes 1970.

Page 111
Depiction of the *Lokator* in the Heidelberger Sachsenspiegal. The *Lokator* is depicted wearing a hat.
https://doi.org/10.11588/diglit.85#0066. Courtesy of Heidelberg University Library.

Page 112
A peasant, accompanied by his dog, sowing corn, depicted in the Luttrell Psalter.
©British Library Archive.

Pages 114–115
Aerial photograph of the site of the rural borough at Newtown Jerpoint, County Kilkenny.
©Ian Doyle.

Reconstruction of an excavated house at Bourchier's Castle, County Limerick. It has been argued that the house itself consisted of two rooms, with a barn attached onto its rear.
©Colin Rynne.

Pages 116–117
Reconstruction of the farmstead excavated at Boyerstown, County Meath.
Courtesy of Libby Mulqueeny.

Aerial photograph of a moated site in the Irish countryside today.
©Photographic Archive, National Monuments Service, Government of Ireland.

Pages 118–119
The motte at Castlemore, County Carlow.
Courtesy of Niall Brady, Project Director, Medieval Rural Settlement Project, Discovery Programme.

Reconstruction image of the rural borough at Castlemore, County Carlow, as it would have appeared in the thirteenth century.
©Discovery Programme, Dublin.

CHAPTER 7:
The Buildings of Dublin's Historic Immigrant Communities

Page 123
Map showing sites discussed in the text.
©IAC Archaeology.

Pages 124–125
Earthworks at Maynetown with Baldoyle estuary to right and Maine River visible.
Air Corps Aerial Photographs Collection Dublin 1932 IE-MA-ACVN-P2-V7 1955. Courtesy Irish Military Archives.

Aerial image showing the Aungier Street excavations in progress.
Image from Google Earth.

Pages 126–127
High-definition orthomosaic image of the sunken-floored structure at the Aungier Street site.
©IAC Archaeology.

Entrance passageway and finds from around the doorway of the sunken-floored structure, Aungier Street, Dublin 8.
©IAC Archaeology.

Reconstruction drawing of the sunken-floored structure at the Aungier Street site.
Courtesy of Matthew Ryan (http://matthewryanhistoricalillustrator.com/).

Page 129
Excavation plan showing the curving boundary ditch, sunken-floored structure (to right), limekiln and later St Peter's church with the plan of Palmerstown church inserted in the suspected location of the early church.
©IAC Archaeology.

Pages 130–131
Excavations in an urban context at a site on Kevin Street, Dublin 8.
©IAC Archaeology.

View north-east of St Kevin's church.
©IAC Archaeology.

Pages 132–133
Early limekiln (eleventh / twelfth century) on left beneath the reconstructed St Peter's church *c.*1380.
©IAC Archaeology.

Red earthenware rooftile from near the church site, an example of imported building materials.
©IAC Archaeology.

St Mary's Abbey gatehouse with diagonal buttresses visible (centre front and upper left).
©IAC Archaeology.

St Canice's church, Finglas, with string course and early gable highlighted and elevation of St Mary's, Glendalough, superimposed for comparison.
©IAC Archaeology.

Pages 134–135
Carved Dundry architectural fragments recovered from excavations across Dublin.
©IAC Archaeology.

The court of the Irish Exchequer in the reign of Henry IV.
Creative commons. Engraving from an original sketch drawn in the reign of Henry IV, which is in the Red Book in the Chief Remembrancer's Office, Four Courts.
https://commons.wikimedia.org/wiki/File:Exchequer_of_Ireland.jpg.

Pages 136–137
Reconstruction drawing of the mason's yard at the Central Hotel (Exchequer) site.
Courtesy of Matthew Ryan (http://matthewryanhistoricalillustrator.com/).

Reconstruction drawing of St Peter's church, *c.*1450.
Courtesy Matthew Ryan (http://matthewryanhistoricalillustrator.com/).

Page 139
Depiction of the last cagework house in Dublin

prior to its demolition in 1813.
Public domain. Published in the Dublin Penny Journal, 1813. https://www.archiseek.com/2012/last-cage-work-house-dublin/.

Pages 140–141
Extract from John Smyth's sketch of Thomas Court.
Public domain. Published in John Harvey's *Dublin,* 1949.

Structural timbers re-used as foundations for mid eighteenth-century fireplace.
©IAC Archaeology.

Page 141
Matt Whyte's Tavern, located on the corner of Newmarket, drawn prior to its demolition in the 1890s.
http://onlinecollection.nationalgallery.ie/objects/6815/vanishing-dublin—a-handwritten-book-with-30-drawings-incl?ctx=57c8b496-633f-4f90-bf52-727b5edcb818&idx=0.

Pages 142–143
Gable-fronted buildings and corner fireplaces along Stephen Street (Aungier Street excavations).
©IAC Archaeology.

House foundation and rear plot fronting Stephen Street (part of the Aungier Street excavations) dating from the sixteenth / seventeenth century.
©IAC Archaeology.

CHAPTER 8:
Beaubec: An alien cell in the Boyne Valley

Pages 146–147
Location map of Beaubec in the Boyne Valley.
©Matthew Stout.

Pages 148–149
Distribution map of alien priories in Ireland and Britain.
©Matthew Stout.

De Bello Becco chapel, Normandy.
©Geraldine Stout.

View of de Bello Becco Abbey, Normandy *c.*1750.
Wikimedia Commons. https://commons.wikimedia.org/wiki/File:Abbaye_de_Beaubec-la-Rosi%C3%A8re.jpg. Plan de l'abbaye de Beaubec-la-Rosière *c.*1750. ©Departmental Archives, Seine-Maritime.

Pages 150–151
Map of de Bello Becco Abbey and its monastic estate based on Deck 1974.
©Matthew Stout.

Medieval drainage system at Beaubec, County Meath.
©Matthew Stout.

Pages 152–153
Excavation of moat with berm and revetment wall.
©Geraldine Stout.

Plank centring in the western culvert.
©Geraldine Stout.

An eighteenth-century avenue runs through the medieval walls.
©Geraldine Stout.

Pages 154–155
Reconstruction drawing of monks' residence after Elizabeth Gardner.
©Elizabeth Gardner.

Medieval louvre from Beaubec.
©Geraldine Stout.

Pages 156–157
Hall-house at Rathumney, County Wexford, after Colfer.
Plan ©Matthew Stout. Photo ©Billy Colfer.

Comparative drawing of Clonshire, County Limerick (right) and Beaubec, County Meath.
©Matthew Stout.

Pages 158–159
La Grava buildings (Baker 2013).
©Evelyn Baker.

Comparative drawings of louvres from other medieval sites.
©Matthew Stout.

Pages 160–161
General view of barn foundations under excavation.
©Geraldine Stout.

Plan of Beaubec barn.
©Matthew Stout.

Pages 162–163
Bective barn.
Image ©Kevin O'Brien.

Monk fishing, from Nuremburg House Books.
Public domain. *Vyscher* or *Fischer* (Fisher), *Hausbuch der Mendelschen Zwölfbrüderstiftung*, Mendel I. Nürnberg 1426–1549. Stadtbibliothek Nürnberg, Amb. 317.2°. http://www.nuernberger-hausbuecher.de/. Image ©City Library Nuremburg.

Monk with hoe, from Nuremburg House Books.
Public domain. *Gärtner* (Gardener) from *Hausbuch der Mendelschen Zwölfbrüderstiftung*, Mendel I, Nürnberg 1426–1549. Stadtbibliothek Nürnberg, Amb. 317.2° Folio 8 verso. http://www.nuernberger-hausbuecher.de/. Image ©City Library Nuremburg.

Detail of image *Türmer* (Tower keeper) showing a cat catching a rat, from Nuremburg House Books.
Public domain. *Türmer* (Tower keeper), *Hausbuch der Mendelschen Zwölfbrüderstiftung*, Mendel II, Nürnberg 1426–1549. Stadtbibliothek Nürnberg, Amb. 317b.2° Folio 7 recto. http://www.nuernberger-hausbuecher.de/. Image ©City Library Nuremburg.

BIOGRAPHIES

DR EDMUND GILBERT is a Lecturer in the School of Pharmacy and Biomolecular Sciences and researcher in the FutureNeuro SFI Research Centre at the RCSI. His research is focused on the genetic footprints of human history.

DR JACQUELINE CAHILL is former Project Director of the Discovery Programme's Late Iron Age and Roman Ireland Project (2011–15) and is currently Vice-Chair of the Historical Studies Committee of the Royal Irish Academy.

PROFESSOR GRAEME WARREN, a specialist in the archaeology of hunter-gatherer communities, especially of Mesolithic Europe, is based at the UCD School of Archaeology. He is President of the International Society of Hunter-Gatherer Research.

GISELLE GONZÁLEZ GARCÍA is a Ph.D. candidate at Concordia University's School of Irish Studies. In 2023 she published *Coffee plantations and Irish migration to Santiago de Cuba: a historical case study of radical environmental transformation*.

DR KIERAN O'CONOR is a Senior Lecturer in the School of Geography, Archaeology and Irish Studies, University of Galway. His research interests include castles, medieval rural settlements and high medieval Gaelic Ireland.

DR SUSAN ARTHURE, who grew up in Co. Meath and now lives in South Australia, teaches and researches at Flinders University, South Australia. Her research focuses on the archaeology of Irishness in colonial Australia.

PAUL DUFFY is an archaeologist, historian and author, specializing in medieval and urban archaeology. He has directed numerous landmark excavations in Dublin and has led projects in Australia, France and the UK.

DR GERALDINE STOUT is the foremost authority on the archaeology of the Boyne Valley. Her publications include *Newgrange and the Bend of the Boyne* (2002) and *The Bective Abbey project, Co. Meath* (2016, with Matthew Stout).

PEIGÍN DOYLE is a writer and editor with a lifelong curiosity about history and heritage of place and how the world might have looked through our ancestors' eyes. She has written on many aspects of archaeology and heritage.